THE SOCIETY FOR THE STUDY OF THEOLOGY

Explorations in Contemporary Theology

Edited by
ALISTAIR I. MCFADYEN
MARCEL SAROT
ANTHONY THISELTON

THE SOCIETY FOR THE STUDY OF THEOLOGY

Explorations in Contemporary Theology

Edited by
ALISTAIR I. MCFADYEN
MARCEL SAROT
ANTHONY THISELTON

The Society for the Study of Theology aims to promote excellence in the study of Christian Theology by facilitating and shaping theological thought, conversation and community. In particular, the Society's object is to identify and to discuss important themes, questions and dialogues which call for theological engagement; to explore the nature of and to foster theological integrity, responsibility and vocation in academy, church and other areas of public life. The life of the Society is centred on its annual conference, which is unified around a particular theme each year. The Society intends to further the discussion of its conference themes by publishing papers from the conference, together with some especially commissioned articles, in a series of books to be published annually.

Forgiveness and Truth

Forgiveness and Truth

Edited by
ALISTAIR MCFADYEN
and
MARCEL SAROT

T&T CLARK
EDINBURGH & NEW YORK

T&T CLARK LTD

A Continuum imprint

59 George Street
Edinburgh EH2 2 LQ
Scotland
www.tandtclark.co.uk

370 Lexington Avenue
New York 10017–6503
USA
www.continuumbooks.com

First published 2001

ISBN 0 567 08777 8

British Library Cataloguing-in-Publication Data
A catalogue record for this book is available from the British Library

Printed and bound in Great Britain by
The Cromwell Press, Trowbridge, Wiltshire

Contents

Short Papers

Invited Essay

Literature Review

Acknowledgements

The essays comprising this volume represent a selection of the proceedings of the conference of the Society for the Study of Theology held in Oxford in April 2000. Also included are an invited essay and a literature review. We wish to extend our sincere thanks to the contributors for their willingness to revise their papers in a form appropriate to this volume, and also to Dr. Gijsbert van den Brink, for his careful proofreading of all the conference papers. Further thanks are due to the committee of the Society for the Study of Theology for their invitation to edit this volume. Finally, we would like to thank the publishers for their assistance in the preparation of the material for publication, and for their patience when it became apparent that we were not able to produce this volume as rapidly as we had promised.

Leeds/Utrecht, August 2001   Alistair McFadyen & Marcel Sarot

1. Introduction

Alistair McFadyen

Forgiveness is at the very heart of Christian faith and practice, centred as it is on God's gracious act of forgiveness and reconciliation. That much might be considered unarguable. But how forgiveness is to be understood – its precise relationship to reconciliation, judgement, justice, penitence and confession; whether it is conditional or unconditional; whether an act or a process – on all of these matters, one finds a great deal of argument. That forgiveness is something argued over is indirectly indicated in the coupling together of forgiveness and truth in the title of this volume. Does forgiveness enact a truthful relationship to the past – rather than covering it over, laying it aside and forgetting it?[1] What must forgiveness be, and how is it to be practised if it is to deal with the past truthfully? These questions have done much to generate pluriform interpretation and assessment of the nature, practice and possibilities of forgiveness within Christianity. Hence, in Nigel Biggar's excellent literature survey (which some readers may wish to read first in order to contextualise the other contributions here), we find a long history of forgiveness being defined, defended and rejected against divergent operating conceptions of what it is and what it involves. The interpretation of forgiveness within Christian faith is neither unarguable nor uniform.

Unsurprisingly, the range and subtlety of divergent Christian views of forgiveness do not inform media representations of Christian faith or the Church. Whether in serious journalism, the melodrama of soap opera or the satire of column, cartoon or comedy show, one finds remarkable uniformity: Christianity obliges victims to instantaneous and unconditional forgiveness, where forgiveness is a kind of forgetting – acting as though no wrong had

---

[1] Peter Sedgwick, below 119–124, draws the chapters into an explicit consideration of the theme of truth in relation to the multiple forms of sin and its forgiveness; in particular, asking how we may know if sin has such a radical hold on us that it distorts all our processes of cognition. Implicitly, his chapter suggests the language deployed to denote what is to be forgiven might be significant. Thinking in terms of the theological language of sin might require us to think of the offence, the harm or the damage quite differently. This point it seems to me does not really depend on the distinction he makes between sin and evil, which I think problematic in suggesting sin is a moral language.

been done – which also involves a letting go of the truth of the situation (hence the couplet in the title of the conference and of this volume). It is this understanding of and emphasis on forgiveness that is the source of a widespread, popular view of Christianity's laughable 'otherworldliness'; its unfitness for handling the realities of a broken and damaged world. The priority of this sense of forgiveness serves as a sign either of Christianity's overly benign, but unrealistic and wishy-washy, optimism; its moral offensiveness; or its lack of psychological, political and interpersonal wisdom and insight.

It is hard to discount such a view of Christian forgiveness as mere caricature, since it has some basis in reality. True, there may be more in the way of variety in the understanding of forgiveness than common public and media representations suggest. But one would not need look far to find repeated confirmation of the priority afforded forgiveness and the sense of forgiveness as unconditional obligation. Indeed, one is likely to find, not just confirmation, but celebration of just these features as distinctively and essentially Christian. In part, what is celebrated is the priority and pre-venience of (forgiveness-bearing) grace, as the wisdom of God over against that of the world. Just as God's forgiveness was freely and unconditionally given, so Christians are enjoined to forgive without recourse to retribution and without waiting for repentance. So understood, forgiveness is an offer of immediate reconciliation, prefigured by this act of unconditional accept-ance of the offender. So the adverse judgement of 'the world' – that this understanding of forgiveness is either offensive or unrealistic, according to the insights and wisdom of 'natural reason,' 'common sense,' secular disciplines, practices and culture – is, in this perspective, more affirming than it is worrying.

When this confident celebration of the distinctiveness of Christian understanding of forgiveness is taken up into theological discourse, it translates into an at least implicit assertion of the priority of positive (if not positivist) theology over other disciplines (though not necessarily to the exclusion of the latter). It is Christian faith that is taken to give the full and proper account of what is true and what is good. Hence, the norms and criteria for discerning the nature of forgiveness and for judging what is realistic, what counts as therapeutic and, indeed, the nature of the pathology to be healed by forgiveness – all are to be found within the circle of Christian faith. That does not necessarily mean that theological accounts of forgiveness of this sort will run counter to or ignore secular accounts. But a discussion of forgiveness controlled by distinctive theological criteria would resist conforming itself to secular understanding of 'truth,' 'reality' and 'the good' unless it can find reasons for so doing internal to Christian faith. 'Natural reason,' 'common sense' and the truth claims of secular disciplines or culture may be made use of, but only in an *ad hoc* fashion, to help extrapolate the account of forgiveness to be found within the distinctive integrity of Christian faith.

Theological positions that celebrate the precedence and unconditional nature of forgiveness in this way – as an instance of the freedom and priority of grace over any preconditions (particularly the recipient's response) – tend to adopt this methodological stance, at least implicitly.[2] Hence, they issue an implicit challenge to alternative theological accounts that work from closer correlations with the insights of secular disciplines or of 'natural reason': that the criteria of truth, reality and goodness they draw on are not hostile to Christian integrity, substituting the rationality of the world for that of faith. Are they giving up on the priority of grace? And on theology, drawing their criteria of judgement about what is good, true, healing, realistic, from other disciplines of enquiry? When H.R. Mackintosh described as 'sub-Christian' R.C. Moberly's insistence on forgiveness being conditional on repentance, he was indicating what he considered to be the methodological dimension of what divided them on the nature of forgiveness, and issuing just this sort of challenge.[3]

Accounts of forgiveness, such as Moberly's, that reject the precedence and non-conditionality of forgiveness issue their own challenge, of course, to those that affirm it. In large part, their wariness of uncoupling forgiveness from repentance reiterates that extant in non-theological and secular cautiousness: is this a truthful and realistic relation to the past? Incidentally, three distinct sources of concern seem to operate, found in various admixtures: moral philosophy, and especially jurisprudential discussions of justice; the rise of the perspective of the victim, especially in liberation and feminist theologies, emphasising also the pathological dynamics and issues of power in the broader context; and psychology and the psychologically informed therapeutic disciplines, with their focus of interest on the psychological condition of the victim and her well-being. But the concern is frequently contextualised in an explicitly Christian emphasis on reconciliation – a concern which, as Nico Schreurs points out,[4] is supra-judicial and is, in some part, attending to the good of the perpetrator. Where, for example, repentance, reparation, judgement are required, these are not presented as alternatives or impediments to forgiveness, but commended as precursors or concomitants for forgiveness to truthfully address the past. All of which is to say that the concern is whether forgiveness, as it is defined and operates

---

[2] Not all apply the methodological stance consistently, however, applying it to prioritise forgiveness, but then adverting to another discipline to define that which is forgiven and the process of forgiveness itself. So one may find evangelical pastoral theology adopting psychological, therapeutic accounts of the harm or offence and of the therapeutic practice appropriate to it.

[3] *The Christian Experience of Forgiveness* (London 1927), 242.

[4] In this volume, 131–138.

in opposing views and practices, can really be an instrument towards that reconciliation – the fully enacted achievement of real forgiveness – that it seeks. Is the Christian obligation to forgive, as advocated by opposing views, the peddling of cheap grace to the perpetrator that abandons the rights and interests of the victim? Are justice, repentance and righteous indignation (even plain anger) abandoned in a headlong pursuit of 'forgiveness' at any price (Alwyn Thompson's account of Conservative Protestants' moral and theological reservations in this regard concerning the Northern Ireland peace process[5] makes sobering reading)? Is reconciliation pursued through strategies that minimise the harm that has been done and what is necessary to heal it? Does the headlong pursuit of reconciliation through 'forgiveness' oblige victims to let go of a proportionate sense of having been wronged or harmed in order to let it go and care for the perpetrator? Is forgiveness a synonym for forgetting or, worse, does it require pretence that nothing has happened? If the answer to any of these questions is in the affirmative, then forgiveness is not only impotent to bring about genuine reconciliation or healing, it is impotent also to bring about genuine forgiveness, which seems to involve a more definite and truthful accounting of the past than this.

Of course, the danger of setting out two polarised options such as these is that they will be taken immediately for a typology. It would be absurdly simplistic to suggest that even the views represented in this volume could be typed according to these two possibilities: affirming or denying the priority and non-conditionality of forgiveness. In each case, much more is going on in the exploration of forgiveness than this affirmation or denial, and it would be an impoverished reading that approached them with an interest only in discerning to which of the two possibilities they assented. What this polarisation might serve to do, however, is to enhance alertness to the way in which forgiveness is being defined and why; that is, in relation to what perceived advantages in this and what perceived dangers in alternative views. One of the reasons that a simplified typology would prove inadequate is that there is no straightforward correlation between the way in which forgiveness is defined (often implicitly, in use) and the position taken on either the priority and non-conditionality of forgiveness, nor the underlying methodological issues. It is not possible simply to read off one from the other. One may find, to select a significant instance, forgiveness being understood as immediately completed act or as somewhat prolonged process in both polarities sketched above. (As Jane Craske helpfully points out, it is not only axiological understandings of forgiveness that may be accused of oversimplification of the messiness of forgiveness in concrete settings.[6]) This antinomy presents itself continually in the contributions to this volume,

---

[5] In this volume, 139–144.
[6] In this volume, 125–130.

as throughout the literature review, as a means of responding to the dangers and advantages of both views. Often, however, it does so slightly beneath the surface as an assumed definition of forgiveness operating either in the writer's own account or as representing the dangers of alternatives.

Positions antagonistic to the priority of forgiveness often assume that the positions they critique work with axiological understanding of forgiveness as a single, discrete act. That does not necessarily follow, however, and the assumption that it does is at least as often projection, revealing the definitions the critique unreflectively works with, as it hits the mark.

Haddon Willmer's contribution, 'Jesus Christ the Forgiven,'[7] is a case in point. He begins with perhaps the most obvious point of departure for a distinctive theological account of forgiveness: Christology. More specifically, the interpretation of the cross: the atonement. But that is perhaps the only obvious and conventional thing about this thoughtful and thought-provoking contribution. In this unconventional experiment in Christology, Willmer probes the nature of forgiveness and of that which is forgiven (sin) by thinking from Paul's statement that Christ was 'made sin for us' (2 Cor. 5:21). In the field of Christology, the traditional attribution of sinlessness to Christ maintains an important distinction between Christ's, on the one hand, being 'made sin' by the action of God and, on the other, his not sinning through his own action (by transgressing divine law). This strongly suggests a mode of attribution of sin that is not dependent on the commission of sin by legal-moral criteria of culpability: Jesus was 'made sin,' but did not 'know sin.'

The crucial emphasis of the Biblical texts on which any atonement theory depends is that the sin that Christ takes on himself and on to the cross is not his own. Willmer presses the contrast suggested in the texts between sin that would have been his own, according to a legal model of sin (as breach of God's law), and that which he is made to *be*, and not just to *have*, on the cross. Perhaps the contrast is a little too quickly played out in terms of modern cultural assumptions. In particular, where one finds a legal definition of sin in the Bible, the concern is often with the forensic and objective conditions pertaining (the law has not been fulfilled), and with how people are to take responsibility for the sundered relationship with God by taking the necessary ritual action, say. It does not necessarily connote any interest in the subjective conditions of action, such as intention, choice or autonomy. And so the Pauline contrast between a legal definition of sin and being 'made' sin is, it is true, probably that between an axiological and non-axiological definition, but this should not be read too quickly as a contrast between that freely chosen and the unchosen.

---

[7] Below, 15–29.

Yet this point does not seem to detract significantly from the thrust of Willmer's meditation. He is undoubtedly right to read this contrast in relation to that which Paul makes between law and faith or grace. Sin then appears as the miserable restriction and constriction of human life from its proper abundance and fullness, found in faithfully and joyfully following the human vocation to glorify – and thence to reflect the glory of – God. It is this, our postlapsarian human condition (in which all our good is in bondage to, muddled up with and disoriented by sin), which Christ takes up and on to the cross. Hence, the persuasiveness of this account of atonement and of sin partly derives from its resonance with the logic of incarnation: it is our humanity, as it is bound into a world of sin, that is taken on to the cross, atoned for and forgiven.

Sin is here defined from God's point of view. Sin is that which falls short of the glory of God; dealt with by God, as it is defined, irrespective of questions as to its agential, causal origin. Hence, this definition is much more comprehensive than a moral-legal one, which recognises as sin only those acts that conform to the criteria for attribution of moral/legal responsibility: that is, that caused by the action of an agent who could have done otherwise. On this reading, sin is not something that is committed by the person as she freely chooses to commit sinful acts. Sin is much more radical than this. It is both the situation the person is in and in the person. Sin is not so much an external object of choice that we may sometimes freely choose to pursue and then actualise, but in relation to which we are free (that is, we could avoid actualising it at any particular point). Rather, sin is already present in us, disorienting our desires and our wills, whilst distorting the criteria by which we make our choices. Our apprehension of what is good, right, normal, true, beautiful or just undergoes a comprehensive confusion. Will is not neutral or free in relation to sin, on this reading, then, but always already bound up and situated in a world of sin, which gives shape to our desires as to the possibilities for action.[8]

Hence, what Willmer regards Christ as taking on when he is 'made sin' is (presumably universally extensive) responsibility for the ways in which human beings are made sin in and through their situatedness. It is in this context that Willmer interprets both the sin which Christ takes on and the responsibility he takes for it. At this point he makes a daring move that he acknowledges goes beyond what is explicitly stated in the texts he draws on. Instead of thinking only in terms of a forgiveness being transacted between God and humanity, he considers the possibility that what happens in the drama of cross and resurrection is the forgiving of Christ, construed as the releasing into a new and transformed life, not bounded by the possibilities

---

[8] See further my *Bound to Sin: Abuse, Holocaust and the Christian Doctrine of Sin* (Cambridge 2000).

of being made sin, though only possible by taking responsibility for it. Hence, the new life does not cancel out the old, but draws it into an amazing new abundance and fullness of life in, with and through God. Forgiveness is not a forgetting or letting go of the past, a denial of its truth, but a drawing of what has actually happened and been done into a fuller truth. It is 'goodness made from sinful humanity.' An essential aspect of that abundance had been prefigured in Christ's taking responsibility for the sin of the world, and that is that his being forgiven is made 'for us' (and here there is perhaps a need to go beyond thinking in terms of a normative narrative of forgiveness, to draw in the significance of Pentecost and the apostolic mission) through the initiation of communal practices and forms of common life that are forgiving. It is this that Willmer identifies as the essential structure of all forgiveness. It is not only a process (rather than an atomic, momentary action), but one that is expansive in human relationships.

This is precisely the point where Christopher Jones takes off, 'the ordering of the life of the Christian community by the dynamics of forgiveness.'[9] Forgiveness is viewed here as a process whereby God's forgiveness forms a forgiving community, which does not only express and witness to that forgiveness, but mediates it in its corporate life and practices. The mediation (here, primarily liturgical) of forgiveness is inseparable from its appropriation.

In working this out, Jones is grappling with a distinctively Christian understanding of forgiveness, in both its substance and its mediation, whilst taking up critically the insights of secular discourse. He is particularly alert to one of the dangers attending modern theological consideration of forgiveness: that, under the lure of psychology, it overly subjectivizes. Forgiveness has its psychological aspects, he confirms, but it is not seen here as a psychological transformation alone. Non-theological disciplines (among them, psychology) can tell us much, and he makes good and extensive use of them, but they are limited, he suggests, simply because they cannot speak theologically. They can therefore bring to articulation neither the deepest realities of the pathology (that which is to be forgiven) nor of the forgiveness appropriate to it. Both are, at bottom, theological realities. That which requires forgiveness is sin, defined in terms of alienation and disorientation in our relationship to God, at once marked by features that incapacitate and inhibit from worship (guilt, shame and impurity). Worship then has a crucial part to play in the mediation of forgiveness that frees from sin by restoring relationships.

Though his formulation that 'The person being forgiven recognises their sins as simultaneously theirs and not theirs' may be a hostage to fortune, the

---

[9] Below, 31–52 (quotation from 31).

context makes it clear that this is a mode of relating to their past in which the past is not forgotten (there is still recognition of sin as really sin and as theirs, and yet as not defining present and future relation and identity – perhaps the same claim could be extended to victims as well as perpetrators of sin to describe what is achieved in forgiving just as much as being forgiven. So again, forgiveness is not a loss of the past, neither does it involve the escapist fantasy of turning of the clock back in the pretence that nothing serious has happened and things can be as they were before. Instead, Jones sees forgiveness as a drawing of the broken past into a new modality of relation through worship. Hence, it may be transformed and transfigured by the energies of worship into the vehicle, not of despair or self-protection borne of shame, guilt and impurity, but of hope. For worship makes available the transformative energies of God through communal practices of mercy, love and holiness and empowers a new patterning of self in relationships (not confined to those predicated on the will's freedom to choose, but those that are given in the fundamental solidarities of our situatedness).

Fraser Watts draws on a single, non-theological discipline in a rather different way and to somewhat different (though not necessarily opposed) ends.[10] The main challenge of his contribution lies in his taking up into a consideration of forgiveness the suggestion that sin be better construed in terms of shame than guilt. What difference would a corresponding category shift in the understanding of forgiveness make? His exploration offers a timely caution over the ways in which theology has tended to simplify secular accounts of shame in its application of them in Biblical scholarship, and points towards a manner of theological appropriation that is at once truer to the subtleties and nuances of secular discourses and to the integrity of specific considerations proper to Christian faith and theology.

Watts helpfully points out the way in which the emphasis on guilt, especially in the modern period, elevates personal culpability into a controlling concept in the understanding of sin. Thus, sin is interpreted primarily in the categories of act, rather than state, situation or relationship: as sins, rather than sin. Indeed, Watts is thinking here of a particular modality of action: *personal* acts that are my fault. Whilst he does not spell it out, he has in mind acts that fulfil the criteria for the attribution of blame on moral-legal grounds (which boils down to: that of which I am the agential cause and that I could have avoided). It is only, he argues, in the controlling perspective of guilt that associates sin with blame, and thereby with personal acts, that original sin appears incoherent or oxymoronic. If, however, we think as well of sin in terms of shame, he suggests, we may see how we may be affected by our being situated in a state of sin for which we

---

[10] In this volume, 53–69.

are not personally culpable, independently of anything we do to situate ourselves through personal action.

Whereas elsewhere in his contribution, Watts speaks mainly of guilt in psychological terms – as the experience or feeling of guilt – here it has objective and forensic, rather than subjective reference. It is being held to account for one's actions; being judged guilty. The contrast between guilt and shame is thus heightened in Watts' handling at this point, in part because – although shame *indicates* an objective state of affairs (alienation in relationship) and may be induced by being shamed by another in relationship – shame *itself* is an internal, psychological reality, albeit one that may elicit desire to change the external state of relationship.

There is much that is persuasive in this commendation to take shame more seriously in our understanding of sin, and a good deal of cautionary wisdom about the dangers of working with damaging concepts of shame, as of guilt. But the question raised through consideration of Christopher Jones' contribution, concerning the limitations of non-theological discourses in rendering an adequate account of that to be forgiven, surfaces here in particularly acute form, given the perceived significance of the doctrine of original sin. Two features of that doctrine seem immediately challenging for a psychological perspective. The first is something Watts is explicitly concerned with: the extension of sin beyond the realm of moral action (sin as well as sins); the second, the doctrine's emphasis on the radical nature of sin. These two aspects of the doctrine are closely interrelated, of course. Its naming of the depth dimension of sin as the universally extensive state or situation we are unavoidably in, which lies behind and stands as the precondition of sinful acts is related to the intuition of sin as having a radical hold on us. Therefore, the capacity of psychological conceptuality to render adequately those aspects of sin that cannot be accommodated to moral-legal notions of blame is called into question wherever the radical nature of sin seems not to be taken seriously. Reliance on the capacity to experience a sense of separateness from God, even if reduced to the sensed alienation of one's self-image from its ideal, seems problematic in this regard. Any account of sin that assumes an innate capacity for reliable knowledge of self (ideal or empirical) or God that is not itself disoriented by the state of sin operates a much less radical estimation of sin than that carried in the doctrine of original sin. Original sin suggests that the social and psychological processes through which we acquire the psychological and moral constituents of personhood (along with our senses of what is right, good and true) are prone to a fundamental disorientation and distortion. This disorientation and distortion is passed on to us in the very constitution of our structures of subjectivity and intentionality – the organs and processes of cognition, desire and will. This means that there are no naturally available, independently reliable criteria for the discernment of true from false self-images, of God and the good, of separation or alienation from God, of healthy and healing from damaged and damaging relationships, even of healthy and unhealthy shame.

To take original sin seriously might therefore involve a commitment to a more positive theological epistemology and method that intrudes specific theological criteria, drawn from the story of God-in-Christ, into the account and use of shame derived from a secular discipline (in this case, psychology). At the same time, the referent and register of the syntax of terms drawn from a secular discipline might be expected to undergo a decisive shift when brought within the sphere of Christian faith and theology. Perhaps that may afford another means of addressing original sin than effecting a distinction between sin associated with guilt, interpreted as moral culpability, and that associated with shame. In Biblical as well as in traditional understanding, sin and guilt are not so easily separated. That does, indeed, present a challenge to our understanding, especially given the hegemony in our context of moral frames and standards of reference in speaking of and attributing responsibility, mixed with assumptions concerning the permanent, inalienable freedom of the individual moral agent. And Watts has done the theological discussion an immense service in using psychology to point this out.

I think Watts is right to see a connection between original sin and the sinfulness of shame. But his intuition here is not quite done justice, if I may be so bold. For what is needed is perhaps not so much a division between sin that is personally attributable and that which is not, as an understanding of personal accountability before God that is not imprisoned by moral criteria. What is needed to make sense of shame as a modality of sin is the same move as required to make sense of original sin, and which is then extendable even to those acts of sin that appear to be amenable to moral evaluation and tempt us to constrict sin within the confines of a moral language. Watts' leads us to ask what form of personal accountability I may have for my shame. That surely leads towards an understanding of accountability (guilt) that does not look backwards, tracing lines of personal causality in order to establish blame. Surely it implies being called to take responsibility for all that we are and have become through our situatedness, as well as for that situation itself, to become guilty for it, and to draw on the transforming energies of God in order to draw it into anticipatory correspondence with the promised kingdom.

Deborah van Deusen Hunsinger's contribution[11] makes searing reading as she too works at the relationship between psychology and theology, this time in relation to survivors of childhood abuse. The focus of this chapter is on healing for the survivor, and the question of forgiveness is raised primarily

---

[11] Below, 71–98.

in this regard: is forgiveness something that contributes towards her psychological healing, or something that is possible only once that has been completed? Yet this is not and must not be read as a mode of psychological or therapeutic reductionism. There is no suggestion here that forgiveness should be defined or deserves consideration solely in terms of its instrumentality for the psychological well-being of the victim. Rather, this focus expresses a therapeutically informed caution about the advocacy of forgiveness that is heedless, if not downright cavalier, about the well-being of the victim and inattentive to what is psychologically possible for her. It probably also reflects concern to avoid the frequent accusation that talk of forgiveness in this context appears more concerned with the needs of the perpetrator than those of the victim. The concerns behind Pamela Sue Anderson's contribution[12] are highly relevant here, since one of the sequelae of abuse is low self-esteem. Is that to take yet another knock by being told that the 'failure' to forgive is something for which the victim may be blamed? That would effect an extraordinary reversal of the true distribution of power and responsibility between perpetrator and victim, appearing to make the victim completely responsible for the future of the 'relationship.'

Van Deusen Hunsinger's focus on the subjective preconditions for and aspects of forgiveness place the subject of forgiveness (the victim) centre stage. And this seems indicative of the understanding of forgiveness that underlies the discussion. Forgiveness is something the victim does. This does not make it a psychological event or achievement, though Van Deusen Hunsinger does present it as requiring a psychological process. Forgiveness itself is neither a psychological nor an interpersonal process. Forgiveness is the actively expressed attitude on the part of the victim. It corresponds, in other words, to the forgivingness of the victim. We may therefore speak of the achievement of forgiveness with reference only to the subject doing the forgiving (and so the victim's being able to forgive is freed from having reference – if not deference – to what the perpetrator does as the precondition of her being and action). It is not therefore necessary to look for something in the perpetrator (say, repentance) or their relationship (say, reconciliation) in order to tell whether forgiveness happens. Forgiveness happens when victims express forgiveness in some way. Hence, forgiveness looks much more like an act of the forgiving subject, distinct from whatever processes it may set in train for the perpetrator or between perpetrator and victim. So forgiveness is here separated, for the purpose of definition, from reconciliation. Reconciliation, Van Deusen Hunsinger argues, is what forgiveness aims at. But it is not part of what forgiveness is. So there can be forgiveness in the absence of achieved reconciliation, even in the absence of its realistic prospect.

---

[12] Below, 145–155.

By speaking of reconciliation as the terminus of forgiveness, she walks what she knows to be a treacherous tightrope in relation to abuse. Part of what constitutes abuse as abuse is the power differential operating between victim and perpetrator. Unless the distorted power dynamics are addressed, they will not only prove resistant to reconciliation and forgiveness, they will distort – and most likely abuse – both. There is an acute danger that reconciliation will mean being reconciled to the abusive relationship and forgiveness be played into its unreconstructed abusive dynamics. As a guard against this, Van Deusen Hunsinger supplies what is, in effect, a criterion of genuine reconciliation, to ensure that reconciliation means the healing of the relationship, not being reconciled to its distortions: reconciliation requires, not only forgiveness, but being forgiven (i.e., the perpetrator's acceptance of forgiveness).

Being forgiving requires a facing of the truth by the victim, which can be difficult and painful when identity and a whole ecology of relationships may have been structured around its denial. Similarly, truth is to be faced by the abuser in order to be forgiven. This in itself seems to indicate the achievement of that healing which forgiveness intends: reconciliation. The relationship is 'healed' to the extent that both parties now share an account of reality. They have faced this truth, else the survivor would see nothing to forgive and the abuser nothing to be forgiven. In the descriptions offered, it would appear that the psychological transactions necessary to be forgiving, and not just for its expression, require to be worked out in direct relation between the parties. This seems to suggest that forgiveness, after all, is a process that only begins with the forgivingness of the victim, aims at reconciliation and requires the acceptance of forgiveness (repentance) by the perpetrator.

Again, there are incredible dangers in this, and one wonders whether it is necessary that forgiveness be so tied to the transaction of face-to-face relationships or with their health being restored. Is the victim to be made responsible for entering the distortions of an abusive relationship in order to forgive and reconcile? Does she have the power to withstand the power dynamics that have previously turned abusive? (That has for long been a feminist complaint levelled against family therapy.) As Anderson might ask, is the inclination to forgive that untruthful minimisation or denial of the reality of the harm done that corresponds to the destruction of self-esteem suffered by an abused self: I am worthless, therefore the abuse is as nothing? There is some real recognition of these difficulties in Van Deusen Hunsinger's indication that the pathological dynamics are not confined to the relationship between victim and perpetrator. The abuser is usually caught in a far wider network of pathological dynamics than can be dealt with by an act of forgiveness or reconciliation between abuser and victim. Whilst that would not in itself account against the possibilities of the victim's being forgiving, even aiming at reconciliation, it does raise questions about the safety of face-to-face transactions if the pathological dynamics of abuse cannot be healed in what can take place between them. Can reconciliation be non-abusive? Can the orientation towards reconciliation be freed from the dynamics of abuse?

These questions are rendered more acute by Van Deusen Hunsinger's recognition that a full reckoning of the realities of abuse require us not only to trace lines outwards from the abuser (his family history, say), but inwards to the victim's innermost subjectivity. She presents the sinfulness of abuse as partly consisting in its manifesting an alienated relationship from God and in its communicating such alienation to victims and survivors. Just as she turns from psychology back to theology, Van Deusen Hunsinger indicates how we are bound into the fabric of sin, even as we are sinned against. It is striking that both the contributors working with psychological expertise find themselves moving onto the terrain of highly traditional theological terminology. In Fraser Watt's case, it was original sin; in Deborah van Deusen Hunsinger's it is the related notion of bondage to sin. She uses psychological conceptuality to give expression to the traditional Christian conviction that we are bound to sin, not only in the mode of perpetrators (in potent agency; pride), but in the mode of victim. Through use of the psychological concept of internalisation, she shows how the dynamics of sin present in abuse may distort and disorient the subjectivities of abusers and victims in all our relations, including that to self. We are bound to sin from within, even as victims of sin. Forgiveness is therefore to be as attentive to the binding of the victim as it is to the binding of the perpetrator in dynamics larger than the self. That is as major and serious a challenge for theology to think through as it is for the therapeutic disciplines.

This seems to press the understanding of sin (that which needs forgiveness) beyond the confines of moral-legal definitions that restrict forgiveness to acts for which one is culpable, based on the freedom of the will. Peter Selby too wants to extend the notion of forgiveness so that it might be directed towards our systemic embeddedness in sin, as victims as well as perpetrators.[13] He begins with a methodologically significant move to ensure that the understanding of forgiveness be not free-floating and unlocated, but given a prime Christological referent: what happens to sin 'in Christ'; the impact on sin of the crucifixion and resurrection of Jesus. His contribution takes us into that heart by a rather different route than Haddon Willmer's, concentrating on the dominant Biblical motif of sin as enslavement by and bondage to debt. The forgiveness of sin achieved by God-in-Christ is thus seen as release from the slavery of indebtedness.

---

[13] In this volume, 99–118.

Selby takes this language with utmost seriousness. The Bible uses debt as
an extensive metaphor for sin against the backdrop of a prevailing sense of
what severe literal, financial indebtedness does to human beings, their
relationships and to society – all in their relation to God. Arguably, we in
the two-thirds world have lost that prevailing sense. Selby's contribution
may be read as an invitation to consider forgiveness once again in relation
to literal indebtedness. Here we encounter an immediate difficulty. Any
thoroughgoing analysis that asks after the conditions that enslave nations in
the two-thirds world with massive and unserviceable debt forces a rethink
as to the location of culpability and therefore the direction of forgiveness.
The language of forgiveness is objectionable if it is directed to the *victims*
of systemic sin, in so far as we assume they are being forgiven sins for
which they are culpable, according to moral-legal criteria, and forgiven by
those whom they have sinned against. Indeed, that would be more than
objectionable in blaming the victims; its real danger would lie in drawing
our attention away from the interests being served by indebtedness, its
systemic and non-accidental character (which he traces to the chaos and
arbitrariness resultant on the ceding of absolute power to order human
affairs to money, under current conditions). Forgiveness directed to the
victims here indicates their release from their bondage to systemic indebtedness destructive of human good. It is accompanied by the refusal to be
drawn into the vicious cycle of 'investing' grievances against the injustice
of the situation – that is, forgiveness of those who are enslaving you through
debt, indicative of a release from the economies of debt into those of grace
and mercy.

The system creates massive indebtedness in its ravages against the human
community, its fundamental bonds and its flourishing, and against the fabric
of creation in its ecological consequences. At heart, all forms of debt bind
our relationship to time, binding the future to servicing the debts of the past.
It is unforgiving and closed. Hence, Selby uses forgiveness to indicate the
opening up in time to the fullness and abundance of life in relationship to
God. This is forgiveness as transformation – of debt into grace and curse
into blessing.

Is this not the purpose of Christian talk of sin and thence of forgiveness,
to assist our drawing the pathological aspects of our human situations into
the energising abundance of life with God, in which the damage, harm and
evil we are enmeshed in is worked through and drawn into a qualitatively
different future? It is a sense of this abundant reality that underlies the
discussions of forgiveness found in this volume.

2. Jesus Christ the Forgiven

Christology, Atonement and Forgiveness

Haddon Willmer

1. All Three at Once

Not all Christologies are shaped by concern for atonement, and not all ideas of atonement have forgiveness as their indispensable centre. And not all forgiveness seeks a foundation or exemplification in Christology and atonement. This chapter discusses possibilities and issues which only arise where the three overlap and are important to each other.

Christ's *being forgiven* is theoretically *imaginable* as part of the way in which these three work together. Historically, however, wherever they have actually been in conjunction, Christ has been seen either as the *forgiver*, or as the cause, agent, medium or justification of God's forgiveness. Christ thus stands on the active, forgiving side of the distinction between forgiver and forgiven.

At least two great traditions of thought about atonement, Christology and forgiveness have prevented Christ's being seen as forgiven. First, there are theories of atonement (like Anselm's) for which it is essential that Christ has no sin of his own requiring forgiveness; hence his death for sin can earn merit for sinners, and it can be seen as a generous undeserved gift to sinners. Christ bears the punishment of sin, the wrath of God, in death and dereliction, experiencing not merely the absence of God, but real desertion by God who turns his face away. Yet because this occurs within the obedience of Christ to the will of the Father, in giving his life perfectly as a ransom for many, the profound picturing of sin under the wrath of God, in the cross, never gives rise to the thought that the crucified might need to be forgiven.[1] In penal theories of atonement, especially, there is a graphic

---

[1] The most recent and notable example is J. Moltmann, *The Crucified God* (London 1974). Repeatedly, Moltmann seems to me to argue in ways which would make it possible to speak of Christ as forgiven. He never does, nor does he see any need to explain why this possibility should be skirted, and yet consistently left unrealised. That is testimony not only to the strong

demonstration through the sufferings of Christ of the power and perversity of sin, because sin blocks the recognition of God and goodness, and works itself out in deadly hostility to them. Yet this demonstration of sin in the cross does not impugn the sinless perfection of Christ. For sin to be seen as sin, Christ must be hated for his goodness. Thus the sin he bears is never his own, although his incarnation is said to realise a genuine identification with sinners, so that he is 'numbered with transgressors' (Isa. 53:12; Mark 15:28; Luke 22:37). He suffers with and for sinners, and because of their sin, but sin does not affect his own being before God.

It may be a general rule that if a purported identification in interpersonal or collective relationships works through representation and vicariousness, it is bound to involve elements of non-identification. The imperfection of identification does not itself undermine a Christology or theory of atonement, since imperfect identification is intrinsic to representation. The question is more specific: in what ways and for what reasons is the Christ, who is one with humanity for its salvation, different from human being generally? Is the difference (that is, the limit of identification) between Christ and humanity indicated by the sinlessness of Christ or does it have some other marker? What precisely is the sinlessness of Christ and what are its implications? A Christology of identification, implying the *full* humanity of Christ, thus competes with the requirement that atonement be achieved through the sacrifice of a *sinless* person.

Another way of linking Christology and forgiveness, in which Christ is placed on the active forgiving side, derives from the synoptic gospels' presentation of Jesus the Lord. He taught that forgiveness was central to the way he modelled for the people of God and was concretely signed by his eating with sinners. Thereby forgiveness was enacted in the accepting fellowship opened to the excluded, breaking free from the pressures of socio-religious correctness and thus was anticipated, in ordinary eating and drinking, the heavenly feast of the Kingdom of God. We may note, in passing, that forgiveness has to work in both directions: it reaches out invitingly to include (embrace) the wrongdoer, the despised and the enemy;[2] and it acts to sign and make a different, better future for all those involved in the present mess. In this double action, enacted reconciliation between persons does not always have to precede change in the arrangements for living. Often people are forgiven through being offered, seduced and even forced into, a better order; only when this stage has been achieved, do they discover that they are reconciled, accepted despite demerit and are called, in turn, to accept others. Forgiving in life is a never-ending leapfrogging of

---

traditional aversion to seeing Christ as forgiven, but also to Moltmann's specific positive purposes.

[2] Miroslav Volf, *Exclusion and Embrace* (Nashville 1996).

these two kinds of action; it is not helpful to make one temporally or logically subsequent to the other. It is certainly wrong to see forgiveness as reconciliation isolated from change to a better, sharable future.

Jesus proclaimed and practised the forgiveness of God and encouraged his followers to forgive even their enemies, as some accounts of his death show he did, thereby giving us an example (1 Peter 2:21–25). It is this example which has inspired the kind of Christianity found in peace churches. They are committed to forgive, as part of the following of Jesus. Often, in their traditions, atonement theory, as shaped by Paul and Anselm, has been brushed aside; with Boso and Socinus, they tend to think that God needs no persuading to forgive and forgiving needs no justification apart from its intrinsic goodness, its harmony both with God as revealed in Jesus and with a respect for all persons, simply as persons.[3] God forgives, so we should forgive; in this tradition, God's forgiveness is communally ethicised rather than metaphysically theorised. This view of Christ the forgiver has had considerable influence in modern Christianity, because a way of life centrally symbolised by forgiving is both distinctive and useful, rare and necessary in the world as we make and suffer it. In this way of thinking, both Christ and his followers are seen almost entirely as forgivers, not as forgiven.

2. Pro-text

Against the weight of these traditions of Christ the forgiver, and with respect for their truth, let us give a moment to explore the notion of Christ the forgiven. In a passage of great significance for Christology and atonement, Paul says that Christ 'who knew no sin, was made sin for us, that we might become the righteousness of God in him' (2 Cor. 5:21). I have found this text encouraging to my quest, though I do not rest on its authority. It stimulates the imagination, rather than proves a theory. That is why I label it a 'pro-text.' It gives place to the sinlessness of Christ, but not in a way that prevents saying that Christ was made sin. If Christ was made sin, but was not left in sin, may we interpret what happened to him next after his being made sin as forgiveness? That would make sense. But Paul does not use the word, perhaps because he was relatively chary with the language of forgiveness, or perhaps because he sensed that it could not be true that the Lord was forgiven. I admit, then, that I am probably saying more than Paul ever would or could. Certainly, to answer my question was not Paul's aim: so I will let his words help me without claiming that he is here in spirit to endorse my judgement.

---

[3] Philip Hallie, *Lest Innocent Blood be Shed* (New York 1994), 34.

My argument so far indicates that theological traditions prevent our seeing Christ as forgiven and that even an early, influential text that suggests the idea does not achieve it. My experiment to make Christ the forgiven plausible and to assess its consequences for theology cannot be carried through unless common ideas of sin and forgiveness are revised and developed. That kind of change is, however, something we should expect in any theological work, certainly in Christian theology. Theology is bound to use ordinary language, because it is the initial intellectual equipment available to all of us – and because theology is obliged to speak intelligibly to ordinary people. But it has to work so that ordinary language serves the gospel, the truth of God, rather than ordinary language, with its everyday limits and even laziness, tailoring the gospel. In dealing with sin and forgiveness, many kinds of revision and development are required, since ordinary language is shaped by many different concerns. For example, the exigencies of the socialising and moral education of children has led to their being taught about sin through discussions of naughtiness ('Christian children all must be, Mild, obedient, good as he' – 'our childhood's pattern'; I accept that nowadays only the grey beards are of an age to have been brought up singing 'He died that we might be forgiven, He died to make us good'). Another example of our being trained in the language of sin and (un)forgiveness is found in newspaper reporting and popular discussion of a handful of criminals, who serve as monstrous icons, alleged to be essentially evil and unforgivable. Theology in the service of the gospel has continually to struggle to redeem and reform words like sin and forgiveness as they are shaped in ordinary languages. The ordinary language of the churches requires similar discriminating pastoral care.

3. Made Sin

My 'pro-text' is clear that Christ *knew* no sin, in contrast to other human beings who sin. The informing law causes them to *know* sin (Rom. 7:7). Law makes sin 'live,' so that it drives people and burdens the conscience. *Knowing* sin is brought about by law, but it is not the primary form of sin. Paul recognises that sin was in the world, and death with it before the law (Rom. 5:12). What the law brought was the *imputing* of sin, whereby God puts it on our account and calls us to account. Thus the counterpart to God's *imputing* sin is our *knowing* sin. Apart from, and prior to, this imputation and knowing, sin and death operate, defining the human condition. So, in Pauline thought, there is an invitation to see sin through its relation with death, as well as through law. Law is insufficient for human salvation and atonement with God, not only because, as Paul interprets it, law is contrary to faith and grace, but also because it encourages a limited moralistic account of sin, in which death as a component and symbol of sin is played down.

Along this way, we have a chance to see how being 'made sin' can be a viable and useful concept. Paul offers a specific explanation of Christ's being made sin: everyone who hangs on a tree is cursed (Gal. 3:13), and though Christ did not break the law, he was hanged on a tree. That was how he redeemed us from the more general curse that is upon all who are under the law but do not obey it perfectly (Gal. 3:10ff.). We may not like Paul's style of argument. His point here depends on his contrast between works of the Law and faith and therefore may require our consent to a whole theology which is alien to us, disliked and feared as dangerous. Nevertheless, even for determined anti-paulinists, it provides a powerfully coloured imaginative background for our investigation.

A similar point is made by Romans 3:23, 'All have sinned and fall short of the glory of God.' The text is usually read as though falling short of the glory of God is the consequence of sinning. But falling short of the glory of God may be another name for sin in itself. For human beings are created in the image of God, and so reflect, and are to reflect, the glory of God. When they fall short of the glory, they fail in their duty to God, which is intrinsic to human being, not realising their essential purpose and not realising the fullness of their created being, as the representatives of God. Sin is dehumanisation: it is found wherever Irenaeus' formula, '*vivens homo gloria Dei*' is discredited by human reality.

Sin is not restricted to disobedience, failing to keep the Law, or to the attempt to be saved by works rather than faith, but is evidenced in a human condition in which the glory of God is neither mirrored nor shared. Sin is then not merely a matter of what we do or fail to do, but rather of what we are. Human misery, mediocrity, manifold failures, confusions, weaknesses compound into sin, for they make up and describe a humanity that falls short of the imaging of God which is the calling of creation. All aspects of our misery make up this sin. But many aspects are not of our choosing; we are made so. The sign of sin in its fullness is death: the disintegration of being, order and community, the destroyer of dignity. Here the mirror that is to reflect the glory of God is turned away and shattered. This unmaking makes us sin. In death, even if nowhere else, sin is shown to be a way of being human which no one who is good could wish or take delight in. Death takes us to the place or condition where God's praises cannot be sung (Ps. 6:5; 30:9). The disfigured, derelict Jesus on the cross falls short of the glory of God, though he knew and chose no sin. He was made sin.

The misery in which human beings find themselves, the misery imposed on them by the experience of life is a better clue to the reality of sin, than the breaking of the law of God on one or many points. For it is the lived reality of our failure to realise the primary command under which human being lives: to image God and to reflect the glory of God. Instead we fall short of it. Even the good do this.

Being *made* sin happens to human beings, even when they do not *choose* it. Some may live all their lives in happy security and virtue, but do not wholly escape this misery. They preserve their immunity only by munitions, by security barriers and social distances, and by looking the other way, defining their humanity inhumanly, radicalising its difference from those they despise. They pay for education to train them to look the other way and for chaplains to give them religion which assures them they are good even when they look the other way. But those perversions are all indices of their misery, their falling short: they cannot bear to be honestly human, sharing with others who have flesh and blood and they are in fear all their lives of the death that comes from being involved with the miserable.

I am mindful of the danger in this argument. That human beings fall short of the glory of God is not to be taken as evidence that all human goodness is a sham or flawed in itself. Bonhoeffer rightly warned us against 'the clerical sniffing-around-after-people's-sins in order to catch them out' as though 'a man can be addressed as a sinner only after his weaknesses and meannesses have been spied out.'[4] In the same letter, Bonhoeffer insisted that we should not let thinking in terms of a merely inward 'good disposition' block and displace 'total goodness' as our theological and ethical measure. What people are in their obvious strong worldliness counts theologically. It is people who are genuinely good who are *made* sin through their involvement in the world, through the frustration and perversion of their good which comes from 'living unreservedly in life's duties, problems, successes and failures, experiences and perplexities.'[5] Some may never be 'made sin' while they live, but death evaporates the glory of God – there is no beauty there that it should be desired (Isa. 53:2).

He was 'made sin': this is especially outrageous for one such as Jesus who so signally knew no sin, but it is not strange for one who was truly human, 'come in the flesh.' For we all are made sin, in the end, and often before it. Hebrews asserts that Jesus was without sin, but also indicates that he struggled against the fear and pains of looming death. His humanity was not sunnily immune from that threat. To be in a position to destroy him who had the power of death, the devil, he shared flesh and blood, thereby freeing those who were all their lives gripped by the fear of death (Heb. 2:14, 15). If sin always involves deliberate choice, death and the fear of death cannot be sin, for death is imposed on us, without our choice. But in the fear that death infuses into our being and living, we fall short of the glory of God, so

---

[4] Dietrich Bonhoeffer, *Letters and Papers from Prison* (New York 1972), 345f. (8 July 1944).

[5] Bonhoeffer, *Letters,* 370 (21 July 1944).

that instead of living the freedom of the children of God, we are all our lives held in bondage.

4. Responsibility

From Abelard and Kant, and in everyday wisdom, 'made sin' is not merely an odd expression, but offensive. The word 'made' is problematic, since intention is held to be essential to sin. Within law, 'made sin' is impossible, because it is unfair: fairness requires that people are free, 'made' means they are not. But life is not fair; yet we think well of, and are often grateful for, those who get on with life positively despite its unfairness. To live well, we have to carry on living, 'for better, for worse.' Being a stickler for law can block life.

The concept of responsibility, it is conventional to say, is required to preserve sin from being confused with mere limitation. If anyone's condition is described as being '*made* sin,' they are not responsible, so it cannot be '*sin.*' They are victims and victims are conventionally, and often in reality, innocent.

I do not want to meet this objection by belittling responsibility, but rather by relocating it. Responsibility is commonly located in causation. We are only responsible for what we cause. And we can only be held accountable for causing wrong when we were competent enough to know what we were doing, knowing that it was wrong and being able to assess its likely consequences as well as free enough to make choices. That is why children who do terrible things, unlike General Pinochet, should not be tried in the adult way.

Anyone who is said to be 'made sin' is not thereby described as a *cause* of sin. Yet if he is made *sin*, he is called to take responsibility for sin, partly because it is in the nature of sin to require responsibility, and partly because our humanity depends always on our taking responsibility for who we find ourselves to be, even though we did not cause what we are. The child who has done terrible wrong ought not to be tried in an adult way, not because he is permitted to be irresponsible, but because the child, in his future living and development, will have to come to take responsibility for what he has been made through his action as a child. The objection to an adult trial is that it will obscure the call to take responsibility, which is essential to maturing personhood, even where the offender cannot be treated as a fully competent sovereign cause. (By taking the example of child offenders, I do not imply that the penal system is highly efficient in helping adults to come to appropriate responsibility. It may also fail many adults by its narrow causative definition of responsibility. Nor do I suggest that the courts should work with any broader notion of responsibility, for that would make their effects even worse. In this age when litigation is expanding in profits and popularity, we need to be reminded that law is ill equipped to do true justice to human beings and should not be allowed to define humanity for us.) More generally, none of us chose to be born and we were already largely shaped before we could begin to understand choice between ways of life which might be feasible to people made as we are. We do not become real, good, mature human beings, unless we take responsibility for much that is not our own work, that is, for our 'selves.' Because we are not our own cause, we can always plausibly blame someone or something else (parents, our times, teachers, ancestors now known as genes, culture) for who and what we are, but that refusal of responsibility is dehumanising. Shuffling off responsibility takes away dignity; like death, it blocks life.

Acting in ignorance, and only finding out afterwards what we have done, is part of being human, with or without the owl of Minerva and her prophet Hegel. In short, we are vulnerable to *being made*, for good and ill. It happens for good in many relationships. To fall in love is precisely to find that one/ we have been 'made' more and differently from what we imagined or planned until that moment. But when lovers stay together, their life involves taking responsibility for what has come upon and been done to them. Older people tut-tut about the irresponsibility of the young, who do not control their lives, but are carried about by whims and fancies, hormones and winds of doctrine. The wisdom of the aged is cautious, constantly asking: Do you *know* what you are *doing*, what you are *causing*, what you are making of yourself? In their view, being responsible means taking care not to cause anything which later we shall have to regret or be ashamed of: 'Marry in haste, repent at leisure.' There is no doubting their wisdom or its folly; human being always needs strong elders, though their attempts to prevent the young getting into trouble are doomed to failure and end up being nothing but a sad background murmur of complaint about human folly. The elders cannot stop life, nor can they supplant the young who have to live through their ignorance and vulnerability, being *made* something before they can *manage* life.

We are *made* not only for good, but also for ill. Most of us are made sin to a far greater extent than we cause sin. We are involved in the life of societies, local and global, moral (to some degree) persons shaped by the necessities and obligations of immoral society. Many who are friendly in spirit and kind to their wives and children, nevertheless run businesses and the world with a restrained or rampant Machiavellian mixture of force and fraud, because they can find no other way to effective action. As Augustine said, even if a war is just, nothing stops it being misery – or hell, as someone else said. Indeed, the misery of being human is deeper when we find that misery comes not only when we do what is wrong, but also when we try to do the right. In such contexts, our virtues, whether we are pagans or Christians, are splendid vices, for we are heroic in trying to do well in an ill world. To see that misery imposed on us is sin, the falling short of the glory of God, illumines what goes on in much of life, where people are made sin against their intention and have to take responsibility for living what they do not approve of. Ethics does not save us from this plight. Ethical instruction may help us to see, for example, that letting die is not the same as killing, but that does not save us from involvement in a world whose structures mean some live while millions are 'let die' all the time. And to be involved in that world, sometimes as beneficiary, sometimes as factotum, sometimes as mere by-stander, is to be made sin, through what we have not chosen or caused. An ethical appraisal thus gives us a more precise analysis of our living, but it does not allow us to excuse ourselves: it serves to explain more precisely how we are made sin.

So we are made sin socially; and we sin when we refuse to take responsibility for what we are made, claiming to be mere victims. Being made sin can corrupt moral judgement, in at least two ways. We may refuse responsibility for what we are. And we may concede the right of the powerful sin making us to define what is right for us. That is when evil becomes our good: when sin, because it shapes life, ceases to be sin for us.[6] To be made sin is to be overcome by an enemy, to have an alien burden imposed, contrary to one's true nature and calling. If we can recognise the burden as alien, as what God has not willed, we do well.[7] But sometimes the burdens are so powerful, they break in upon the spirit. The Stockholm syndrome, in which hostages form an emotional attachment to their captors, is well documented: a violence that was initially resented and opposed produces a dependence, even a willing co-operation, in which the hostage comes to see and even favour the captor's point of view. It has also been noted that where young women are groomed by a pimp, often in a long process mixing charm and violence, the victim has great difficulty in recognising that she has been ill-treated and deprived of her freedom and identity, and so is unable to resist or even wish to get free of the destroyer she euphemises as the 'boy-friend.'

However, while these examples show how the extraneous can become part of inner identity, they may be inadequate as explanations of 'being made sin.' The victims in these examples suffer psychological distortion, so that they cannot see that their acceptance of the extraneous burden is wrong. What has happened is that people are so determined by wrong or sin done to them, that they no longer see what they suffer and accept as sin and cannot take responsibility for it as such. Instead of seeing that they have been made sin, they work with another reading of the whole experience, in which they accept what has been done as the norm.

---

[6] Dietrich Bonhoeffer, *Ethics* (London 1964), 75–78 ('The Successful Man').
[7] Karl Barth, *How I changed my Mind* (Edinburgh 1969), 86.

An example where being made sin is lived and thought with clear-sighted responsibility within and for the situation is given by Desmond Tutu, describing the effects of apartheid first on his father and then on himself as a father. When Desmond took his children to play on the beach in East London, they went to the less attractive part reserved for blacks. His youngest child looked at the swings in the white section and said she wanted to go to play on them. 'And I would have to reply in a hollow voice, a dead weight in the pit of my stomach, "No, darling, you can't go." What was I to say when my baby insisted … how could I tell her she could not go because she was not the right kind of child? I died inside many times and was not able to look my child in the eyes because I felt so dehumanised, so humiliated, so diminished. Now I probably felt as my father must have felt when he was humiliated in the presence of his young son.'[8] This is clearly an account of oppression and injustice, of being sinned against. But that is not all. The deepest pain was not the suffering of the black adult, Desmond's father, at the hands of white shop girls who called him 'boy,' but the failure of these fathers to be father to their children, in the way they wished, and to be seen as truly father, by the children. In order to do the best thing in the circumstances for the child, the father had to deprive the child, not of a relatively trivial consumer good (a swing on the swings) but of an effective parent, of one in and through whom the child could see and so learn directly what human dignity and caring and loyalty are. What the child sees here is the father who is forced to give a stone instead of bread. The child may well have an intelligent affection for, and trust in, the parent, so that she knows that the parent is not being true to himself in this behaviour. She may be sure, as Tutu says he was of his father, that the parent is a genuinely good parent (knows no sin, in the language of this chapter) but the child sees this parent being made sin, tailoring the parenting to accommodate the power of sin in the situation. And it is a being made sin because the parent knows what is happening and does not pretend that it is other than it is: he 'dies inside.' Living in the body of this death (Rom. 7:24), he does what he does not want to do, not because he has an evil will or perverted taste, but because the duties, goods and responsibilities of life require him to struggle through conditions where doing unalloyed good, without being shaped by the evil and sin in the situation, is impossible. He cannot get out of living in the real situation and thus within its terms. To live is to act and then to know what one is doing. And sometimes this is to be made sin.

Here is an example of taking responsibility for and within what is imposed on victims and so discovering that one is made sin, involved in doing ill, in letting others down. It would be foolish to suppose that this occurs only rarely, in special places like Golgotha and apartheid South Africa.

---

[8] Desmond Tutu, *No Future without Forgiveness* (London 1999), 19, cf. 14.

Being 'made sin' is not then a misnomer for conditions which are really nothing but innocent victimhood. It is being placed in a situation by reality, and by the goodness which does not deny incarnation and involvement, for which one must take responsibility, and in which one finds that one is, in some form, doing or sharing in sin, falling short of the glory of God, being dead rather than alive. 'Being made sin' reflects an aspect of human being, in the negative, which falls out of sight when our vision is merely binocular, seeing only causative evildoers and innocent victims.

I know hardly any theological texts which speak for me here. More than thirty years ago, R.C. Moberly's presentation of Christ as the perfect vicarious penitent[9] gave me a push on the road I have been travelling since. But on re-reading him now, I see how far I have strayed from his way. For Moberly, to be the true penitent is an achievement of supreme virtue; it is the work of a good and sensitive person. And he makes it pretty clear that his model for Christ the vicarious penitent is the Victorian mother, inter-ceding for her wayward child while submitting to the doubtless righteous anger of the punitive Victorian Father. Over against the naughty child, both parents in that world were unquestionably righteous. Though he quotes 2 Corinthians 5:21 as one of his texts in the crucial chapter VI, he is unable to give any serious meaning to 'made sin.'

Bonhoeffer's *Ethics* offers more. That is not surprising, since he did his theology in a world, beyond Moberly's, where 'reality lays itself bare' and there are 'once more villains and saints.' The remarkable *Ecce Homo* sequence describes the Man 'in whom the world was reconciled with God.' Bonhoeffer works through three moments of an outline theological narrative of the life of Jesus: incarnate (against the despising of humanity), condemned (against the pretensions of successful humanity), risen (against the idolisation of death). This sequence not only offers a Christological sketch which does not shy away from the 'made sin,' though it does not discuss it explicitly; it also gives a penetrating moral and spiritual analysis of the evil and sins of Nazism, which is unmistakable, though no names are mentioned.

The second section, on the Successful Man, begins:

Behold the man sentenced by God, the figure of grief and pain. That is how the Reconciler of the world appears. The guilt of humankind has fallen upon Him. It casts Him into shame and death before God's judgement seat. This is the great price which God pays for reconciliation with the world. Only by God's executing judgement upon Himself can there be peace between Him and the world and between man and man. But the secret of this judgement, of this passion and death, is the love of God for the world and for man. What befell Christ befalls every man in

---

[9] R.C. Moberly, *Atonement and Personality* (London 1901), 109ff.

Him. It is only as one who is sentenced by God that man can live before God. Only the crucified man is at peace with God. It is in the figure of the Crucified that man recognises and discovers himself. To be taken up by God, to be executed on the cross and reconciled, that is the reality of manhood.[10]

5. Forgiven

Forgiveness is a change in the relations, circumstances and possibilities of sinners, including those 'made sin,' such that while the sin is truthfully recognised for what it is, it does not have the power to determine the future or final worth and being of the sinner. This change does not consist in overlooking the wrong or treating it as trivial or tolerable. To be forgiven is not to be freed of responsibility but is a way of taking responsibility with hope for good rather than despair.

If 'being made sin' calls those who live within that 'making' to take responsibility for sin, they are eligible for forgiveness. It is not an inappropriate category, even for Jesus Christ. Forgiveness is a response to sinners which does not abandon or disown them, so that they have no other possibility but to live with their sin and its consequences. The forgiven are given friendship and other practical help in finding a new and different future from the one marked out by the sin. Christ was not disowned by God, nor was he left in Hades, the place of death. His story is thus of one who is forgiven. This reading requires giving resurrection a significant role, and not trying to find the forgiveness of sins solely in the cross, through the full perfect sacrifice there offered.

Paul, and all Christian theologians after him, did not present the vindication and exaltation of Jesus (designated to be the Son of God in power according to the spirit of holiness by his resurrection from the dead, Rom. 1:4) as being forgiven. The links between resurrection and Paul's preferred language of justification are suggestive, but were never developed in the direction of a Christology of the forgiven. Paul might be seen as going in another direction in presenting the death of Christ as the death of sin and the 'old humanity,' so that resurrection signifies a quite new and different humanity. The discontinuity between the two humanities, achieved radically by the break between death and resurrection, prepared the way for moralising interpretations of Christianity, like Kant's, in which forgiveness is, at best, belittled, out of fear of its moral generosity.[11] It is perverse, however, to

---

[10] Bonhoeffer, *Ethics,* 75.

[11] Immanuel Kant, *Religion within the Limits of Reason Alone* (New York 1960, ET by T.M. Greene & H.H. Hudson) 66ff.; cxxxi–cxxxiv.

read Paul as though he were suspicious of the grace which abounds much more than sin, coming from the love by which Christ died for his enemies. There is reason to look for other explanations of Paul's language, to understand why he never got near seeing Christ as forgiven, without implying that it would have been impossible in his theological imagination.

To see the one made sin as forgiven depends on understanding that forgiveness is not a dropping of charges; it is not an empty freedom from the wrong done and from guilt as the ground of accusation and punishment. An empty freedom, a mere letting off, waits for seven devils worse. The substance and manifestation of forgiveness is the fullness and power of new and better life. Paul the persecutor was not forgiven through an act of absolution – no one said to him: 'you are free from guilt.' His being forgiven was not a discrete act in which his past was washed away, or written off. He was forgiven in the positive, future-constituting event of his being made an apostle to the Gentiles, being set apart to suffer for the Lord he had persecuted (Acts 9:13–17; Gal. 1:13–16). His being forgiven was a meaning of his being the apostle, part of its content and power. The word forgiven may not be used, because the concrete form of forgiveness is a new way of being, to be named and celebrated by its own qualities, not by its achievement of freedom from the past. To grasp this point about the language of forgiveness and how it works in practice would save us from much sterile pedantry.

That Christ, who was made sin, is forgiven, may be understood on similar lines. Christ's own forgiveness is realised in his saving work, which is enabled and endorsed by God. The forgiven one forgives and in forgiving his being forgiven is actualised. Christ was made sin to reconcile the world to himself in new creation; he was made sin 'for us,' in order that we might be made the righteousness of God (justified, forgiven). Christ's whole story is for and with others. If he is forgiven, it is not as though he were an individual sinner, responsible simply for himself, who is raised to renewed individual life, freed from personal guilt. He was raised for *our* justification (Rom. 4:5). The first Adam was made a living soul (with life *in himself*); the second Adam a life-*giving* spirit (1 Cor. 15:45), being what God gives him to be in giving life to others and having it in them. The suffering Servant is forgiven in that the one who bore the sin of many and was cut off from the land of the living, ('Who could have imagined his future?' as the New RSV has it) justified many (Isa. 53:8,11). If the one made sin were to ask: 'Am I forgiven?' the answer would be: 'Look at all these who are forgiven and renewed because of you.' To be forgiven is not an individual possession or benefit; it is given to persons through participating in some way in a movement which gathers many people together and opens the way to a better shared future.

6. Forgiveness as Christological Narrative and Ontology of New Creation

The idea of Christ the forgiven one might in itself be defensible, without its having a significant effect on the overlapping of Christology and atonement at the core of the Christian understanding of salvation. I am unable, not merely for reasons of space, to deal with the issues arising here. I can only indicate further speculative possibilities which might be worth at least an hour's discussion – an easy burden, when compared with the centuries of polemic which some theories on these topics have generated.

Christ as forgiven invites us to read God's forgiveness in a fully Christological two-natured way. God's forgiveness is not only God's active work in Christ, but it is also what is definitively received in Christ. God in Christ is God for and towards human being, and also, equally, God in and as human being, so that Christ is and represents truly human being before God and humanity. If that is so, God's story in Christ shows how God forgives, not from a world-transcending throne, but through the suffering of flesh. And further, it shows how forgiveness affects and transforms human being from within, giving life in the glory of God instead of, and despite, sin-death. If the story of Jesus, crucified and raised, is the exemplary or paradigmatic case of forgiveness, forgiveness cannot be a subjective indifference to wrong, or a mere change of attitude on the part of an offended party who gives up resentment.

It also follows that forgiveness is defined by God in Christ as well as dispensed by God in Christ. If God only actively forgives in Christ, the nature of being forgiven is to be found by looking at human beings other than Christ. And that presents us with a vast range of more or less satisfactory ideas of what it is to be forgiven, and so of what God – or any forgiver – is doing in forgiving. If Christ is also the forgiven, it can be taken as a normative picture of what forgiveness is – if we want such a picture. Christology thus gives us a normative narrative of being forgiven. This is in addition to an account of the way in which God actively forgives through a complex process, adequate to human need and to the divine purpose.

Furthermore, if Christ was made sin and is forgiven as the risen one, in whom there is new creation, we are given a perspective in which to read all reality. In this perspective, there is no reason to pretend we have no sin, or even that sin is less grievous than it is. Seeing what sin is in Christ who was made sin will help even the most pious to consider the weight of sin, and to see it through what happens in the public, organised and disorganised world of humanity, not in the precious inwardness of religion. It is forgiveness which enables us to be honest and realistic about our own sin and the sin of the world. If there is no forgiveness, we will make our working arrangements, even our peace, with the dominant evil – and end in being unable to name it as sin. The forgiven Christ (seen, for example, in Bonhoeffer's way) keeps us faithful to the human calling which has been realised in Christ, since we can never, for ourselves or for others or for the world, accept that the story of humanity ends with sin, dominant or even condemned. That is not the full story of how God has lived for us in Christ.

In Christ there is new creation. Paul says that. I have argued for the extension: In Christ *the forgiven* there is new creation. The new creation is good and secure, thus reflecting the glory of God. This secure, because constantly renewed, goodness is the outcome of forgiveness; it is goodness made from sinful humanity. Commonly, we deal with humanity without giving a central place to forgiving, as a significant kind of change. Good is good, bad is bad, so they should be distinguished and kept apart. Some words of Jesus encourage this way of thinking: the good tree brings forth good fruit, the bad, bad. From this may be derived a simple ontology where things are what they are; and they produce only after their own kind. But if the whole new creation holds together in Christ the forgiven, its goodness or righteousness is the outcome of continuous ontological transformation. Forgiveness means that good comes from what is wrong and bad, through change within the continuity of the living of persons. Everything is what it is in the moment of transformation, it is the old made new, the sin forgiven, the memory of wrong present as the disempowered foil to the good which itself is the substance of forgiveness. Part of the good is precisely the forgiving power which achieves such a transformation, the amazing grace perceived and received in the transformation, the justice which validates the transformation. Goodness is not a perfect quality, unforgiving because it is beyond the reach of what needs forgiving; goodness is rather the sufficiency of forgiveness to realise the promise of goodness. Forgiveness does not forget or deny the sin. Creation is not new because it has no history, but because the history of sin is forgiven. Forgiveness is simultaneity, but not equality between the sin and the good given beyond sin: *simul peccator, simul iustus*.

So forgiveness is the clue to the ontology of new creation. And the new creation is signed sporadically in the old creation. Wherever human living is good, it is simultaneously truthful about, and hopeful for, human being – that is, it is forgiving. But it is only so by living, engineering, suffering and sharing the transformation linking the truth of sin and the hope of the glory of God (whatever name it goes by).

One last debt I must mention: I cannot say how much I owe to Barth's *Church Dogmatics* IV/1. In some respects, this chapter is little more than a faint, distorted, clumsy echo of it. Barth of course is careful to guard Christ-who-was-made-sin, from being treated as a sinner eligible for forgiveness. The Son's way into the Far Country is traced, without discovering Christ the forgiven and its implications. In transgressing at that point, I seem to be on my own, a sign that I am probably making a serious mistake somewhere.

3. Loosing and Binding

The Liturgical Mediation of Forgiveness

Christopher Jones

1. Confusing Unscientific Preface

'We confess one baptism for the remission of sins.' Thus the Nicene-Constantinopolitan Creed of 381 articulates both the evangelical promise of forgiveness and the need for its reception in the life of the Church. The theologian seeking to explore how this actually happens faces some formidable obstacles. *First*, the complexity and opacity of the process challenge any attempt at comprehensive or definitive understanding. To try to interpret one's autobiographical experience of being forgiven by God is problematic: how much more to generalise about the corporate experience of the Church. *Second*, the Lord's Prayer, the whole direction of Jesus' teaching and life which the prayer sums up, and the narratives of Jesus' death all make clear that being forgiven and forgiving others are inseparable. Therefore the mediation of forgiveness is not a private transaction between God and the individual but the ordering of the life of the Christian *community* by the dynamic of forgiveness – divine and human, received and offered.

Third, there is a pervasive temptation to engage in idealising description which evades the depressing reality of the churches' *failure* to mediate forgiveness in their worship and corporate life. I recall a young man in a Remand Centre many years ago who was baptised and confirmed while there, but returned some months later facing new charges, and asked, 'That Church that the New Testament talks about – where is it?' Any treatment of the subject must wrestle with the scandalous nature of liturgical and religious practice, acknowledging their self-negating potential; though a survey of theological criticism of worship in the Bible would show this to be no new anomaly but part of the ambiguity of being a people dedicated to God.

Finally, there is a surprising dearth of modern theological literature in which the subject is treated both explicitly and satisfactorily. On the one hand, much discussion of forgiveness is focused on individual experience or interpersonal relationships, and its concerns are often ethical and therapeutic rather than theological or liturgical.[1] On the other, much analysis of liturgy is either purely historical or flatly descriptive, lacking insight into the theological dynamics of worship and tending to be stronger on the affirmative aspects of shaping identity than the disturbing and apparently negative elements of judgement, penitence and forgiveness. It might be salutary to ponder the reasons for these lacunae in contemporary reflection. Historically, the divisions of the Reformation may have contributed to a breaking-apart of the liturgical mediation and the personal appropriation of forgiveness. While Catholic practice and theology carry the danger of sacramental 'automatism,' Protestant practice and theology sustain the lurking misconception that liturgical and sacramental acts are no more than the outward representation of spiritual events which happen in the experience of the individual.

More recently, the erosion of public rites of confession and penitence in modern Western society has helped to produce a pervasive cultural incompetence in handling issues of guilt and forgiveness: witness the bifurcation of fiercely censorious and self-righteous patterns of criticism in public life, and the proliferation of denials of responsibility and culpability legitimated by the discourse of victimisation.[2] What the Christian gospel joins – judgement and compassion – much of modern society puts asunder, with incoherent results which place increasing constraints on the Church's ability to shape its own practices of forgiveness and discipline, such as the regulation of the remarriage of the divorced.

This selective distaste for 'being judgmental' is doubtless – among other things – a reaction against theologies and liturgies which seemed to portray God as a demanding father who could never be satisfied[3] and ecclesiastical habits of scapegoating the unpopular and the vulnerable. However, the tendency in liturgy and spirituality to accentuate the positive leads to repression of the dark side of human (and divine?) life and the promotion of false peace, thereby inhibiting the search for forgiveness. The liturgical mediation of the gospel must render accessible the truthfulness of divine judgement, indivisibly from the depth and power of divine forgiveness.

---

[1] An outstanding exception to this generalisation is the study by L. Gregory Jones, *Embodying Forgiveness: A Theological Analysis* (Grand Rapids, Michigan 1995), but even he is frustratingly elusive in explaining how liturgy shapes what he calls 'habits of forgiveness' in the Christian community.

[2] For an influential critique, see Christopher Lasch, *The Culture of Narcissism: American Life in an Age of Diminishing Expectations* (New York 1979).

[3] See H.A. Williams, 'Theology and Self-Awareness,' in: A.R. Vidler (ed.), *Soundings* (Cambridge 1962).

2. Action, Structure and Mediation

A creative summary of these initial apprehensions may be found in St Paul's statement – itself the fruit of much painful experience – 'We have this treasure in earthen vessels' (2 Cor. 4:7). Christian worship, like every aspect of Christian life, has a dual character. It is necessarily a human activity, conditioned by the worldly particularity both of the people who participate in it and of their context. Yet it is also intrinsically an orientation to that which transcends worldly particularity, namely the mystery of God: not only that, but it is experienced as participation in that mystery *in response to the divine initiative*. This chapter is governed by twin convictions. First an adequate account of what is going on in Christian worship must recognise the presence and activity of the Triune God because it is only in this interpretative framework that the event of forgiveness is adequately articulated. And second, light can, and must, be shed on this event by knowledge of the social and psychological processes that structure human perceptions and behaviour. To refuse the knowledge yielded by empirical study of the Church and its members would be to risk colluding with the tendencies already identified towards ideological distortion and self-deception. Nevertheless, a hermeneutic of suspicion should be pursued by theological and not merely anthropological critique, and must be held in tension with the hermeneutic of trust which orientation to God requires.

The 'un-liturgical' approach to forgiveness which I criticised above, represented by even so fine and sensitive a theologian as Hugh Ross Mackintosh,[4] tends to assume that forgiveness is essentially an *unmediated* interpersonal transaction, either between God and the individual human being or between human beings, whose dynamics are inward and psychological. The correct perception that forgiveness is not mere pardon or remission of punishment but restoration to fellowship is undermined by the abstraction of personal relationships from the complex situations in which forgiveness is either needed or practised. Forgiveness as a human experience is inescapably spatio-temporal and embodied, because it is a creative response to estrangements which are embedded not merely in the human self but in the history of inter-personal and group relations, institutions and social structures. A theology grounded in personal subjectivity which fails to acknowledge the *socially* mediated character of experience is tempted to romanticise the event of forgiveness because it underestimates the constraints on human action – a lesson taught all too well by Reinhold Niebuhr in his reaction against theological liberalism.[5]

---

[4] H.R. Mackintosh, *The Christian Experience of Forgiveness* (London 1927).
[5] Notably in *Moral Man and Immoral Society* (New York 1932).

But if we must abandon an epistemological idealism grounded in human subjectivity, we ought not to rush too quickly to adopt the fashionable alternatives, which deconstruct and de-centre the human subject. These may re-centre communication in *language* – as do those postmodernist dogmas which reduce all of life to discourse, and insist that language 'speaks in us' because structure is everything and subjectivity nothing. Alternatively the brunt of mediation may be borne by *communal traditions* – as in those forms of postliberal theology which speak uncritically of traditions and practices 'shaping' believers, of the 'collision of narratives,' 'the absorption of the world by the text' and 'the grammar of faith.' These commonly fail to recognise the externality of the metaphors and sometimes imply that the appropriation of tradition is no more than the unproblematic reception of predetermined meanings and norms. A more adequate account would complement the enabling and constraining influence of tradition-bearing communal life with the active and subjectively mediated response of the participants, as the 'symbolic interactionist' school of sociology has done.[6]

However, when social, subjective and even *linguistic* mediation have been acknowledged, a fatal omission remains. To be a Christian is not merely to be socialised into the practices and norms of the Church, nor is it simply to achieve an integrated personal identity. It is first, and above all, to know God and to grow in 'the grace of our Lord Jesus Christ, the love of God and the fellowship of the Holy Spirit' (2 Cor. 13:14). Sitting among the husks of their rationalist inheritance, contemporary theologians have become increasingly aware that beliefs about God are not universally available intellectual and cultural constructs, but are generated and sustained by association with particular religious communities and centrally by participation in communally regulated acts of public worship.[7] I take as my guide in tracing the liturgical mediation of forgiveness Claude Welch's comprehensive assertion that the dependence of the Church on the activity of God is to be understood 'both as the determination of the creative memory, hope and loyalty of the community through the historical event of Jesus Christ, and as the continuous act of God in grace and love, to which the unifying faith and love of the Church are a response.'[8] I will argue that this entails an explicitly Trinitarian dynamic, which is actualised in worship as the source and the reconstitution of the Church's sociality. In other words, liturgy is both the

---

[6] George Herbert Mead, *Mind, Self and Society: From the Standpoint of a Social Behaviorist* (Chicago 1934).

[7] A point made polemically by Aidan Kavanagh, *On Liturgical Theology* (New York 1984), and temperately by Daniel W. Hardy, 'The Foundation of Cognition and Ethics in Worship,' in: *God's Ways With the World: Thinking and Practising Christian Faith* (Edinburgh 1996), Ch.2. See also James B. Torrance, *Worship, Community, and the Triune God of Grace* (Carlisle 1996), Chs.1–3.

[8] Claude Welch, *The Reality of the Church* (New York 1958), 74.

expression and the matrix of the experience of being forgiven: worshipping communities both *structure* and *are structured by* their liturgies.

There are striking parallels to these debates on 'ecclesial epistemology' in the field of social theory, which is not surprising since they revolve around the same issues. There is a broad division between the approaches of structuralist-functionalist sociologies which understand social order on the analogy of a complex mechanical system or self-regulating organism, and 'interpretative' or action-oriented sociologies which give a constitutive role in shaping societies to the meanings perceived and created by social agents. In recognition of the systematic incompleteness of each of these approaches, many attempts at synthesising their insights have been made, prominent among them Anthony Giddens' theory of structuration.[9]

Giddens' concept of 'structuration' seeks to explicate the manner in which social practices located in space and time constitute both acting subjects and social institutions. His main methodological objective is to demonstrate what he calls 'the duality of structure and agency' within a framework of interaction. *Structure* is defined as the 'rules and resources recursively implicated in social reproduction'[10] and it is pivotal to his thinking in so far as the structural properties of social systems are 'both medium and outcome of the practices they recursively organise.'[11] Social agents draw upon rules and resources in the production of their action, while their action in turn contributes to the development of the rules and resources which comprise the structure of the particular social practice. There are considerable affinities between this concept of structure and the Christian understanding of tradition, particularly when we note that Giddens uses 'structures' in the plural to denote the sets of rules and resources which focus relations of mediation and transformation in social systems, and that he refers to their 'structural properties' as the institutional features which give solidity to their life across time and space (ecclesial examples would be Scripture, liturgies, creeds and ministerial order).

What does Giddens mean by 'rules' and 'resources'? He defines *rules* of social practice as techniques or generalisable procedures used in social action (with explicit and articulated rules treated as a derived subset). It might appear that Giddens is according primary importance to practical knowledge, but he does not dismiss the cognitive dimension of action. He stipulates that rules have two primary roles: the constitution of meaning and the sanctioning of action. The test of understanding a rule is the ability to apply it successfully rather than the ability to articulate it fully: the most

---

[9] Anthony Giddens, *The Constitution of Society* (Cambridge 1984); id, *New Rules of Sociological Method* (London 1976); see also David Held & John B. Thompson (eds.), *Social Theory of Modern Societies: Anthony Giddens and His Critics* (Cambridge 1989).

[10] Giddens, *Constitution of Society*, xxxi.

[11] Giddens, *Constitution of Society*, xxxi.

influential social rules are intensive, tacit, informal and weakly sanctioned. The strength of Giddens' interpretation of rules lies in highlighting their normative character for social learning and conditioning. However, we need a richer account of the role of conceptual and theoretical learning to do justice to religious and liturgical practice.

Here many theologians have found the thought of Michael Polanyi illuminating.[12] Like Giddens, he is concerned with the practical orientation of knowing, which is a skilled activity, but he goes beyond him in suggesting how personal knowledge is structured so as to guide action. He argues that human frameworks of knowing are like tools, because they become assimilated to our bodies as instruments of perception and action: we 'indwell' them so as to understand and act through them, and in monitoring this process we modify them in the direction of what we judge to be increasing adequacy and universal validity. Central to Polanyi's epistemology is the distinction between 'focal awareness,' in which attention is concentrated on the object of our perception, and 'subsidiary awareness,' which denotes our 'indwelling' of the frameworks of knowledge *through* which we perceive.

Liturgy provides an excellent example of this distinction: its purpose is to focus attention on the mystery of God, but worshippers are subsidiarily aware of the words and actions by means of which this attending and knowing happens. If we become focally aware of the words in the book or the actions taking place in front of us, we are unable simultaneously to attend focally to God. The value of routinization in worship is that it enables participants to 'indwell' the liturgy so that it becomes a vehicle for the apprehension of God rather than a distraction from it. Another relevant application of Polanyian epistemology is its distinction between 'explicit' and 'tacit' knowledge, which means that the knowledge which we articulate at any moment is conditioned by and associated with much more that remains unexpressed: 'we know more than we can say.'[13] This is not only a recognition of the limits of comprehension in worship, but a reminder that we constantly rely on tacit knowledge to interpret situations.

Returning to Giddens: *resources*, as distinct from rules, refer to the transformative capacities on which agents draw in order to get things done in social life. Giddens distinguishes between *authoritative* resources, which generate power over other persons and social agents, and *allocative* resources, which generate power over objects or material goods.[14] At first sight this

---

[12] Michael Polanyi, *Personal Knowledge: Towards a Post-Critical Philosophy* (London 1958), esp. Ch.4. See also Daniel W. Hardy, 'Christian Affirmation and the Structure of Personal Life,' in: Thomas F. Torrance (ed.), *Belief in Science and in Christian Life* (Edinburgh 1981), Ch.4; Colin E. Gunton, *Enlightenment and Alienation* (London 1985), Ch. 3.

[13] The maxim popularised by Michael Polanyi, *The Tacit Dimension* (London 1967).

[14] Giddens, *Constitution of Society*, 33.

may not seem relevant to understanding liturgy, but worship is an *embodied* practice which draws on *symbolic* resources, requiring social space, and human and material resources, for its effective reproduction. William Cavanaugh's recent study *Torture and Eucharist*[15] chillingly demonstrates the inseparability of the violation by torture of the bodies of Catholics in Chile during the Pinochet regime and that regime's attack upon the Catholic Church as a *social* body (and the Church's collusion with both forms of 'disappearance').

Liturgy is therefore to be understood as the embodied set of focal practices in which the members of the Church both appropriate the rules and resources which structure it as a human community and reproduce those rules and resources in their ongoing life. The adjective 'focal' indicates that in worship believers encounter in maximally explicit and concentrated form the presence and activity of God which they know otherwise in relatively tacit and diffuse modes. Individual participation in worship reinforces and deepens Christian identity in at least two ways. First, worshippers learn to appropriate the rules and resources of the Christian tradition in the continuing structuring of action (sin is, among other things, failure to do this). And second, the framework of knowing through which the worshipper interacts with God and other people is continually extended and revised. Receiving and offering forgiveness is a fundamental element in the process of learning and growing which constitutes discipleship.

Finally, it is axiomatic to the Christian understanding of worship that God is not the inert object of human activity but its active source and goal (Father), mediator (Son) and medium (Spirit). When at worship Christians are not drawing solely on the rules and resources of the human community but 'indwelling' the movement of God's own life and love. To social, liturgical, linguistic, symbolic and subjective mediation, we must preface *theological*, in recognition of Karl Barth's principle that 'God is known through God.'[16]

As a thought-experiment, consider what it might mean to treat God as the ultimate example of the duality of structure and agency: that is, both self-structuring and structuring all else. We might then conceive of the Father as the generator and destination of the divine rules of ordering and the divine resources; the divine rules of ordering as communicative Word and instructive Wisdom; and the divine resources as the liberating and trans-formative energy of the Spirit (noting that interdependence of ordering and resources makes the characterisation of their distinction problematic). This is a more sophisticated Trinitarian 'social analogy' than is customarily

---

[15] William T. Cavanaugh, *Torture and Eucharist: Theology, Politics and the Body of Christ* (Oxford 1998).

[16] Karl Barth, *Church Dogmatics* I/1 (ET Edinburgh 1975), esp. 5 & 6.

essayed, and it is congruent with my interpretation of ecclesial and liturgical mediation. On this account, we need to reckon not only with double agency – divine and human – in the life of the Church but 'double structure': 'the Church being both a society and a society supernatural'[17] – the household of God, the body of Christ and the temple of the Holy Spirit.

3. Liturgy and the Memory of Jesus

My initial paradigm for understanding the liturgical mediation of forgiveness is the appearance of the risen Jesus to his disciples in John 20:19–23. It is an assembling marked by disorientation, guilt and fear in the aftermath of the scattering of the disciples and the crucifixion of their Master, but the account carries liturgical echoes.[18] Here in archetypal form is the 'gathering, upbuilding and sending'[19] of the Church: its orientation to God through the risen Christ who identifies himself as the Crucified One, and as such the cause of rejoicing; its vocation to bear the peace won through Christ's faithfulness in the enlivening and empowering energy of the Spirit; and the offer of forgiveness as integral to this vocation. Here also are the beginnings of the 'shape of the liturgy': gathering, greeting, gospel, praise, communion, blessing and sending. In this structured encounter, the community of disciples is drawn into the reconstituting activity of God, from the purposeful directing of the Father, through the embodied communication of the Son, in the recreative energy of the Spirit.

The liturgical encounter with Jesus Christ is not direct in the same sense: post-ascension Christians are those 'who have not seen and yet believe' (John 20:29). Yet Jesus continues to make himself known through the correlation of memory, presence and anticipation. First, the Church's *remembering* is 'sedimented' in the canonical Scriptures, liturgical texts (such as the Lord's Prayer) which order the offering of praise to God through the mediation of Christ, and symbolic actions in which the meaning of Jesus' work is communicated. Second, the presupposition of participating in liturgical worship is receptivity to the divine *presence* in the expectation that the covenantal promises of God to his people will be fulfilled. The presence of Christ is promised to those who gather in his name, inseparably from that of the Father and the Spirit. It is in the Spirit that worship is evoked (hence the Spirit is *invoked* at the beginning of the Eucharist and on other liturgical occasions), through the Son that it is

---

[17] Richard Hooker, *Laws of Ecclesiastical Polity*, I.xv.2.

[18] Raymond E. Brown, *The Gospel According to John*, vol. 2 (London 1966), 1019–1020.

[19] The threefold characterisation of 'the Church as event' employed by Barth in his Doctrine of Reconciliation, in *Church Dogmatics*, vol. IV/1, 2 & 3 (ET Edinburgh 1956–62).

focused, and to the Father that it is directed. Third, faith in the promises of God advertises the element of *anticipation*, which is ultimately bounded by the expectation of Christ's 'coming again' to consummate his work, and which through the forward-moving abundance of the Spirit enables worshippers to 'abound in hope' (Rom. 15:13).

In accord with the methodological axiom of the dual character of worship, both its divine orientation and creaturely contextualisation must be fully acknowledged. The three temporal dimensions of worship are interdependent: without memory, the presence of God is dangerously unidentifiable; without presence, the activity of worship is simply a human projection; and without anticipation, it becomes an introverted celebration lacking transformative potential. The complementary specification is the set of particular relations between the worshipping community and the wider world to which it belongs, in which the Triune God is at work as Creator and Redeemer.[20] The insight that informs much contemporary ecumenical theology, that the Church worships and prays on behalf of the world, means that the liturgical mediation of forgiveness includes a vicarious element which arises from solidarity with the world, in blessing, in sin and in hope. This solidarity is expressed primarily in the activities of *thanksgiving* (celebrating the dependence of all creation upon both divine and human goodness), *confession* (acknowledging shared responsibility for evil and shared desire to 'make good')[21] and *intercession* (proceeding from the sense of solidarity in good and evil to articulate the desire for God's will to be done in the life of humanity and the cosmos).

Liturgy is a structured and cumulative sequence of interactions in which the self-presentation of God and the response of worshippers are enfolded in an expanding dynamic of praise, thanksgiving and exchange.[22] It is structured in a temporal series of differentiated actions because we cannot 'take it all in' instantaneously. It is cumulative because the forward movement of the rite integrates the memory of earlier elements into perception of the later. It would make no sense to read from the Bible *after* the sermon, or for the confession to *follow* the celebration of the Eucharist, or for communion to be administered *before* the interpretative ministry of the Word. Within this differentiated sequence, the memory of Jesus Christ is presented in two distinct forms. These correspond to Hans Frei's account of the

---

[20] I am grateful to Professor D.W. Hardy for making this point in discussion, though I fear I have been unable to take account of it adequately.

[21] Another relevant activity or genre is that of 'lament', in which modern liturgies are often deficient; on this, Claus Westermann, 'The Role of the Lament in the Theology of the Old Testament,' *Interpretation* 28 (1974), 20–38; Robert Davidson, *The Courage To Doubt: Exploring An Old Testament Theme* (London 1983), Ch.1.

[22] I here follow the broad outline of the interpretation offered by Daniel W. Hardy & David F. Ford, *Jubilate: Theology in Praise* (London 1984), esp. Chs. 4 & 8.

complementarity of 'intention-action' and 'self-manifestation' descriptions.[23] The first type of description answers the question 'What is he like?' and renders Jesus' character in narrative form, interacting with people, situations and events. Conversely, the second type answers the question 'Who is he?' and expresses the continuity of Jesus' identity through time in integral form, e.g., in titles, metaphorical images or symbols. It is of crucial importance that this identification of Jesus depends wholly upon his being embodied: embodiment is an indispensable element of theological as well as ecclesial mediation.

The *narrative* mediation of Jesus occurs at three major points in the liturgy: first in the reading of the Gospel; second in the recitation of the Apostles' or Nicene Creed; and third (at the Eucharist) in the Great Prayer of Thanksgiving. Each provides what might be called a 'moving focus' in which the congregation follows the direction of the story of Jesus. While the reading of the Gospel is an 'intensive' focusing on a small segment of the story; the Creed is an 'extensive' focusing which places the story within the wider narrative of Trinitarian action from creation to consummation. The Eucharistic Prayer, finally, is a combination of the previous two, in which the narrative of institution is bracketed by thanksgiving for creation and redemption and prayer for the eschatological consummation. It is notable that each of these 'moving foci' is followed by 'fixed-focus' liturgical actions which help the congregation to interpret, assimilate and 'indwell' what they have just followed: the sermon following the Gospel, prayers or praise following the Creed, and the breaking of bread and distribution of communion following the Eucharistic Prayer.

Through this interweaving of narrative, praise, prayer and sacrament, worshippers know Jesus both as a character identified by his words, actions and relationships ('intention-action') and as an integral mediator whom they can approach and 'indwell' ('self-manifestation') – as the Anglican Prayer of Humble Access pleads. We are now in a position to specify the field of mediation of forgiveness in liturgy. Focal knowledge of Jesus as mediator depends upon indwelling the awareness derived from the Gospel narratives and other interpretative material. Identifying Jesus as the 'friend of sinners,' which is a 'self-manifestation' description, depends on knowledge of specific encounters with sinners. The cognitive and emotional power of the image of Jesus thus constructed will depend upon understanding, and identifying with, the dynamics of particular narrated encounters. Interaction takes place between worshippers' knowledge of Jesus in these two modes and their self-knowledge given through the narrative construction of personal identity as memory, self-presence and self-projection. Thus interpretation of Jesus

---

[23] Hans W. Frei, *The Identity of Jesus Christ: The Hermeneutical Bases of Dogmatic Theology* (Philadelphia 1975), Chs. 9, 10, 12 & 13.

and self-interpretation become mutually implicating, while prayers of confession articulate the fusion between focal awareness of God *through* Jesus and awareness of oneself as a sinner. Liturgy resolves this interaction in a number of ways (and not just one).

The field of interaction can be mapped in terms of three inter-related features of human alienation, all of which inhibit access to God in worship: guilt, shame and impurity. I make two general points. *First*, each of the three arises from social processes of attribution which take specific religious forms. *Guilt* is concerned with the attribution of moral responsibility for acts of wrongdoing, and its removal is widely (but wrongly) supposed to be the sole purpose of forgiveness. *Shame* is the negative component of the attribution of status, and identifies its object as deviant in relation to prevailing norms, often with the result that the person is subject to some form of deprivation of status or expulsion from a community, and feels humiliated. *Impurity* is created by cultural processes of ordering which seek to control the physical body as a means of defending the boundaries of the social body.[24] Such processes identify particular objects or persons as dis-ordered, that is, incomplete or ambivalent or displaced in relation to accepted classifications. There are commonly symbolic associations between attributions of disorder and physical uncleanness – 'dirt is matter out of place' – with consequent reactions of aversion and disgust (e.g., in stigmatisation of criminals, racial prejudice or homophobia).

Second, each of the three may be present in genuine or inauthentic forms, through internalisation of the effects of disordered human relationships. Guilt may be healthy or unhealthy depending on the truth of a person's perception of their responsibility for wrongdoing, and its magnitude. Shame may be appropriately or inappropriately directed, and shaming all too easily becomes an expression either of hostility and estrangement, or self-negation. Impurity is more difficult to evaluate because it reflects particular systems of ordering, but attribution to others is usually a manifestation of the desire to control, and its self-attribution may have obsessional or traumatic roots (e.g., the experience of sexual abuse).

Jesus of Nazareth was experienced and remembered as the mediating agent of a divinely authorised and divinely energised reconstitutive dynamic that embraced and transformed each of these aspects of alienation from God and from other human beings. In his ministry, he reached out in God's name to the guilty, the ashamed and the impure, thus disturbing those who were self-righteous, proud or supposedly pure. In his conflicts with authority and finally in his dying, he identified with human guilt, shame and impurity, accepted the negative projections and violence of those unable to accept

---

[24] Mary Douglas, *Purity and Danger: An Analysis of the Concepts of Pollution and Taboo* (London 1966), esp. Chs. 1, 3, 6, 7 & 8.

their own guilt, shame or impurity, and by his trust in God's mercy, love and transforming holiness contained the destructive power of these projections at the cost of his own life. In Jesus' resurrection, God affirmed his actions and made the reconstitutive dynamic of his life available to those who had followed and then betrayed him, but now found themselves reclaimed and redirected by the power of forgiveness.

Rowan Williams has shown how in the resurrection narratives the risen Jesus generates hope by resolving the ambivalence of the disciples' memories: they are confronted by their victim as their judge, but his judgement is merciful and healing, the source of repentance and newness of life. 'If forgiveness is liberation, it is also a recovery of the past in hope, a return of memory, in which what is potentially threatening, destructive, despair-inducing, in the past is transfigured into the ground of hope.'[25] Because Jesus is the pure victim – and we should observe that the term 'victim' belongs to all three spheres of guilt, shame and impurity – he has broken the spiral of self-protection, retaliation and violence, and is able to draw his followers into the counter-dynamic of self-giving, forgiveness and peace-making. Through appropriation of the 'counter-memories' of Jesus' work and the projection of the new order which he has inaugurated in 'counter-imagination,' human memories can be healed and their power to perpetuate destructive patterns of behaviour contained and overcome.[26]

The purpose of liturgy, therefore, is to recapitulate the story of Jesus' work in overcoming the forces of alienation and to reappropriate the transformative energy of mercy, love and holiness released by it, by directing attention to the God who is the source and goal of both, so that the Christian community and all in whom God is at work may share in the divine restructuring. This is effectively (if obscurely) a paraphrase of Ephesians 2:13–22, where by an extraordinary juxtaposition of metaphors it is emphasised that the site of the liturgical mediation of forgiveness is no longer the Temple, but the crucified and risen body of Jesus Christ.

4. One Baptism: A Matter of Death and Life

To return to the very beginning of this chapter: why does the Creed link the forgiveness of sins with baptism rather than any other vehicle of mediation? In the New Testament, the baptism of John is declared to be 'a baptism of repentance *for the forgiveness of sins*' (Mark 1:4) while Peter calls the crowd on the day of Pentecost to 'repent and be baptised ... in the name of Jesus Christ *for the forgiveness of your sins*; and you shall receive the gift of

---

[25] Rowan Williams, *Resurrection: Interpreting the Easter Gospel* (London 1982), 32.
[26] I here rely on Charles Elliott, *Memory and Salvation* (London 1995), Chs.11 & 12.

the Holy Spirit' (Acts 2:38). If we apply to baptism the model of a rite of passage (defined by the anthropologist van Gennep as a sequential movement from an initial act of separation through a transitional state of 'liminality' to an act of incorporation or reaggregation[27]), John's baptism is an incomplete rite. It initiates an act of separation, by means of symbolic washing, from the sinful past, out of the solidarity of disobedient Israel, but does not complete the transition to incorporation. John acknowledges the incompleteness: 'I baptised you with water, but he (the one who is to come) will baptise with the Holy Spirit.' The sign prepares for, and awaits, the coming of God's Anointed, and its anticipated fulfilment comes at Pentecost when a new community is constituted by the Spirit who is both the life-giving energy of the new order and the agent of incorporation and participation.

Between these events, however, there is a bridge: Jesus the Anointed One. It is Jesus who embodies the meaning of John's sign by undergoing baptism on behalf of disobedient Israel, experiencing his own initiation as God's obedient Servant in the power of the Spirit. Not only this, but Jesus' whole life becomes an embodied interpretation of the meaning of baptism pointing towards a climax of suffering in which the symbolism of immersion in water takes on the sinister overtones of drowning, of being overwhelmed by an ordeal of testing and judgement (Mark 10:38; Luke 12:50). Jesus' life is an extended rite of passage from baptism through death to the resurrection which is (for him) aggregation with the life of the new order. The rite of Christian baptism which defines the new community of the Church is co-extensive with it, symbolically integrating a range of 'baptismal' events and images into a single action. Baptism embraces repentance, purification, the descent of the Spirit, obedient service, dying and being raised up, fused in an act of ritual washing which now incorporates repentant, forgiven and believing sinners into the fellowship of the Spirit. Repentance – expressed by confession of sin, renunciation of evil and turning to Christ in faith – is a necessary element of being baptised and receiving forgiveness, but it is a response to the promise of new life in the name and character of Jesus Christ, and in the power of the Spirit who anointed him and raised him from the dead. Incorporation into Christ is identically incorporation into the community which is the embodied sign of his presence and activity, that is, his body.

That being so, there are two senses in which baptism anticipates future forgiveness. First, its association of the candidate with the death (and burial) of Christ is not merely metaphorical. 'Christ being raised from the dead dies no more' (Rom. 6:11), but this is not true of those being baptised, whose death still lies ahead of them. 'We *have been* united with him in the likeness

---

[27] Arnold van Gennep, *The Rites of Passage* (1909; ET Chicago 1960), Chs. 1, 2, 6.

of his death ... we *shall certainly be* united with him in the likeness of his resurrection' (Rom. 6:5). Baptism is a preparation for death in the sense that it dedicates the whole of a life to God in the expectation that the work begun in baptism will be brought to a gracious completion.[28] Conversely, the liturgy of death, in which we commend the departed to God's mercy 'in sure and certain hope of the resurrection to eternal life,' should be seen as the fulfilment of baptism.

Second, the rite is anticipatory in providing a paradigm for subsequent passages from the unforgiven to the forgiven state: further acts of repentance which are analogously liminal in their transition between relapse into the old sinful identity and return to the 'fount of grace.' It is unrepeatable because no future sin short of apostasy can undo the baptismal transition, but it models a life in which the old self is continually renounced and left behind in order to grow into the fullness of the new life. In that sense, every act of confession is a recapitulation of baptism but not a repetition of it. Christian life is lived between the judgement of the cross and the eschatological judgement which corresponds to it; repentance and forgiveness are part of the continuing process of reorientation and reconstitution which is the direction of that life.

All this is effected by incorporation into the worshipping community whose life is bounded by 'the washing of water with the word' (Eph. 5:26). The baptismal identity is emphatically *social*, instituting new patterns of solidarity which are not humanly chosen but *given* in shared dependence on God's gracious action:[29] 'neither Jew nor Greek, slave nor free, male nor female, but you are all one in Christ Jesus' (Gal. 3:28). This means not only that the baptised share a common life with those whom *God* has chosen and adopted, but that the patterns of relationship and interaction into which they are called to grow are those of Jesus Christ, not those of guilt, shame and impurity. Ephesians 4:1–16 gives a portrayal of 'redemptive structuration' in which the dynamic of the Trinitarian life is manifested in the baptismal unity of the community, the harmonious exercise of diverse gifts and a process of 'making bodily growth and upbuilding in love' (4:16). The rules and resources on which the community is exhorted to draw are those of Jesus, who gives the community his own baptismal character and orientation. Incidentally, this demonstrates that the human body (and by extension the body of Christ) is a natural analogue of Giddens' concept of structuration, being both medium and outcome of the processes it recursively organises.

---

[28] See Wolfhart Pannenberg, 'Baptism as Remembered "Ecstatic" Identity,' in: David Brown & Ann Loades (eds.), *Christ: The Sacramental Word: Incarnation, Sacrament and Poetry* (London 1995), 83–84.

[29] A principle highlighted by Rowan Williams, 'Sacraments of the New Society,' in: Brown & Loades (eds.), *Christ: The Sacramental Word*, 90–94; see also Peter Selby, *Be-Longing: Challenge to a Tribal Church* (London 1991).

The character of the Church as the embodied sign of God's presence and activity draws attention once again to the reciprocal relation between worship and the life of Christians in the world. Christian baptism, it has been suggested, is a rite of passage symbolising the transition from human solidarity in sin to solidarity in the hope of redemption. As such, it reveals God's purpose not only for the Church but for the whole universe whose destiny is to be 'summed up in Christ' (Eph. 1:10) and it acts as a sign of promise for all human beings in their subjection to the forces of estrangement and their struggle to find forgiveness and achieve reconciliation. In their baptism, members of the Church follow Christ first in their confession of solidarity in sin and then in their participation in the life of the Resurrection. The life and worship of the Church embodies the confrontation and contradiction between the old patterns and structures of estrangement – epitomised in Ephesians by the division between Jew and Gentile – and the new dynamic of Christ's risen and reconciling humanity. Since Christ is not only the head of the Church but the prototype of redeemed humanity (the 'firstfruits,' in the language of 1 Cor. 15:20–23), the baptismal calling of Christian is to participate in working out forgiveness wherever the need for it arises, to encounter the risen life of Christ through immersion in the world's conflicts. Worship should be the expression and the reaffirmation of that calling.

Baptism is therefore the primary sign of the decisiveness and comprehensiveness of God's act of forgiveness in Jesus Christ and of the new identity and calling which baptism initiates. The unrepeatability of baptism rests upon the singularity of what it signifies, and the unconditionality of what it effects. We can now identify any further liturgical mediations of forgiveness in the Church as 'recall to baptism' and regard with suspicion any tendency to make penitential rites independent of baptism (or the Eucharist). The danger of isolating confession and absolution as a liturgical act is the loss of its *evangelical* character. The prevenience and decisiveness of divine grace may be eclipsed by the sense that the offer of forgiveness depends on human acts of repentance and contrition. We have then regressed to the incompleteness of John's baptism rather than 'the fullness of Christ.'

We have begun to establish a 'hierarchy of mediation' of forgiveness with baptism at the apex. The justification for this is that – as Luther realised with unequalled clarity – baptism is the sacramental απαξ ('once for all') which embodies and safeguards the απαξ (Heb. 9:26, cf. 10:10) of Christ's self-offering. The assumption that it needs to be supplemented by other rites of penitence carries the perpetual danger of making baptism an episode in the spiritual autobiography of individual Christians rather than the over-arching sign of the redemptive accomplishment of Jesus Christ and of the constitution of a community living by grace and forgiveness. It has always been tempting to conclude 'that as Christ did institute Baptism to give life, and the Eucharist to nourish life, so Penitency might be thought a sacrament ordained to recover life, and Confession a part of the sacrament'[30] but the ambiguity of penance – as Luther again discovered – is its tendency to become a cuckoo in the ecclesiastical nest, displacing the two chief rites of forgiveness to which it should remain ancillary. The growth of the Western system of private penance, displacing the mediation of the Eucharist, threatened to 'immobilize'[31] the gracious freedom of God in Christ and subject the gospel to moralistic redefinition and manipulation.[32] Unfortunately, what the Reformation unmade, it only partly re-made: its semi-restoration of the Eucharist left a penitential vacuum.

It remains the case that Christians need systematic help in appropriating Christ's forgiveness, and that sacramental confession, spiritual direction and self-examination have great value in encouraging disciplined exposure to the liminality of repentance. It is particularly welcome that contemporary liturgies of confession and reconciliation explicitly address the corporate as well as the individual dimension of sin, and that in the Roman Catholic Church the ethos of penitential rites is now evangelical and pastoral rather than juridical. However, such means of grace can never be other than recapitulations of baptismal incorporation and aids to Eucharistic participation. They lack the dramatic representation of the wholeness of forgiveness in Christ which the two great sacraments of the Gospel convey by their socially embodied character and their access to the mystery of Christ's death and resurrection.

What then of the 'power of the keys' (which is a legitimate inference from John 20:23)?[33] At the heart of the event of forgiveness is a crucial ambivalence, which may be called 'penitential liminality.' The persons being forgiven recognise their sins as simultaneously theirs and not theirs: *theirs* in the past, as a matter of sober truth and sincere confession, but *not theirs* in the future, by their intention to accept the forgiveness of God in Christ and to 'lead a new life, following the commandments of God and walking from henceforth in his holy ways.'[34] This is true repentance, and

---

[30] Hooker, *Ecclesiastical Polity*, VI.iv.3. (Hooker did not share this opinion.)

[31] I owe this expression to Rowan Williams, 'The Nature of a Sacrament', in: John Greenhalgh & Elizabeth Russell (eds.), *Signs of Faith, Hope and Love: The Christian Sacraments Today* (London 1987), 32, rpt. in: *On Christian Theology* (Oxford 2000), Ch. 13.

[32] The theologically disastrous effects of reasoning back from individual penitence to the interpretation of atonement and forgiveness are manifest in Richard Swinburne, *Responsibility and Atonement* (Oxford 1989).

[33] J.A. Emerton, 'Binding and Loosing – Forgiving and Retaining,' *Journal of Theological Studies* 13 (1962), 325–331, argues that John 20:23 and Mat. 16:19/Mat. 18:18 are variant forms of a saying derived from Isa. 22:22, 'opening' in the original being applied to permissive rulings ('loosing') in the Matthean tradition, and to the declaration of forgiveness ('remission' or 'release') in the Johannine.

[34] Church of England, *Book of Common Prayer*, 1661/2, Order for Holy Communion, Invitation to Confession.

when liturgically expressed in confession, it leads to the declaration of absolution: the forgiven sinner is released from past complicity in sin and the 'binding' consequences which that entailed. The ambivalent orientation to God, to other people, and to the past and future, is resolved by the authoritative declaration, and typically a new sense of freedom and joy is experienced. Yet 'the power of the keys' ought not to be restricted to sacramental absolution. It surely includes the communal and mutual forms of confession advocated by Dietrich Bonhoeffer,[35] general confession and absolution, preaching (which the magisterial Reformers regarded as the pre-eminent use of 'the keys'), counselling, friendship and all the means by which Christians share Christ's 'releasing' work.

It may be observed summarily that the major conflicts over post-baptismal sin and penitential discipline in the early Church[36] sprang from two errors: first, failure to grasp the implications of the decisive, eschatological orientation of baptism, and second, failure to distinguish rites of penitence from rites of excommunication and restoration.[37] Churches may need in extreme circumstances to exclude those whose impenitence threatens the integrity of the community, but such acts of excommunication should be a last resort, and not simply a defensive reaction to scandal or discomfort. Expulsion, and readmission, are boundary activities, and therefore quite distinct from the bounded penitential life of the Church. Baptism remains an indelible and irrevocable sign both of the forgiveness offered by God and the forgiven life to which the baptised are called. It is accompanied by prayer for the impenitent to be reconciled, that 'all things belonging to the Spirit may live and grow in them'[38] as members of Christ's body.

5. Eucharist: Energy and Embodiment

There are clearly major differences between the roles of baptism and the Eucharist in structuring the life of the Church. Baptism is a rite of incorporation, administered only once to each individual. The Eucharist, in contrast, is a regular rite of participation, in which all fully initiated members may join. There is another contrast between the two rites, namely their respective historical origins in relation to the common life of Jesus and his disciples. Baptism developed from the ministry of John the Baptist, and was no part of Jesus' own practice – except, paradoxically, in totally defining it. The

---

[35] Dietrich Bonhoeffer, *Life Together* (ET London 1954), Ch. 5.

[36] The history is summarised conveniently in William Telfer, *The Forgiveness of Sins* (London 1959), Chs. 1–6.

[37] Robert W. Jenson, *Visible Words: The Interpretation and Practice of Christian Sacraments* (Philadelphia 1978), 183–184.

[38] Church of England, *The Alternative Service Book 1980*, The Baptism of Children, §59, 249.

Eucharist was instituted at a 'defining moment' in his relations with his inner circle of associates, and was deliberately intended to be an expressive ritual of solidarity with him. Thus he bequeathed to his followers a rite which more than any other single practice gave access for the community he founded to the 'core meaning' of what he had done. My main contention here is that the celebration of the Eucharist is the primary condition of the continuing embodiment of the Church as a sign of the forgiveness of Jesus Christ, because it structures the embodied Trinitarian social dynamic derived from Jesus' ministry, death and resurrection.

I propose to explore this by taking seriously the implications of eating and drinking as means of 'participating in the body and blood of Christ' (1 Cor. 10:16). It is a commonplace of social anthropology that ritual creates symbolic correspondences between the human body and the social body: in this case we have to add a third term, the body of Jesus Christ, which co-defines the other two. The physical body is 'mapped' on to the social body, and vice versa. A body may be defined as a bounded system of interactions and energy transformations, and its functioning is critically affected by events which occur across its boundaries. The physical body is sustained in its interaction with its environment through respiration (analogous to the Church's participation in the Holy Spirit, the Life-Giver), nutrition (which I shall argue is analogous to the Eucharist), work (the service of God) and excretion (the necessary process of expelling sin from its life).

The energy exchanges and transformations which constitute the body can be summed up in the cycle of *nutrition* and *work*. In eating and drinking, ingestion provides the supply of energy for the body's physiological processes, to offset the entropic tendencies of the system. Conversely, metabolism effects the conversion of that energy in order for the body to act negentropically in relation to its environment, producing both increase in ordering of the environment and loss of energy to the body. The analogy is obvious, as it was to the author of St John's Gospel. 'Do not labour for the food which perishes (*entropic*), but for the food that endures to eternal life (*unbounded negentropic effects in the abundance of the eschatological Kingdom*) which the Son of man will give to you' (John 6:27). We understand the 'Eucharistic energy cycle' too restrictively, because we are apt to view it exclusively from the standpoint of consumption, but we ought to ask whence the energy comes and whither it goes (cf. John 3:8). Its origin is the *work* of Jesus, namely that costly reordering which he undertook in obedience to the Father's purpose and by the Father's energy, leading him to the disorder and entropy of the cross ('My food is to do the will of him who sent me, and to accomplish his work,' John 4:34). Its destination is the service of God and the world which is expressed in the post-communion prayers: 'We thank you for feeding us with the body and blood of your Son

Jesus Christ ... Send us out in the power of your Spirit to live and work to your praise and glory.'[39] Central to this service is the energy, or labour, of forgiveness and reconciliation, which in a disordered world cannot be effective except through sacrifice.

The metaphor of the body compels us once again to trace the continuity between the liturgical gathering and the dispersed life of the Church. The Eucharistic configuring and transformation of energy underscores the physical embodiment of the Christian community and its consequent interaction with other human bodies, both individual and social. Just as members of the Church share the common human need for food and drink, they belong to a complex network of relationships characterised both by creative and destructive flows of energy. The energy of forgiveness is the energy of the Creator God seeking to fulfil his good and wise ordering of creation, and that energy must be expended in work in opposition to the forces of estrangement and destruction. The Church gathers for worship in order to experience the concentration of the energy of divine goodness – blessing, forgiving, healing – but also to be receptive to the continuing outpouring of that energy in the life of the world. But the direction of energy requires intentional embodied action, which is the principle of the Incarnation, and part of the liturgical mediation of forgiveness is the preparation of worshippers to enter into interactions and exchanges within which the divine goodness and mercy is active to forgive, restore and perfect human relationships.

We must next move from the physical to the social body, for eating and drinking are social and ritual as well as physical activities. The Eucharist itself is based on a symbolic meal which commemorated the making of a covenant and maintained the identity of a people by reference to a once-for-all redemptive act of God – the Jewish Passover. Jesus no doubt intended these connotations to be preserved and extended in the remembering of his own action, but conveyed to the elements of bread and wine a new signification of his self-giving to death, his blood 'poured out for many for the forgiveness of sins' (Mat. 26:28). At the heart of the Eucharistic Prayer, the narrative of institution, worshippers are relocated in the upper room, identified with the unfaithful disciples on the night of betrayal, but are also symbolically linked with the memory of Jesus' other meals – feasting with tax-collectors and sinners; feeding the multitudes; turning water into wine at a wedding; eating and drinking in renewed communion with the disciples after his resurrection. This context is amplified by the anticipation of feasting in the Messianic kingdom where forgiveness will be consummated: we 'proclaim the Lord's death until he comes' (1 Cor. 11:26). The baptismal

---

[39] Church of England, *Alternative Service Book 1980*, The Order for Holy Communion Rite A, §53, 145.

liminality is revisited: the renewed confrontation with the ambivalence of judgement and forgiveness, guilt and hope, occurs in the presence of Jesus – but now in the form of 'Eucharistic liminality.' The response of repentance and trust, in grateful and humble reception of the symbols of Jesus' self-giving, brings renewed participation in his reconstituting work: 'Love is that liquor sweet and most divine/Which my God feels as blood; but I, as wine.'[40]

The Eucharistic action is both personal and corporate: as a shared experience of celebration and participation in Christ, it expresses and deepens reconciliation between members of the body, symbolised in the giving of the Peace. The assimilation of worshippers to Christ's body is also their assimilation to one another, the permeation of whatever social, cultural or other boundaries may exist between them: 'It is the mystery of yourselves that you receive.'[41] Thus Gerd Theissen has argued that Paul's instructions to the Corinthian church were intended to be a correction of socially-disruptive eating practices in the Lord's Supper which nullified 'the symbolic accomplishment of social integration'[42] and brought divine judgement on those who ate and drank without 'discerning the body' (11:29). The 'recon-stitutive dynamic' embodied in Jesus' self-giving to death and his raising by God in the power of the Spirit is brought into critical confrontation with the divisions produced by social structures and reproduced in human action to bring worshippers to a common identity as forgiven and a common calling as forgiving.

The Eucharist therefore creates a symbolic social space in which the reordering work of Christ can be enacted as a sign of the vocation of the Church to enact forgiveness in the social space beyond its boundaries. It reflects the Church's threefold solidarity with the world, in the blessings of creation, in the travails of sin and in the hope of redemption, and therefore generates diverse forms of embodied response in the life of societies. Sometimes this will be affirmative, working with the grain of existing institutions and practices in order to pursue shared goals – as in the broad support of South African churches for the work of the Truth and Reconcilia-tion Commission[43] or the commendation of the peace process by the leadership of most of the Northern Irish churches. Sometimes it will be explicitly nonconformist in seeking to subvert destructive patterns of human interaction and to give concrete expression to the God-given peace and unity of which the Eucharist is a sign, foretaste and pledge. William Cavanaugh shows graphically how specific forms of resistance to oppressive practices

---

[40] George Herbert, 'The Agonie.'

[41] St Augustine of Hippo, *Sermon* 272.

[42] Gerd Theissen, 'Social Integration and Sacramental Activity: An Analysis of 1 Cor. 11:17–34', in: *The Social Setting of Pauline Christianity* (Edinburgh 1982), 167.

[43] Now chronicled by Desmond Tutu, *No Future Without Forgiveness* (London 1999).

in Pinochet's Chile can only be understood as attempts to 'make visible the body of Christ' in a situation where the order and discipline of the gospel were in direct competition with the order and discipline of the coercive State for sovereignty over human bodies, both physical and social.[44]

Most frequently the Church lives in an ambiguous relation to its social environment: both conforming and resisting; at different points endorsing and challenging the practices of unforgiving structures and institutions. When I was a prison chaplain, this was symbolised for me by the windows of the prison chapel, in which the metal bars were wrought into the recurrent pattern of the cross. Was the gospel of Jesus Christ being co-opted into the system of control, or did it stand in judgement and promise over against that system, as the Eucharist was celebrated at a table open to everyone in the midst of a culture of recrimination and coercion? Whatever the particular context, the Eucharist perpetually reminds the Church that it has no option but to seek to embody in human relationships and structures the gospel by which it lives. The stark truth is: no embodiment, no forgiveness.

6. Seeking Signs

'Were we led all that way for/Birth or Death?'[45] Some readers may have found the journey into the labyrinth of mediation wearisome and perplexing. However, it was necessary to proceed through the outer courts of the Temple (so to speak) in order to reach the Holy of Holies. Failure to complete the journey not only hinders access to the mysterious gift of forgiveness but leaves us unable to perceive and understand distortions in the process of mediation. We live in a world mis-structured by the vicious processes of recrimination, scapegoating and stigmatisation from which Jesus came to deliver the human race, and to the extent that we fail to understand the scope and dynamics of forgiveness, we remain bound. Churches as institutions and communities embedded in particular contexts share in that mis-structuring, with the result that the mediation of forgiveness frequently goes wrong – sometimes appallingly wrong – as those who claim to *possess* the freedom for which Christ has set us free (Gal. 5:2) not only celebrate their un-freedom but impose intolerable burdens and indignities upon others.

The complexity of mediation means that the promise of divine forgiveness is always in danger of being 'impaled and bent/Into an ideological instrument.'[46] Intertwined as they are with human dependence and

---

[44] Cavanaugh, *Torture and Eucharist*, Ch. 6, 'Performing the Body of Christ.'

[45] T.S. Eliot, 'Journey of the Magi', *The Complete Poems and Plays of T.S. Eliot* (London 1969), 104.

[46] Edwin Muir, 'The Incarnate One,' *Collected Poems* (London 1963), 228.

vulnerability, the 'means of grace' by which forgiveness is communicated are always ambiguous and potentially oppressive. They are all too easily co-opted into anxious, restrictive or exploitative human projects, thereby becoming alienated from the life-giving dynamic which they represent. Nevertheless, at the heart of the 'semiotic cathedral'[47] stand two signs which are peculiarly resistant to manipulation and assimilation because they are signs of *bodily dispossession*: the sign of the cross (1 Cor. 1:22–25), the presence of God's forgiveness at the heart of human violence and estrangement, and the 'sign of Jonah' (Mat. 12:38–40), which is the assurance of God's unbounded desire and capacity to re-make the world. These two signs continue – despite all – to interrogate, liberate and re-form the Church, and offer to compromised human beings the possibility of reconciling the demands of truthfulness and mercy. To complete St Paul's phrase with which we began, 'we have this treasure in earthen vessels, *in order to show that the transcendent power belongs not to us but to God.*'[48] Worship and forgiveness both embody visitations of that transcendent power, but we may sometimes wonder whether the alienating and destructive dynamics of our world are such that we shall never find our way through the labyrinth. Yet the last word must rest with the leading authority on the subject: 'It is not those who are well who have need of a physician, but those who are sick.'

---

[47] Gerd Theissen, *A Theory of Primitive Christian Religion* (London 1999), 17–18.

[48] Hooker, while describing the reconciliation of penitents as conveying 'treasure,' is at pains to magnify 'God the giver of grace by the outward ministry of man, so far as he authorizeth man to apply the sacraments of grace in the soul, which he alone worketh, without either instrument or co-agent': *Ecclesiastical Polity*, VI.vi.11.

4. Shame, Sin and Guilt

Fraser Watts

1. Introduction

This chapter is a contribution to an ongoing research project that might be called 'theology through the emotions.' Different human emotions each raise interesting and important theological issues. For example, anger and jealousy raise the interesting issue, which exercised Lactantius, of why anger seems to be acceptable for God, but not for us. Hope, which is in some sense an emotion, carries us deep into eschatology. Depression raises issues about the presence and absence of God. Indeed, there are perhaps few theological issues that could not be approached from the perspective of one emotion or another. However, the emotions of shame and guilt that are the focus of this chapter raise particularly interesting theological issues concerning sin and salvation.

It needs to be made clear at the outset that approaching theology through the emotions does not amount to reducing it to a matter of the emotions. Most theology is concerned in some way or other with the relationship between God and humanity, and can be approached from one or other starting point. Some people think it makes a huge difference to theology where you start from, but I suggest that involves a confusion between the place from which you begin the journey of exploration, and what you eventually give primacy of place to. There is no reason at all why they should be the same. To begin an exploration of sin from the human emotions of shame and guilt in no way commits us to giving humanity pride of place in the theology that emerges. Emotions simply provide one possible vantage point from which to undertake the theological task of elucidating the relationship between God and humanity.

2. Current Theological Interest in Shame

There are good reasons at the present time for re-evaluating the respective
contributions of shame and guilt to the theology of sin. Pressures to do so
come from two rather different quarters, New Testament studies, and pastoral
theology. Scholars in both areas appear to be suggesting that the theology of
sin has been too much concerned with guilt and not sufficiently with shame.

New Testament scholars, drawing on recent cultural anthropology that has
suggested that the Mediterranean world is a culture concerned with honour
and shame, have brought this perspective to the reading of the New Testament. There is a case that Christians through the centuries have read the
New Testament too much through the eyes of subsequent cultures more
concerned with guilt. We may have read St Paul too much through the lens
of what Stendahl controversially called the 'introspective conscience of the
West.'[1] If we are now once again living in a shame culture rather than a
guilt culture, we may have the opportunity to return to reading Paul from a
perspective rather like that of the shame culture in which his Epistles
originated.

From a very different quarter of theology, pastoral theologians have
noted that, though concern with guilt in our culture is fading, we live in a
narcissistic culture in which shame is a predominant and troubling emotion.
The problem, from this perspective, is that the Christian theology of sin and
salvation has been largely addressed to problems of guilt and to release
from it, but has had little to say about shame and its healing. Stephen
Pattison has provided a very helpful critical overview of what recent
pastoral theology has had to say about shame.[2] The majority of recent
religious books on shame focus mainly on shame as a pastoral problem.[3]
However, the theological implications of a focus on shame are sometimes
very much to the fore. For example, Donald Capps has argued that we need
a theology of sin that addresses itself to our culture of shame rather than to
guilt.[4] Similarly, Robert Albers has proposed a theology of the cross as
'God's shame-bearing symbol.'[5]

If you put these two perspectives together, we seem to have something
rather exciting in prospect. New Testament theologians are suggesting that
the gospel originated in a shame-based culture. Contemporary pastoral
theologians are saying that we have returned to a shame-based culture.
There thus seems to be a possibility of the New Testament speaking in a

---

[1] Krister Stendahl, *Paul among Jews and Gentiles and Other Essays* (Philadelphia 1976).

[2] Stephen Pattison, *Shame: Theory, Therapy, Theology* (Cambridge 2001).

[3] E.g., John Patton, *Is Human Forgiveness Possible?* (Nashville 1985); Lewis Smedes,
Shame and Grace (London 1993); James Fowler, *Faithful Change* (Nashville 1996).

[4] Donald Capps, *The Depleted Self: Sin in a Narcissistic Age* (Minneapolis 1993).

[5] Robert H. Albers, *Shame: A Faith Perspective* (New York 1995).

fresh way, from one shame culture to another, leaping across the centuries of guilt-oriented Christian theology that have intervened.

Though there is something attractive about that grand vision, you will not be surprised to hear me say that things are not so simple. There are various problems with it. One is that the concept of shame is a slippery one and the distinction between shame and guilt is made in a variety of different ways. In particular, when scholars say that the New Testament came out of a shame culture they are drawing on an older anthropological literature about shame than the one on which pastoral theologians are relying when they say that we are currently living in a shame culture. The two sets of theologians may mean something completely different by shame. It is a gross over-simplification of the psycho-history of the Christian centuries to suggest that through most of those centuries human experience and Christian theology have been almost exclusively concerned with guilt and not with shame. The historical story is more subtle and complex.

3. The Concept of Shame

Those who write about guilt and shame are divided on the question of whether or not the distinction between the two is important at all. Some, such as Joseph Amato, think it is not.[6] However, there has been a growing conviction, which I share, that this is an important distinction. That is not to say that the words are always used in same ways. The point is that there is a significant conceptual distinction, for which the words 'guilt' and 'shame' are rough markers. I am certainly not espousing a kind of essentialism about emotions, that each of these two emotions has taken exactly the same form in different times and different cultures. There may be some primitive emotions, such as disgust, that are relatively invariant across cultures, though even that is debatable. When you come to complex emotions such as guilt and shame, it is clear that they take different forms in different cultures.

There are two main approaches to the distinction between guilt and shame, in social anthropology and psychology. The key source of the anthropological distinction is Ruth Benedict's book, now fifty years old, *The Chrysanthemum and the Sword*.[7] Here the distinction focuses essentially on public versus private transgressions. We may feel guilt about transgressions that only we know about, but those transgressions that are committed in the public gaze lead to shame. It seems that we are vulnerable

---

[6] Joseph Amato, *Guilt and Gratitude: A Study of the Origins of Contemporary Conscience* (London 1982).

[7] Ruth Benedict, *The Chrysanthemum and the Sword: Patterns of Japanese Culture* (London 1946).

to being 'shamed' by others in a way that does not apply to guilt. Psychologists have more recently made the distinction in a different way, and the key source here is Helen Block Lewis' *Shame and Guilt in Neurosis*.[8] The idea is that we feel guilt about particular behaviours that we regard as transgressions, but we feel shame about our very selves. Shame is thus a much more pervasive, less differentiated emotion than guilt.

The fact that there are two different ways of distinguishing between shame and guilt in the literature has caused enormous confusion. Many authors simply set out one distinction without apparently being aware that another very different approach is available. That is true for example of Gabrielle Taylor's otherwise impressive philosophical book, *Pride, Shame and Guilt*.[9] Patricia Greenspan gives an account of the distinction between shame and guilt that is similarly blinkered. Particularly remarkable is her comment that 'the central point that distinguishes guilt from shame ... seems to be self-alienation. Shame does not seem to divide the self against itself in the way that guilt does.'[10] That seems to me the reverse of the truth, and it is very strange to make such a claim that flies in the face of much of the current literature, without even pausing to note that it does so.

Which is the right way to make the distinction? It is clear that recent Anglo-American empirical research favours Block's distinction of behaviour versus self rather than the older anthropological distinction of public versus private transgressions. June Price Tangey, in a recent review, says flatly that 'empirical research has consistently failed to support the public/private distinction.'[11] She bases that conclusion largely on the results of systematic empirical data about how the terms are used. However, that is not the last word. There can be a tendency for such empirical data to confirm what the researchers expect to find. Also different results might have been obtained in research carried out in the Mediterranean rather than America.

I am content to agree that there is confirmation of the idea that shame relates to the self whereas guilt relates to behaviour. So, Bonhoeffer was essentially on the right lines when he remarked that 'man feels remorse when he has been at fault; and he feels shame because he lacks something.'[12] (I am assuming that remorse is a synonym for guilt.) On the other hand, I prefer to be agnostic, rather than as dismissive as Tangey, about the idea that guilt is private whereas shame is public. It is important to retain an

---

[8] Helen Block Lewis, *Shame and Guilt in Neurosis* (New York 1971).

[9] Gabrielle Taylor, *Pride, Shame, and Guilt: Emotions of Self-Assessment* (Oxford 1985).

[10] Patricia Greenspan, *Practical Guilt: Moral Dilemmas, Emotions, and Social Norms* (Oxford 1995), 134.

[11] June Price Tangey, 'The Self-Conscious Emotions: Shame, Guilt, Embarrassment, and Pride,' in: Tim Dalgleish & Mick Power (eds.), *Handbook of Cognition and Emotion* (Chichester 1999).

[12] Dietrich Bonhoeffer, *Ethics* (London 1955), 145.

adequate appreciation of the social contextuality of all emotions, including guilt and shame, even if the old ideas about shame cultures and guilt cultures, stemming from Benedict, did not get it quite right. Let me just note that the most promising social theorising about shame in the current literature is that of Thomas Scheff, who sees shame as signalling a state of alienation in relationships.[13]

This issue clearly bears on the idea of bringing New Testament scholars and pastoral theologians into conversation with one another on this topic. Pastoral theologians are alerting us to the claimed tendency in contemporary society for people to feel a pervasive shame about themselves rather than guilt about specific actions. On the other hand, New Testament scholars are alerting us to the fact that many of the scriptural books concerned came out of a culture in which people felt shame when their transgressions became public and they were thus dishonoured. The two literatures are using shame in different, though not incompatible, senses.

In addition to this, much of the New Testament work that purports to make use of the anthropological work on Mediterranean culture as one of honour and shame does so in rather loose way. This emerges, for example, from the volume of the Journal *Semeia* devoted to *Honour and Shame in the World of the Bible*. After a number of Biblical contributions making use of the honour and shame idea, there are two responses by anthropologists, which are as dismissive of the anthropological quality of the work as politeness permitted. John Chance comments on the dated and limited quality of the anthropology on which the Biblical scholars draw. Gideon Kressel goes into more detail about specific papers and is particularly critical of the contribution to the volume of most potential relevance to this paper on sin, i.e., Neyrey's paper on the shame of the cross in John's Passion narrative. Kressel comments that 'the anthropological model of honour and shame selected here as a template for reading John 18–19 is not appropriate to the assignment.'[14] That confirms my own judgement that the links being made here between anthropology and Biblical studies use the anthropological model in a way that is rather impoverished, and which does not really shed any fresh light on the Passion narratives. One of the key problems with most Biblical applications of the honour and shame culture is that gender differences are so central to the honour and shame paradigm, but not to the New Testament.

---

[13] See, e.g., Thomas J. Scheff, *Microsociology: Discourse, Emotions, and Social Structure* (Chicago 1990).

[14] Gideon M. Kressel, 'An Anthropologist's Response to the Use of Social Science Models in Biblical Studies,' *Semeia* 68 (1996), 159.

4. The History of Shame and Guilt

Some historical cautions also need to be added about the idea that Christian culture has for long been preoccupied with guilt rather than shame. We do indeed seem to have moved recently from an age very preoccupied with guilt to one less so preoccupied, as Bonhoeffer, among others noted in the middle of the twentieth century. However, it is easy to over-generalise this into a sweeping historical meta-narrative. Not everyone who has been concerned with the history of shame and guilt has even bothered to make the distinction. Jean Delumeau, in his vast cultural history of sin, simply remarks that 'No civilisation has ever attached as much importance to guilt and shame as did the Western world from the thirteenth to the eighteenth centuries.'[15]

Ruth Benedict told a more specific story, suggesting that 'the early Puritans who settled in the United States tried to base their entire morality on guilt ... But shame is an increasingly heavy burden ... and guilt is less extremely felt than in earlier generations.'[16] However, John Demos of Yale has persuasively argued that this is a misreading of New England Puritanism, which was, in fact, a culture of shame rather than guilt.[17] He documents his claim that the issues they were concerned with were narcissistic ones. In conflict situations they instinctively sought to shame their opponents and defend themselves against shame.

By the nineteenth century, however, things were different. Drawing on the work of Anthony Rotundo, Demos suggests that it was then that guilt replaced shame as the dominant motif. His claim that guilt becomes prominent in the nineteenth century is persuasive, but it would probably be a mistake to suggest that shame was marginalised. Rather, it seems that the character of shame was changing, and becoming focused more on private feelings and less on public roles.[18] It was probably in the nineteenth century that people began to experience the kind of personal shame with which we are now familiar.

Caution also perhaps needs to be entered about the claim, made for example by Christopher Lasch, that we live now in a narcissistic culture in which shame predominates.[19] Commenting on Lasch's position, Charles Elliott remarks sharply, but justifiably, that 'he presents no serious evidence

---

[15] Jean Delumeau, *Sin and Fear: The Emergence of a Western Guilt Culture: 13th–18th Centuries* (New York 1990), 3.

[16] Benedict, *Chrysanthemum*, 223–224.

[17] John Demos, 'Shame and Guilt in Early New England,' in: Carol Z. Stearns & Peter N. Stearns (eds.), *Emotion and Social Change: Toward a New Psychohistory* (New York 1988).

[18] Norbert Elias, *The Civilising Process* (Oxford 1994); Richard Sennet, *The Fall of Public Man* (London 1986).

[19] Christopher Lasch, *The Culture of Narcissism: American Life in an Age of Diminishing Expectations* (New York 1978).

for the claims that (a) this condition is 'new'; (b) that it is common; or (c) that it is so common that it can be taken, not simply as metaphor, but as constitutive of a social condition.'[20] It is indeed easy to make exaggerated claims here, and I am wary of the idea that we live in a narcissistic culture or a shame culture.

Though I am forced to say this without evidence, I think it is probably correct that we live in an age when narcissistic personality problems are rather common, and that shame-proneness is prominent among them. Shame may not be as ubiquitous as some commentators such as Lasch claim, but I suggest that, while the tides of guilt are receding in our society, the tides of shame are conspicuously not doing so. There is probably sufficient truth in the claim that contemporary experience is more of shame than of guilt for it to be worthwhile to pursue a theology of sin that speaks to the experience of shame rather than of guilt. That is what I will attempt in this chapter.

5. The Fall

One text that has played a key role in the theology of sin is, of course, Genesis 3, that we know as the story of the Fall. Though it is a story that, in our post-Augustinian world, we have come to read through the lens of a theology of sin, it is worth noting that neither the Jewish community nor the Eastern Orthodox Christians read it in that way. In fact the text has next to nothing to say about sin, as James Barr noted in his admirable little book, *The Garden of Eden and the Hope of Immortality*.[21] Attention has tended to focus on the sinful, disobedient act of eating the apple, a reading that feeds into a guilt-oriented theology of sin. However, heard with fresh ears, the story of Adam and Eve is a story of shame rather than of guilt, as Fowler has pointed out.[22] Indeed, guilt is not mentioned, nor even implied. Adam and Eve did not apparently feel guilt or remorse about their disobedient act. Rather, they felt shame about their nakedness; after eating the apple, they wished to hide. To try to avoid being seen by eyes that will leave you feeling exposed is a prototypical shame theme. Because of their sense of shame, they resorted to the their fig leaves, but found that God is a being from whom you cannot hide in such a way.

What then precipitated the sense of shame? You can read the story as saying that it was the act of disobedience, but equally well you can read the precipitant of shame as lying in the nature of the apple that was eaten. It came from the tree of knowledge of good and evil, and represented a new

---

[20] Charles Elliott, *Memory and Salvation* (London 1995).

[21] James Barr, *The Garden of Eden and the Hope of Immortality* (London 1992).

[22] Fowler, *Faithful Change*.

kind of consciousness. In the story, Adam and Eve come to have a new and more differentiated consciousness, enabling them to discriminate between good and evil more clearly, to have a new sense of the difference between themselves and God, and a new sense of 'self' that led to their sensing how naked and inadequate they could appear on the eyes of another. The new consciousness that came from eating the fruit of this tree, though in some ways representing an advance into a more discriminating consciousness, and in that sense being a 'fall upwards,' also brought a new sense of separateness from God and a vulnerability to narcissistic injury. I am indicating this reading only briefly. There is a fuller treatment of the role of shame in the development of religious consciousness, relating it to Genesis 3, in works by James Hans and Mario Jacoby.[23]

Incidentally, I would want to suggest that Genesis 3 is, in part, talking in its mythological way about evolutionary developments in consciousness that must have actually occurred over long periods of time. Though, of course, I would not want to take the story literally, I do not think that need lead to seeing it as making only static, ontological points about human nature. The story is about change, and its core meaning is lost if the theme of change is neglected, however gradual the change may have been.

6. Shame and Sin

But how well does this reading of Genesis 3, emphasising the shame of Adam and Eve, sit with a theology of sin? Sin, like all worthwhile theological concepts is multi-layered. Seward Hiltner, in a helpful taxonomy, suggested that there are three main strands of thinking about sin, each based around a core metaphor. The first is a proud and angry rebellion against God. Secondly, there is sin as alienation, estrangement or isolation from God. Thirdly, there is sin as error or missing the mark.[24]

The traditional Augustinian reading of Genesis 3 links most closely with sin as rebellion. It focuses on the act of disobedience to which guilt is the appropriate response. However, it seems to me that the sense of shame links most closely with sin as estrangement. It is of the essence of shame that it builds on a sense of separateness from another being, and in this way depends on the development of a sense of self. Without a developed sense of self, you cannot feel estranged. (The idea of sin as missing the mark is probably

---

[23] James S. Hans, *The Origins of the Gods* (New York 1991); Mario Jacoby, *Shame and the Origins of Self-Esteem: A Jungian Approach* (London 1991).

[24] Seward Hiltner, 'Christian Understanding of Sin in the Light of Medicine and Psychiatry,' *Medical Arts and Sciences* (1966), 33–49.

more neutral in relation to the distinction between shame and guilt; a sense of having made a moral error can lead to either shame or guilt.)

The distinction between shame and guilt also relates to the distinction between sin as state and as act. Remember that guilt is a response to discrete actions, particular things that you should not have done, whereas shame relates more generally to your very self, to what you are. With this in mind, I would suggest that a guilt-oriented theology of sin tends to be limited to particular sinful acts, and to have difficulty in broadening out to give an adequate account of the estrangement of humanity from God. In contrast, that sense of estrangement would be centre-stage in a shame-oriented theology of sin. The concept of 'original sin,' is, of course, largely concerned with sin as state rather than sin as act. In trying to preach the Christian faith, I find that there is a resistance to the concept of original sin, which is understandable but nevertheless misplaced.

It is understandable that people who have a strong sense of shame find an emphasis on original sin as 'rubbing salt in the wounds' of their sense of inadequacy. Christian teaching on sin is inevitably heard differently now from how it was heard before the nineteenth century when, as I have noted, guilt became more prominent and shame became more personalised. It raises interesting issues about the development of Christian doctrine that, as society and human consciousness evolve, the same teaching comes to have a very different resonance. In the climate of the last 150 years, much Christian teaching about sin is now heard as seeking to shame people, in a way that it used not to. Christians have not adequately appreciated the extent to which they have, often inadvertently, contributed to the present sense of shame in our society.[25]

Nevertheless, considered rationally, resistance to the idea of original sin seems to arise from a conflation of two different lines of thought about sin. Ideas of blame-worthiness that properly belong only to sin as *act* are extrapolated and mis-applied to the *state* of sin. It is crucial to the idea of original sin that we are caught up in sin, but it is not specifically our personal fault in the way that specific sinful acts are our fault. Indeed, heard in this way, the doctrine of original sin may in fact liberate people from a sense of personal blame. Talk about sin tends now to be heard as intended to give us a bad conscience, though I suggest that is to mishear the theology of sin through 'the introspective conscience of the West,' just as Genesis 3 has so often been misheard in the West. A theology of sin that focused on shame rather than guilt might help to lead us away from the link between sin and blame. A shame-oriented theology of sin would focus on *un*worthiness rather than on *blame*-worthiness.

---

[25] Pattison, *Shame.*

7. Sin and Inflation

But just what is *wrong* with sin, in this shame-oriented theology? In a guilt-oriented theology, sin is transgression, and it is clear what is wrong with that. Even accepting that shame may arise from the sense of separateness from God, what exactly is wrong with such separateness? My suggestion is that, in a shame-oriented theology, the counterpart of wrong action is the adoption of a false self-image. Nathanson has suggested that shame arises 'when one member of a dyad assumes a self-image unjustified by what can be validly accepted within the relationship as previously agreed.'[26] It is the function of shame to modulate the relationship when such a false image arises. Shame, I would suggest, arises in our relationship with God when we adopt a false self-image that God in his truthfulness cannot accept. It is especially serious when we adopt a self-image that falsifies our relation to God and which therefore does violence to our relationship with him.

Such false self-images are usually inflationary. It was an inflationary act for Adam to eat the apple which the serpent had said would make them like God, though the text is unclear about how much that hope was the motive for eating the apple, or whether it was eaten for the more innocent reasons that it was 'good for food, a delight to the eyes, and ... was to be desired to make one wise.' However, if the fruit was eaten because it could, as the serpent promised, make them 'like God, knowing good and evil,' it arose out of a false self-image and an inflated pretension.

Adopting an inflated self-image is, of course, close to the sin of pride, which has often been seen as the core sin. The interesting thing about pride in this context is that it is less a matter of behaviour than any other sin, and more a matter of self image and attitude. Pride would, if anything, have an even more central place in a shame-oriented theology of sin than a guilt-oriented one. Hiltner sees pride as being linked to sin as rebellion rather than sin as estrangement, but that does not convince me. Shame arises from a confusion about relationships, about proudly wanting to be at one with the other, but painfully recognising that you are not at one with them because you have fallen short.

There is an essential ambivalence here, which Bonhoeffer brings out well in his remarks about shame in the *Ethics*. He sees that shame 'implies both a positive and a negative attitude to man's disunion.'[27] In disunion from another, you can have a positive experience of fellowship, realising the importance of union with another through the shame that cuts you off from it. Equally, in fellowship, you can have a strong sense of disunion, realising

---

[26] Donald L. Nathanson, 'A Timetable for Shame,' in: Donald L. Nathanson (ed.), *The Many Faces of Shame* (London 1987), 32.

[27] Bonhoeffer, *Ethics*, 146.

the essential gulf between yourself and the other even in the moment of fellowship. In the core experience of separateness out of which shame arises there is still a sense that union with the other is the right and desirable state of affairs, even while there is also a sense that such union has been rendered impossible by unworthiness.

8. Healthy and Unhealthy Shame

However, shame is a complex and multi-faceted emotion, and to get further we will need to make some distinctions. One key question to ask in approaching a theology of sin from the vantage point of human shame is whether there is any constructive form of shame. It is clear that much shame is intertwined with pathology, often arising from personal abuse, and making fulfilling relationships virtually impossible. However, there may be a constructive shame too, as Schneider has suggested.[28] In the theological literature Hardy and Ford, drawing mainly on Biblical material, have also distinguished between right and wrong forms of shame.[29] Right shame is a proper recognition of being in a false position but it does not cut us off from the promise of joy. Wrong shame in contrast is a 'radical distortion of the ability to respect and praise' (p. 91) in which we can too easily remain trapped.

A useful distinction can be made between, on the one hand, 'being ashamed,' in the sense of feeling disgraced in front of another person and, on the other hand, having a 'sense of shame' in the sense of having an intuition of what it is proper to be private and reticent about. Many languages have different words here, and English having the same word for both causes some confusion. Though feeling disgraced by another seems to be a harmful state, a sense of discretion and privacy can be a virtue. Plato speaks of 'that divine fear which we have called reverence and shame'; the Talmud remarks that 'a sense of shame is lovely in a man; whoever has a sense of shame will not sin so quickly'; and even Nietzsche said that 'the shame with which nature has concealed herself behind riddles and enigmas should be held in higher esteem.'[30] Though in our contemporary society there is too much sense of shame as disgrace, it might be reasonable to say that we lack an adequate sense of privacy and discretion that is also in a different way a sense of shame. There is no virtue in being shameless.

---

[28] Carl D. Schneider, 'The End of Shame,' in: Stephen Kepnes & David Tracy (eds.), *The Challenge of Psychology to Faith* (Edinburgh 1982), 34–39.

[29] Daniel W. Hardy & David F. Ford, *Jubilate: Theology in Praise* (London 1984).

[30] See Carl D. Schneider, 'A Mature Sense of Shame,' in: Nathanson (ed.), *Many Faces*, 199.

A particularly interesting question here is how the sense of shame as privacy is intertwined with a sense of the presence of God. Ana-Maria Rizzuto has made the interesting suggestion that the sense of God arises as children develop the need to keep things private from their parents.[31] In this context it becomes especially helpful for them to have God as a constant companion. He is always present, but not in a way that intrudes on privacy in the way that another human being would. A sense of the presence of God thus arises from, and facilitates, the development of a proper sense of shame as privacy. We can commune with God privately, and this privacy is a crucial and unique aspect of the relationship.

In contrast, to be shamed by another involves a kind of violent assault on the self that is more likely to separate the person from God than to draw them close. However, God does not to seek to disgrace or humiliate us in the way that human beings may do. This is a key prerequisite of the unique kind of trust that people can place in God. He may discipline and correct in his loving way, as the scriptures say at many points, but he does not 'name and shame.' Though he sees all, what he sees is private with each person. Though he sees all, he loves rather than ridicules what he sees. I suggest that it is one of the distinctive features of the religious life that it can foster a sense of shame (as discretion and privacy) without shaming us.

However, the sad fact, as Pattison points out, is that those who are locked in shame all too easily feel that the gaze of God deepens their shame, and they long to escape from it.[32] There are two ways of trying to remould this destructive, theologically inappropriate, but all too real, experience. The one to which I feel inclined is to work harder to correct the idea to which Christian teaching has often contributed, that God shames those on whom he looks. However, an alternative, which Pattison develops in an interesting way, is to emphasise the theme of how God 'hides' his face from us. Both approaches have strong Biblical roots, and both have the potential to be pastorally helpful.

Intertwined with a sense of privacy and discretion is a sense of boundaries. Shame presupposes that we can tell the difference between ourselves and the other. Until consciousness has emerged sufficiently to enable us to make that distinction, we can know no shame. Also, once consciousness has developed sufficiently to permit shame, shame functions to maintain and enforce the boundary between ourselves and the other. We need shame to remind us of our distinctness, and one of the problems with contemporary society is perhaps that the sense of boundaries is often very fragile. In so far as we have shame in relation to God, that sense of shame can serve to maintain a sense of the boundary between ourselves and God, a sense of his transcendent beauty and otherness. It provides a bulwark against inflationary

---

[31] Ana-Maria Rizzuto, *The Birth of the Living God: A Psychoanalytic Study* (Chicago 1979).
[32] Pattison, *Shame*.

acts such as that of Adam and Eve in the myth of the Garden. Looked at in this way, it is clear that shame can prevent us from the ultimate sin of confusing ourselves with God.

Shame can also remind us of our humanity, bodiliness and mortality. We instinctively feel shame about our bodily functions and wish to be private about them. That is not to say that our bodies are sinful, only that our bodies remind us of our limitedness and our humanity. It is a key feature of the new kind of consciousness, characterised by shame, of which Genesis 3 speaks, that we know that we have to endure all the problems and limitations described in verses 16–19, the pain, toil, sweat and, ultimately, mortality. These things are, of course, a heavier burden the more you are conscious of them. It is one of the consequences of the more advanced consciousness of humanity that we know pain more acutely than do other animals. That is part of the burden that comes with the 'fall upwards' that also enables us to know the difference between good and evil, between ourselves and God, and to experience shame so intensely.

Another important distinction arises within the different ways of feeling shamed, and the most helpful way into this is via Kohut's concept of the bipolar self. Kohut distinguishes between the grandiose self that is infantile and exhibitionist, and the idealised self.[33] When our grandiose self is shunned or humiliated we experience shame. However, there is also the idealising self that aspires to the best, and some theorists such as Morrison have claimed that there is another kind of shame that is experienced when we fall short of our ideals.[34] Though much recent thought about shame has, with Kohut, emphasised the falling short of the grandiose self rather than the ideal self, I would prefer to say that shame of different kinds can arise in relation to the grandiose and idealised self. The shame that arises from falling short of our ideals is more likely to be constructive than the shame that arises from falling short of our grandiosity.

9. Pruyser on Shame, Guilt and the Atonement

This notion of shame as a falling short of the ideal self leads into a discussion of an important paper written by Paul Pruyser back in the 1960s, when thinking about shame was less developed than it is now. Pruyser maps the experience of guilt and shame onto theories of the atonement.[35] Just as

---

[33] H. Kohut, *The Analysis of the Self* (New York 1971).

[34] Andrew Morrison, 'The Eye Turned Inward: Shame and the Self,' in: Nathanson (ed.), *Many Faces*, 271–291.

[35] Paul W. Pruyser, 'Anxiety, Guilt, and Shame in the Atonement,' *Theology Today* 21 (1964), 15–33.

theologies oriented to shame and guilt emphasise different aspects of sin, so they emphasise different interpretations of the atonement. Pruyser's key insight here was that the three classic theories of the atonement speak to different human emotions. In particular, he suggested that satisfaction theories that are influenced by the Roman judicial process speak to people with a sense of guilt. In contrast, theories that see Christ's act on the cross as moral example rather than sacrifice speak to those vulnerable to shame. (For completeness, I should mention that he also sees a link between ransom theories and anxiety, but I find that the least convincing linkage, and it is in any case outside the subject of this chapter.)

Pruyser also connects the distinction between guilt and shame to the Freudian concepts of super-ego and ego ideal. Briefly, guilt arises from an oppressive super-ego, and the work of Christ on the cross can be seen as liberating us from such guilt. To put it more circumspectly, it is those who are in the grip of guilt arising from the super-ego who will most welcome an understanding of the atonement in which Christ shoulders the burden of our guilt. In contrast, Pruyser suggests that shame arise from the discrepancy between the ego and ego ideal. In as far as Christ on the cross represents the ultimate ego-ideal, that accentuates the sense of discrepancy between the ego and ego-ideal, and can induce a sense of shame about ourselves that motivates us to become more Christlike.

I have summarised Pruyser's mapping between concepts in theology and psychology baldly, but I hope I have not misrepresented it. I find it an intriguing and mostly convincing piece of mapping in which each discipline retains its proper autonomy. Theology is not being reduced to psychology; rather the attempt is to co-ordinate the two disciplines in a way that elucidates the psychological resonance of Christian doctrine. However, there is one aspect of Pruyser's mapping of doctrines of the atonement onto guilt and shame about which I am very uncomfortable, and it arises from an asymmetry in the way the mapping is done that you may have noticed.

The cross is seen as liberating people from guilt, but it is seen as accentuating their shame and changing them by so doing. The work of Christ on the cross is seen as shaming us into trying harder. That seems an inadequate understanding of the cross, though to be fair the moral example theory has seldom been advanced in isolation. Unfortunately, when such theories of the atonement are used in the pulpit, they often descend to something that is little better than moral blackmail. Surely this will not do. What Christ does for us on the cross needs to be seen as gift and liberation, rather than simply as moral pressure. The Augustinian 'Christ did so much for us – what can we do for him?' seems to sit very uneasily with the Pauline emphasis in Romans 5 on Christ's work on the cross being a free gift.

In fact it seems unsatisfactory to see the cross *either* as relieving people of their guilt, *or* as harnessing their shame for moral ends. It might be more appropriate to speak of how the cross can heal and reshape both guilt and shame. A basic assumption here is that there are different forms of both guilt and shame. There are forms that arise from estrangement from God and reinforce that estrangement; there are other forms which can draw people closer to God and arise in a proper and constructive way in the course of life with God.

10. The Healing of Guilt and Shame

Guilt is a concept that has been the subject of much confusion. Though feeling guilty is an emotion, guilt itself is not. Theological claims about the effect of the cross on human guilt are essentially claims about whether or not we can properly be held guilty. However, it seems to me that that must in turn have implications for whether or not we feel guilt. A removal of guilt that had no implications at all for feelings of guilt would be very strange. There is also an important distinction to be drawn between realistic guilt and neurotic guilt. The former is discrete and circumscribed, whereas the latter is exaggerated or pervasive. Indeed the pervasive character of what is called neurotic guilt suggests that in some cases it may be more appropriately called shame. Realistic guilt is a proper response to discrete transgressions, and has been valued in the Christian tradition as a preliminary to repentance. Neurotic guilt has been a cause of concern to psychologists and therapists as the source of a good deal of human distress. Though there has sometimes seemed to be a clash of values between theologians and psychotherapists about guilt, I think it is clear that the focus in the two traditions has been on different kinds of guilt; once that is clarified the apparent conflict melts away.

The question arises of how these different kinds of guilt relate to sin. What implications for guilt would Christians expect to see flowing from the saving work of Christ? I suggest that it would be a reshaping of guilt. There might, first, be a release from the pervasive guilt that is sometimes a sad feature of the human condition. On the other hand, people might be convicted of their proper guilt, though with the possibility of receiving forgiveness for it. There has been less talk in the Christian tradition of the reshaping of guilt than one could wish. In one vein, there has been talk of human sinfulness in a way that implies guilt and blame. In another vein, there has been talk of the work of Christ relieving us of this burden of guilt. I suspect that mixed messages have often been heard, leading to confusion. I would wish to talk more clearly about the reshaping and narrowing of guilt, from the destructive guilt that is so pervasive that it could almost be called shame, to the more differentiated, focused guilt than can readily lead on to penitence, forgiveness and amendment of life.

There is a similar need for the reshaping of shame. The sense of discrepancy between ego and ego-ideal which Pruyser sees as the basis of shame is characteristic of a rather limited kind of shame, quite different in character from the more toxic shame associated with the sense of falling short of the grandiose self. In fact some have felt that it is over-extending the concept of shame to call the former shame at all. We can have a sense of our inadequacies, of falling short of what we ought to be and would want to be, without that sense of wanting to hide or sink through the floor that is the hallmark of deep shame. A sense of shortcoming is also more differentiated than shame proper, more focused on specific areas of inadequacy; it need not involve that devastating sense of the unworthiness of our whole being. It is also more private, less relational. We can be aware of our shortcomings without feeling that another has shamed us. The sense of falling short of the ego ideal can be constructive, as Pruyser implies. On the other hand, it is the shame that relates to the grandiose self that is especially damaging and from which we need to be released, because of the way it ruptures relationships and makes us want to hide.

Pruyser's approach lacks any account of how God's saving work can release us from this burden of shame. Again, I would want to talk of healing and reshaping, of how the destructive shame that arises from the grandiose self can be reshaped towards the more constructive self that arises in connection with the ideal self. The key difference, I suggest, concerns relationality. In the myth of Genesis 3, the grandiose act of Adam and Eve ruptured their relationship with God and led to a primitive sense of shame. However, when there is a shameful rupturing of relationships, there is usually a longing for restoration, and that restoration heals the shame. Albers has it right when he says that 'the guilt-laden person needs to interpret and experience grace as a word of forgiveness and pardon for culpability, the shame-based person requires an experiential encounter with grace as unconditional acceptance.'[36]

It is this restoration which was God's work in Christ. The first essential stage of that work in Christ was incarnational; the God who had been a distant figure became Emmanuel, God with us. I would also see this restoration of the relationship with God as depending essentially on the gift of the Spirit. If the Spirit is given to dwell within us, we are finally healed of the shameful sense of our unworthiness and separateness. Also, this gift of the Spirit is comprehensive in the sense of being for the Gentiles as well as the Jews, drawing together those who were far off with those who were near, to use the Pauline language. Again, separateness is overcome and shame is healed through God drawing close to us.

---

[36] Albers, *Shame*, 92.

It may seem strange to place such a strong emphasis in soteriology on the gift of the Spirit, but that gift is inseparable from the resurrection, and the resurrection is in turn inseparable from the cross. It is perhaps part of the residue of the liturgical celebration of these things on separate occasions that we have come to separate them too much in our thinking. In any case, I am only talking about a strong emphasis on the gift of the Spirit as healing our shame, not an exclusive emphasis.

A gift requires reception; God gives the Spirit, but we need to receive it. That has important implications for the grandiose self out of which a primitive and destructive sense of shame arises. The grandiose self has to be willing to receive the gift, and is healed as much by that willingness to receive as it is by the gift itself. The giving and receiving are inseparable aspects of the healing of primitive, grandiose shame. However, the more differentiated, constructive shame that arises in relation to the ideal self continues. To use more Pauline language, if we are a temple for the Spirit, there is a need to make ourselves a fit temple. That links to a proper sense of shame at how unfit a temple we are. Thus, our shame is healed and reshaped.

Though I would see God's drawing close to us as the central feature of a soteriology that speaks to humanity locked in shame, there are other strands that are relevant too. There is the example God provides of not standing on his dignity. Rather, he 'emptied himself' (Phil. 2:7) and 'endured the cross, despising the shame' (Heb. 12:2). Shame is all too easily accompanied by various self-defeating strategies for protecting the ego. God in Christ gives humanity an example of how it can be liberated from all that.

I hope that in this chapter, I have clarified the nature of shame and harvested that clarification in a way that points towards a theology of sin and salvation in which shame rather than guilt is centre-stage. Such a theology emphasises sin as separateness from God, a separateness which is experienced as shame, and which is healed by God's gift of the Spirit to us. Thus healed, we retain the sense of self that was initially intertwined with our shameful sense of separateness. We now retain our distinctness, but now in the context of the restored relationship that God has bestowed on us.

5. Forgiving Abusive Parents

Psychological and Theological Considerations

Deborah van Deusen Hunsinger

Are adults who were abused by their parents when they were children obligated to forgive them? When an adult Christian undergoes therapy and begins to recover memories of painful abuse which lie at the very heart of her suffering, and when she realizes that those who abused her were none other than her own parents, is she still obliged to 'honor them in the Lord?' If she actually confronts her parents and they minimize or deny their culpability, is she justified in cutting them off, in turning away from them and having nothing further to do with them? Or must she forgive their trespasses against her, knowing as she does the unfathomable depth of the mercy and forgiveness of God toward her own sins? If she attempts to forgive them, what is she to do with her rage and outrage, with the feelings of hurt and betrayal that keep emerging? Questions like these burden those who seek to heal from the emotional wounds of childhood and to live faithful lives of Christian discipleship. For innumerable Christians, these questions are not merely theoretical, but have tremendous practical implications for their most intimate relationships and for the living out of their faith. In this chapter I want to examine a nexus of questions about the nature of forgiveness with this particular situation in mind: the adult who is seeking to heal from genuine harm committed by his parents when he was a child. What is the relationship between the healing he seeks and a Christian understanding of forgiveness? I ask this question as a Reformed pastoral theologian who, as a practicing pastoral counselor for nearly fifteen years, faced the question of human forgiveness in many guises.

It is important to begin with a description of what I mean by abusive parents, particularly because, as Marie Fortune has observed, the word 'abuse' is sometimes used so loosely that anything that is considered harmful or which lowers a person's self-esteem is labeled abusive, making the term too broad to be helpful.[1] First, situations of abuse are those 'situations which are dominated by fear'[2] where, in the case of physical abuse, parents subject their children to physical violence and use force, threats and intimidation to make their children obey them. Second, children who grow up in homes where they are sexually violated are victims of incestuous abuse. Sexual abuse would not only include sexual touching of the child, but also having the child touch the parent sexually. It would also include sexualized talk, showing a child pornographic materials or some kind of intentional parental exhibitionism in front of the child.[3] Third, the phenomenon of psychological abuse, is 'a pattern ... which occurs over time and which instills in that person a sense of their worthlessness and their inability to take care of themselves.'[4] Repeated shaming and humiliating comments, efforts at keeping the child totally in control (basically not see-ing the child as a separate person with a will of his own), while attempting to isolate the child from outside sources of help, all contribute to this kind of abuse. Such patterns of psychological abuse are familiar to us from literature on cults (which we think of as 'brainwashing'), as members are systematically taught not to trust their own perceptions and thus lose their capacity for independent judgment and initiative and become dominated by fear and dependency.[5] The suffering of persons subjected to extensive psychological abuse has also been compared to the anguish of hostages and prisoners of war.[6]

Perhaps it goes without saying that all such abuse, whether physical, sexual or psychological, is sinful. Nevertheless, the following proviso speaks to the complexity of our topic. Though taken from an essay on the relationship between addiction and sin, similar questions about the relationship between social breakdown, systemic chaos, psychopathology and the question of personal responsibility can be raised.

None of us knows the degree to which other human beings bear responsibility for their behavior, the degree to which they 'could have helped it.' That is one important difference between us and God. So even

---

[1] Marie Fortune, 'The Nature of Abuse,' *Pastoral Psychology* 41 (1993), 275–288.

[2] Fortune, 'Nature of Abuse,' 276.

[3] Mic Hunter, *Abused Boys: The Neglected Victims of Sexual Abuse* (New York 1990), 8–9.

[4] Fortune, 'Nature of Abuse,' 277.

[5] Cf. Steven Hassan, *Combatting Cult Mind Control* (Rochester, NY 1988) 55–56. Hassan makes a distinction between 'brainwashing,' which is a coercive process undertaken by an enemy, and 'mind control,' which is a more subtle process involving hypnotic techniques undertaken by one perceived to be a friend or peer. In the latter case, the victim participates in his own victimization as information which he voluntarily gives is used to manipulate or deceive him.

[6] Fortune, 'Nature of Abuse,' 277. See also Margaret Z. Kornfeld, *Cultivating Wholeness: A Guide to Care and Counseling in Faith Communities* (New York 1999), 262.

if, for the purposes of discussion, we call an addict's immoral acts sin, we do so provisionally. Perhaps, if we had all the facts, we might downgrade some of these acts to the more general status of moral evils. Indeed, when one observes the rifts and scars of children whose parents took turns slapping, deriding, ignoring, bullying, or, sometimes worse, simply abandoning them; when one observes the wholesale life mismanagement of grownups who have lived for years in the shadow of their bereft childhood, and who attempt with one addictor after another to relieve their distress and to fill those empty places where love should have settled, only to discover that their addictor keeps enlarging the very void it was meant to fill ... one hesitates to call all this chaos sin.[7]

Because we never know the extent to which another human being 'could have helped' their harmful deeds, Christians are always aware of the provisional nature of their own judgments about sin and righteousness. They remain acutely aware of their own need for God's merciful judgment, and of the same for all persons. Nevertheless, in so far as we view every person as responsible for his actions in life, such abusive behavior clearly betrays not only a gross failure to love his nearest neighbor, but more fundamentally indicates a gaping abyss between the person engaging in such abuse and God. The distortion and rupture in the abuser's primary relationship with God has disastrous effects on his interpersonal relationships with those in his family. Such sin is particularly troubling in the context of the parent/ child relationship because that relationship is meant to shower God's own blessing on children. Recall that through their relationship with their parents, children are given God's express promise of blessing. The fifth commandment reads, 'Honor your father and your mother, as the Lord your God commanded you, that your days may be prolonged, and that it may go well with you, in the land which the Lord your God gives you' (Deut. 5:16). In explicating the obedience, honor and gratitude that children owe their parents, Calvin emphasizes that since God himself places their parents in authority over them, 'it makes no difference whether they [the parents] are worthy or unworthy of this honor.'[8] But later he goes on to say that

> we ought in passing to note that we are bidden to obey our parents only *in the Lord.* (Eph. 6:1). This is apparent from the principle already laid down. For they sit in that place to which they have been advanced by the Lord, who shares with them a part of his honor. Therefore, the

---

[7] Cornelius Plantinga, Jr., 'Sin and Addiction,' in: Robert C. Roberts & Mark R. Talbot (eds.), *Limning the Psyche: Explorations in Christian Psychology* (Grand Rapids MI 1997), 255–256.

[8] John Calvin, *Institutes of the Christian Religion* II.8.36; ed. John T. McNeill Vol. I (Philadelphia 1960), 402.

submission paid to them ought to be a step toward honoring that highest Father. Hence, if they spur us to transgress the law *we have a perfect right to regard them not as parents, but as strangers* who are trying to lead us away from obedience to our true Father.[9]

'We have a perfect right to regard them not as parents, but as strangers.' . Parents who dishonor God by abusing their children are putting their children in terrible jeopardy, the worst of which may be in leading them away from trusting faith in God. In our world today, we have plenty of evidence showing how abusive fathers can lead their children into the temptation of questioning the very goodness of God. Certain contemporary feminist readings of the gospel, for instance, call the loving fatherhood of God into question because of the abusive practices of human fathers.[10] But Calvin's argument is based on diametrically opposite presuppositions as such arguments. He assumes that since God is the true Father, all human fathers (and mothers) are but pale and distant reflections of that fatherhood. Human parents who reflect the light and goodness of God's fatherhood (that is, the tender and watchful providential care of his children), are worthy of their children's honor precisely because they point beyond themselves to God, the One whom parents and their children are both called to honor. It is not that an abusive father is capable of calling into question the goodness of God as Father, but rather that God calls into question the fatherhood of that parent who abuses his children. Karl Barth takes a line of thought similar to Calvin's. He writes:

No human father, but God alone, is properly, truly and primarily Father. No human father is the creator of his child, the controller of its destiny, or its saviour from sin, guilt and death. No human father is by his word the source of its temporal and eternal life. In this proper, true and primary sense, God – and He alone – is Father. He is so as the Father of mercy, as the Father of His Son, of the Lord Jesus Christ. But it is of this Father's grace that, in correspondence to His own, there should exist a human fatherhood also. And the fact that the latter may symbolise the father-hood of God in a human and creaturely form is what lends it its meaning and value and entitles it to respect.[11]

Though children seeking to honor God might justly regard their parents as strangers, there are in fact serious problems in attempting to do so. First,

---

[9] John Calvin, *Institutes* II.8.38, 403–404. Emphasis added.

[10] See, for example, Joanne Carlson Brown & Rebecca Parker, 'For God So Loved the World ... ?' in: Carole R. Bohn & Joanne C. Brown (eds.), *Christianity, Patriarchy and Abuse: A Feminist Critique* (Cleveland OH 1989), 1–30.

[11] Karl Barth, *Church Dogmatics* III/4 (Edinburgh 1961), 245.

because of the way that we grow psychologically and develop as human beings, it is literally impossible to sever this primary relationship. Second, when we view the parent/child relationship in the context of the intergenerational family system, any attempt at cutting off a member only exacerbates the problem, not only for the victim, but for the entire extended family. And third, cutting another off in this way actually reinforces a pattern of mutual alienation, hostility and lack of trust. If we are created to live in glad fellowship with God and each other,[12] then any decision which perpetuates the alienation of those meant to live as a sign of God's Kingdom would also perpetuate sin. Nevertheless, it is nearly impossible to imagine how anyone would have the ability to forgive the kind of violence done in situations where the abuse has been extreme and the harm far-reaching. It seems as if only an appeal to miracle could account for any real human capacity to forgive in these kinds of situations.

Those who have little acquaintance with the effects of childhood abuse sometimes have difficulty in imagining the extent of the suffering caused by it and may consequently minimize its effects. A great deal of additional harm is done, however, if such persons recommend that the sufferer 'put it behind him and get on with his life,' or suggest that he should not spend so many useless hours solipsistically focusing on past events that he can't change anyway. Such comments have the effect of shaming the person for doing the one thing that might actually bring some healing, namely, paying attention to the effects of the trauma in his life and allowing himself to feel the profound grief related to it. But minimizing the extent of the suffering may be a temptation hard to avoid, simply because facing the magnitude of the harm which is done to children is so painful. Some have aptly called it 'soul murder.'[13]

In order to provide a particular focus to our discussion, let me describe the situation of a woman who sought psychotherapy in adulthood in order to heal from having been raped by her father when she was three. Like most persons healing from sexual abuse, it took her many years even to learn the nature of her most intimate suffering, for she had repressed all memory of the traumatic event itself as a way to survive. I will not quote her description of the rape, but rather of its protracted effects as she was growing up. While each person's experience is unique, the kinds of symptoms and

---

[12] Karl Barth argues that the crown of our humanity is in our gladness and joy in being in relationship with God and with other human beings. In *Church Dogmatics* III/2 he says that to be human is to engage in mutual seeing, mutual speaking and listening, offering one another mutual assistance and doing it all with willing gladness. See *Church Dogmatics* III/2 (Edinburgh 1961), 250–274.

[13] Leonard Shengold, *Soul Murder: The Effects of Childhood Abuse and Deprivation* (New York 1991).

experiences Gizelle (a pseudonym) describes are fairly typical for persons
who have undergone traumatic sexual abuse.

> The effects of the abuse manifested through my body. I sleepwalked. I
> had high fevers that were life threatening. And they could never find a
> cause. I had nightmares. I had severe asthma. I would just stop breathing.
> I was at the doctor's all the time. I was in the bed, always sick. My legs
> were turned out so badly that I could not walk without tripping over my
> own feet. I had to wear corrective shoes. It all fits now...
>
> I split my father into two different people, because there was no other
> way to sit across the breakfast table from him. The man who came down
> and sat at the kitchen table was my father. The man who came in the
> middle of the night and molested me was a shadow. I made him into
> someone else.
>
> And as I split him into two, I split myself into two. There was the little
> girl whose father taught her to ride a bike, who got A's and became a
> perfectionist. And then there was the little girl who played in the attic,
> felt that she was dying, wanted to commit suicide, had nightmares. But I
> never could speak of her. Her voice had been taken away.
>
> I felt caught, trapped in my body. That's continued into adulthood. I
> never heard any messages from my body. I would be really sick and I'd
> stagger around and go to work. I made a lifetime dedication of not listening
> to my body, because if I had, I would have had to hear that I was raped,
> and I couldn't do that and survive.
>
> I developed an eating disorder when I was eighteen, which they now
> call anorexia nervosa. I was at college. I felt obese if I weighed over
> ninety-five pounds.[14]

And then as Gizelle grew into adult life:

> I remember very distinctly that when my daughter was the age I had been
> when I was raped, I began to distance myself from her. She came to me
> in tears and said, 'Mommy, you don't like me anymore.' ... I didn't ...
> remember the rape at all ... When Adrienne was five, I developed chronic
> hip and back problems. I became crippled by the pain ... I had anxiety
> attacks so bad I couldn't move. I was in severe depression ... One
> morning when I was thirty-eight and my daughter was almost twelve, I
> took a lot of pills. I never said anything to anybody. I just knew I
> couldn't go on in the kind of pain I was in, that I had tried everything I

---

[14] Ellen Bass & Laura Davis, *The Courage to Heal: A Guide for Women Survivors of Child
Sexual Abuse* (New York 1988), 448–449.

could think of. As I said it was not just the physical pain, but the terror that hooked into the physical pain. The two completely overwhelmed me.[15]

Gizelle tried to commit suicide on four different occasions. Her last attempt very nearly succeeded. After recovering from the fourth attempt, she got herself into therapy. After a long and arduous process, she was eventually able to remember what had happened to her nearly forty years earlier. She experienced immense relief once she was able consciously to remember what had happened. She says:

> Since it's come out, it's been the difference of night and day, of living in hell and living on the earth ... For so much of my life, I have fought death wishes. Now I feel grounded, very connected to the earth, very determined to stay ... My strength and energy to deal with my life is returning. My neck has begun to unlock. I've begun to feel a looseness in my hips that I never felt before ... I really can't tell you how far my body can heal ... But I do know that I will heal physically enough to be able to lead a productive, full, and happy life, even if I have residual pain.[16]

While the symptoms of physical and psychological abuse may be different from some of these which are specific to sexual abuse, they can also be both severe and prolonged, and can also lead to such mental anguish that the person may attempt suicide.

How might someone like Gizelle heal from trauma of such immensity? What are the steps she would need to take in order to find any kind of peace or wholeness or restoration? Would forgiving her father be a necessary step for her to become fully healed? Would it somehow help promote her healing process? Or is it rather the converse, that emotional healing would somehow facilitate her ability to forgive? Or are healing and forgiveness not related to each other in either of these ways? If not, how then are they related?

Two contemporary schools of psychological thought may be of help to us in thinking about the issues of healing, forgiveness and reconciliation. One school is more oriented toward the internal dynamics of the self while the other is more oriented toward the outer relationship with the parents. Both perspectives provide insight into the question of forgiveness in so far as it is a matter of human growth and maturity. That is to say, being able truly to forgive a person is, among other things, a matter of a certain measure of psychological maturity. The first approach, known generally as 'family systems,' focuses on the wider implications of abuse, both its origins and its consequences, for the extended family. Any 'symptom,' such as abuse,

---

[15] Bass & Davis, *Courage to Heal*, 449–450.
[16] Bass & Davis, *Courage to Heal*, 456.

comes into being over a period of generations, so that an adequate theory must take into account more than one generation. Family systems theory may be especially pertinent to the church, not only because the church itself is obviously a system that can be analyzed, but even more because the theory can facilitate a glimpse into the communal nature of sin, into the ways that sin arises in specific relational contexts and involves a vast hidden web of complex circumstances and relationships. Just as grace is passed from one generation to another as God blesses persons through families rich in love, so also is sin mysteriously visited on children and children's children unto the third and fourth generation. Family systems theory, when placed into a Christian theological context, enables a glimpse into the hidden truth of our human solidarity in both sin and grace.

The second approach, known generally as 'object relations' theory, has to do with the developmental process each of us undergoes as infants, as we learn in our earliest years about love and hate, guilt and reparation, and as we respond to both the gratifications and the frustrations of being completely dependent upon another human being to meet all our needs. This theory is pertinent to our subject, not only because it shows the psychological capacities which are needed for forgiveness to take place, but also because of its specific focus on the relationship between children and parents. Learning to forgive our parents has enormous implications for our emotional and spiritual growth, perhaps more than any other relationship we have, for the simple reason that our parents are internalized parts of our own personality in a unique sense. In so far as we achieve a more harmonious relationship with our parents in the outer world, it simultaneously affects our inner world as well, that is, our relationship to ourselves. If we experience forgiving our actual mother and father for the hurt they caused us, the internalized representations of our parents would also change, allowing for less need to split off or repress painful aspects of the self. Our 'inner' parents would become far less persecuting and more supportive as a consequence. While such psychological concepts, though very important, are not sufficient for understanding the complexity of what is involved in the event of forgiveness, at least not from a Christian perspective, they can nevertheless help illuminate certain crucial features. I will proceed first by looking at a family systems approach by drawing on the work of Murray Bowen and then turn to an object relations perspective, drawing on the work of Melanie Klein, before putting both into a theological framework.[17]

The first step that many survivors of abuse take is a literal one away from the abuser; that is to say, they put as much distance between themselves and

---

[17] I am greatly indebted, as the reader will see, to a book by David W. Augsburger, *Helping People Forgive* (Louisville 1996), in which Augsburger features each of these psychological theories in relation to their implications for the process of forgiveness.

their parents as is physically possible. Angry, hurt, betrayed and at last free of the household where the abuse took place, they are eager to begin a life of their own as far away from that home as possible. Particularly in a mobile society like the United States, a decision to distance themselves from their family of origin and simply cut off contact, has not only been possible but, by virtue of the advice given by much popular therapeutic 'self-help,' has also been widespread. Thus bonds of kinship already frayed by economic considerations that take grown children to faraway locations are further strained as children intentionally distance themselves, both physically and emotionally, from their parents and siblings. In the cultural ethos of the United States during the past thirty years or so, there have been advocates for this kind of radical dismembering of the family. Cutting off their parents, seeking to dissociate themselves from a 'dysfunctional' family and avoiding the 'toxic' relationships of their family of origin have all been recommended to survivors of abuse as a way of coping with its ongoing painful effects. Underlying such recommendations is an implicit portrait of emotional maturity as a matter of separateness and autonomy. 'Maturity is ending dysfunctional relationships, writing off controlling persons, distancing from dominating people, getting out of trapped or manipulative relationships, becoming an autonomous self-reliant individual with freedom from co-dependence.'[18]

Murray Bowen and other family systems therapists, however, would strongly contest such an understanding of emotional maturity. Human maturity for Bowen is not a matter of becoming more and more 'independent' or autonomous, but rather a matter of growing from the infant's original emotional fusion with the mother toward becoming a fully differentiated self in relation to those in his family. A mature, differentiated adult would be capable of taking a clear 'I' stand while remaining emotionally linked to significant others; that is to say, he would be able to stand alone and claim who he is while also remaining closely connected to those whom he loves. He is differentiated from others without being separated, cut off or isolated from them. This is more difficult to do than it might at first seem. It is difficult to state with conviction what one believes, thinks, feels and values in a clearly differentiated way to those with whom one is emotionally close, particularly when one's feelings, ideas and values diverge from others in the family. The 'togetherness forces' in a family exert strong pressure either to 'fuse' with others, blending one's own values and identity in with theirs, or are so strong that one feels compelled to distance oneself by reactively taking an opposite position. Staying connected to one's family is a matter of

---

[18] Augsburger, *Helping People Forgive*, 47. It should be noted that this sentence does not represent Augsburger's own view of maturity, but rather is his depiction of how some people might conceive of it.

knowing how to stay centered and non-anxious, how to interact non-reactively with family members, especially when 'taboo' topics are raised, those issues which arouse shame, guilt, anxiety or grief. Those in the family who are anxious about human separateness would tend to gloss over differences in situations of conflict or anxiety, seeking to re-establish some kind of emotional fusion.[19] Those anxious about human closeness would seek to distance themselves from others or to cut them off as a way of dealing with the anxiety involved in being in a conflictual or painful relationship with them. The goal of human maturity would lie midway between these two poles of compulsively moving either toward or away from intimate others. Those who are emotionally mature would be able to tolerate the anxiety of being close to others without losing their identity, on the one hand, and the anxiety of being separate from others without feeling isolated or abandoned, on the other.

When confronted with wrongdoing, those who normally distance themselves under stress would tend to give an account or offer an explanation, in an effort to excuse the wrong, rather than facing it frankly and acknowledging it openly. By contrast, those whose anxiety is activated by separateness would tend to appease or placate the other, negate any rightful claims they may have, and generally give up their own point of view as a way of seeking reconciliation at any cost. Fully mature adults, in contrast to both of these positions, would be able to take responsibility for their own point of view, values and actions, could stand up for them vigorously, but could also openly admit it when they have acted contrary to their values, and apologize to whomever they have wronged. When entering into a process of reconciliation with one they have harmed, they would neither attempt to appease the other nor to exonerate themselves, but would be capable of offering a true apology. A true apology 'offers no defense or excuse, gives true sorrow or regret for the injury, pledges full change in a clear appeal to the whole person ... [and involves] a painful embracing of [their] deeds and their consequences.[20]

Families in which abuse has occurred, by definition do not have clear boundaries safeguarding each member's physical and emotional space. Human closeness is experienced as being extremely dangerous because to be close *means* to be violated. Therefore, in such families the temptation to move compulsively away from the other is very great indeed. Unfortunately, cutting off from their family of origin not only fails to resolve the problem of how to cope with intimacy but also transfers it to the next generation. When such compulsive distance is maintained between an adult and her

---

[19] Augsburger, *Helping People Forgive*, 42.
[20] Augsburger, *Helping People Forgive*, 42. See page 42 for a chart, which vividly differentiates these three options sought by those attempting to reconcile.

extended family, 'the cutoff tends to make emotional forces in the nuclear family system implosive, with the result that the reactivity of its members becomes more automatic.'[21] Cutoffs in one generation, in other words, have the effect of increasing overall family anxiety and intensifying emotional fusion in the following generation. When abused children become adult and cut off relationships with their family of origin, the unresolved emotional issues that belong with their parents unwittingly get transferred in some form to their children. This transfer process usually happens outside of awareness. If they are distant or detached from their family of origin, for example, they would likely become overly invested in and emotionally enmeshed with their own children, making it difficult for the children to grow normally. The children would likely feel engulfed by the over-closeness of their parent, and would typically react by disconnecting and pulling away, thus perpetuating the cycle into yet another generation. Cutting off parents apparently does not resolve the relational impasse; it merely displaces it. Augsburger asks several questions that go right to the heart of the matter:

> If the frozen grief is denied and mourning is displaced onto subsequent generations, what will be the new shape of this system? How will the pain trickle down? With what long-range increase in enmeshment? What payments will be charged to the children, what emotional story of repetition without reparation, recapitulation without reconciliation be turned in a new direction?[22]

It is an observable psychological phenomenon that whatever is not emotionally confronted and worked through in one generation will be passed on to the next. 'Repetition compulsion,' or being compelled to repeat unconsciously what cannot be faced consciously does not happen simply in the lives of isolated individuals. It is rather an intergenerational, complex social reality.

> If parents fail to do this [embrace their own unconscious wounds], they unwittingly pass on the weight of unhealed suffering to their children. It is not the psychic wounds of the parents which are, themselves, toxic to the children, but the lack of conscious encounter with those wounds that pervades the family unconscious and gets transferred to the next generation. If the previous generation hasn't consciously suffered, the pain will be handed on, often unconsciously, to the next generation.[23]

---

[21] Edwin H. Friedman, *Generation to Generation: Family Process in Church and Synagogue* (New York 1985), 26.

[22] Augsburger, *Helping People Forgive*, 30–31.

[23] Phillip Bennett, 'Family Complexes and Individuation,' *The Round Table Review* 1/5 (May–June 1994), 9.

Lasting resolution, it would seem, happens only when adult children decide to confront the impasse with their parents, only when they stop running away and face the depths of their own pain. And because the pain from the abuse is both an interpersonal and an intrapersonal phenomenon, it can be approached either externally or internally.

Let us turn, then, to the same set of issues from an intrapsychic perspective. From an object relations point of view, 'reconciliation ... comes about as a result of peacemaking *within* – resolving intrapersonal relationships – leading to peacemaking *between* in personal harmony.[24] Intrapsychically, reconciliation with our parents is an event, which is unique in kind because the very building blocks of our psychic make-up are the primary internalized objects of our mother and father. Given the way that human beings develop, the internalization of our parents inevitably forms an integral part of our identity. Our peculiar psychology is substantively shaped by what we have introjected of our parents (assuming that they were our primary caregivers), by what we have taken of them into ourselves, into our own sense of self. We piece together an identity by internalizing them, their way of speaking, their way of holding and feeding us, and our feelings about how they move and smell and taste. We drink in their eyes and the way they look at us. We become finely attuned to their emotional state of being. We absorb everything about them and weave fantasies about everything they do (or fail to do) from the earliest beginnings of our lives. If we later turn away from them and reject them because they have hurt us, we are also thereby rejecting and 'cutting off' an essential part of ourselves. The distinctively Christian perception that we 'are members one of another' is applicable not to our ecclesiology alone. In an analogous way, it is also a profound psychological truth pertaining to what it means to live in a family, to have a mother and a father whom we have internalized even before we consciously knew who they were. Melanie Klein describes this process of internalization as follows:

> The baby, having incorporated the parents, feels them to be live people inside its body in the concrete way in which deep unconscious fantasies are experienced – they are, in its mind, 'internal' or 'inner' objects, as I have termed them. Thus an inner world is being built up in the child's unconscious mind, corresponding to actual experiences and impressions gained from people and the external world, and yet altered by its own fantasies and impulses. If it is a world of people predominantly at peace

---

[24] Augsburger, *Helping People Forgive*, 53.

with each other and with the ego, inner harmony, security and integration ensue.[25]

The reverse of Klein's statement is unfortunately also true. If the world that we internalize is one where the people are predominantly at war with each other and with us, then inner disharmony, insecurity and disintegration or splitting occur. Because the normal process of human bonding and attachment entails the psychic introjection of our parents, our relationship with them occupies a unique place in our psychology. They become the prototype or template, so to speak, of all subsequent relationships. Working things through with our parents therefore has the potential to affect all our relationships profoundly, even our relationship with ourselves. Because the internalized image of our parents is so formative of our own sense of self, we are mistaken if we think that we can rid ourselves of our parents simply by putting distances of time or space between them and ourselves. Decades, indeed a whole lifetime, can go by without seeing them but our relationship with them will not cease to live on inside our own minds. Even if we have consciously 'forgotten' them, they are nevertheless operative and present to us unconsciously, i.e., outside of our awareness. In so far as we successfully dissociate ourselves from them inwardly, all that we actually accomplish is to split them off from our ego awareness; unfortunately, in doing so we also cut off any possibility for growth, change or healing to take place in relation to them.

From an intrapsychic perspective, a person needs to reach a certain minimal level of emotional maturity in order to have the psychological capacity to forgive. In Klein's understanding of normal development, every infant goes through stages from a phase of primary attachment where the mother and infant are one and the mother is internalized as all good (ages 1–3 months, the so-called schizoid position), to a second phase where the mother and infant begin to separate and the splitting of the mother into good and bad begins, (4–6 months, the so-called paranoid position). In this second phase of development, the baby experiences intense love toward the gratifying object and intense hate toward the frustrating object, not yet realizing that they are one and the same person. Just as the emotions split, so also does the mother; she is perceived by the infant as the idealized 'good' mother, who satisfies her every need, on the one hand, and the persecuting 'bad' mother, who frustrates the infant in her wishes and desires, on the other. Finally, if all goes well, the infant is able to achieve the so-called depressive position (at about age six months to three years) when she can perceive the mother as a unified whole, at once the persecuting 'bad'

---

[25] Melanie Klein, *Love, Guilt and Reparation and Other Works 1921–1945* (New York 1975), 312–313. Cited by Augsburger, *Helping People Forgive*, 54.

mother and the gratifying 'good' one. And just as the mother is eventually perceived as a whole person, so the child also begins to experience herself as a separate whole person with contradictory feelings toward one and the same mother.

> When love and hate are experienced together, a new set of feelings emerges for the first time: guilt, sadness, depression, and grief: guilt that one's hostile feelings have hurt the other, sadness at the loss, grief and depression in consequence. This emotional position – the depressive position makes possible feelings of concern.[26]

The transition to the depressive position is what enables the child to make reparations to the parent. The infant becomes anxious that her hate may be too powerful for the parent, that her bad feelings will outweigh the good ones and that she may even have the power to annihilate her mother's goodness. If the mother survives the infant's destructive impulses and fantasies and does not retaliate, but continues to love and nurture the child, then feelings of gratitude and love will well up in the child. The child would then wish to repair any damage she has done in her imagination and would desire to reconcile her mother to herself, safeguarding 'the good object' outside her and restoring the good object representation within. As the infant's earliest experience of the mother's forgiveness, this primitive psychological process forms the rudimentary underpinnings of the adult capacity to forgive. The child who has this kind of experience with a mother in the earliest months of life will have the psychological capacity for building relationships where forgiveness is emotionally possible.

> True reparation, rising out of psychic realities between infant and mother, allows the experiencing of real pain and grief and a genuine desire to reshape the inner world of love, hate, and guilt into a new unity and to respond to the external reality in bonding ways ... Authentic forgiveness ... is marked by a reconciliation in which there is movement by both parties toward each other, cessation of continuing animosity over the injury, and a reopening of the future in trust as each accepts both the good and bad parts of the self and the other ... [Thus] the capacity to forgive another's offenses is directly related to the ability to deal with one's inner offender. As a person learns to deal with the bad objects within, bad objects in others become less troublesome. The ability to deal with the internal is requisite for dealing with the external.[27]

---

[26] Augsburger, *Helping People Forgive*, 57; see also figure 3.2, 58.
[27] Augsburger, *Helping People Forgive*, 60–61, 64–65.

A person who lacks this kind of emotional maturity would tend to split both the self and the other as he regresses to earlier stages of development (the paranoid and schizoid positions). Such splitting accounts for the well-known phenomenon of seeing himself as 'all good' and the other as 'all bad,' while the other carries the 'unowned, unacceptable parts of the self ... As we see these traits in the face of the foe, projections though they are, they disappear in the self. Anxiety and guilt, aided by selective perception and recall, now diminish and disappear.'[28] The other is perceived to be all-powerful (like the formerly all-powerful parent) and the self is perceived to be little and helpless (like the infant he used to be and with whom he is unconsciously identified in this regressed state). Augsburger's observation at this point corroborates the conclusion already reached from a family systems perspective, namely that 'the degree to which one blames one's parents is the degree to which one is still stuck in the family of origin, is still a child.'[29] Harsh though this judgment may sound to those adults unable to forgive their parents for the wrong done them, it nevertheless points to the central impasse where people find themselves 'stuck' in both an inner and an outer sense. They are unable genuinely to come to terms with the past in such a way that they can prevent repeating it in another form. If they are psychologically still children blaming their parents, they will inevitably repeat the past in some form. Child psychotherapist Dorothy Martyn captures the essence of the dilemma:

> Psychological distress in itself is not erasable because there is no way to start over. We are caught in an infinite series of mirrors in which repetition of man's error is inevitable because internalization from one's relational matrix is axiomatic.[30]

The normal psychological phenomenon of human functioning, psychic introjection, is thus responsible for the fact that the inner world and the outer world of our interpersonal relationships actually mirror each other. Thus our attitude toward the outer abuser is intimately entwined with our attitude toward 'the inner abuser.' The 'inner abuser' would be the internalized representation of the person with whom we have a primary relationship with in the outside world. He (or she) becomes an integral part of the self, with both good and bad characteristics. Growth or development in the outer relationship would inevitably have a powerful impact on our inner world; and coming to terms with the reality of the abuse inwardly

---

[28] Augsburger, *Helping People Forgive*, 63.
[29] Augsburger, *Helping People Forgive*, 63.
[30] Dorothy Martyn, 'A Child and Adam: A Parable of the Two Ages,' *Journal of Religion and Health* 16 (1977), 278.

could empower us to approach the parent in the external world. Inner and outer reality are mirror images of each other. As Augsburger points out,

> Our special relations [e.g., intimate relations with family] contain deep involvements, profound loyalties, intimate feelings, and covenantal obligations that connect us to inner layers of the soul, former selves in the developmental process, and other persons in our family systems ... We become systemically interrelated with the whole person and the other as a totality is connected with us.[31]

Because our parents live inside us as part of our own psychic constitution, cutting them off would be something like trying to excise a liver or heart or kidneys, a part of our body essential for life. 'Cutting off' parents as a way of managing anxiety and pain may provide temporary relief, but as an attempt at a permanent solution it is bound to have deleterious effects on everyone: on the perpetrator of the abuse, who never gets confronted with the effects of his sin; on the victim, who not only remains in a victimized position vis-à-vis her parents, but is also seriously split (i.e., cut off from herself) in so far as she avoids facing the internalized representations of her parents; and also on the whole extended family, who are adversely affected by the taboos and secrets related to the abuse, even if they themselves have no direct knowledge of it.[32]

In so far as forgiveness and reconciliation are a psychological possibility, they involve processes of emotional maturing. From an interpersonal perspective, they require a person to be able to take a clear differentiated stand. In terms of the concrete situation that we are considering, taking such a stand would be a matter of the victim taking her own suffering seriously enough to stand steadfastly with the emotionally traumatized child that she once was (and who therefore still lives inside her). It would involve a capacity to confront the abuser in some way with a description of the suffering she has undergone as a result of the abuse. It would include the recognition that what was done to her was unjust and intolerable. Taking steps toward some kind of reconciliation with the abuser therefore would not mean that she was offering him 'cheap grace.' Even if she were the one initiating the encounter (i.e., without his prior repentance) she would confront him precisely as a way of giving him the opportunity truly to repent the wrong he has committed. She would not be interested in hearing explanations that

---

[31] Augsburger, *Helping People Forgive*, 34.

[32] 'Secrets function to divide a family, as an avalanche would a community ... The most important effect of secrets on a family's emotional system is that they exacerbate other pathological processes unrelated to the content of the particular secret, because secrets generally function to keep anxiety at higher energy levels ... [Secrets] are never on the side of challenge and change. Secrets are very serious stuff.' Friedman, *Generation to Generation*, 52–54.

sought to deny his responsibility because of possible extenuating circumstances. In other words, even if the abuse arose out of the abuser's own terrible inheritance of twisted relationships, he nevertheless would need to take responsibility for his own actions. In recounting her suffering to the one who has harmed her, she would be giving the perpetrator an opportunity to begin genuinely to make amends. Far from being retaliatory or vindictive, confrontation in this sense would be one of the most loving and generous actions a victim could undertake.

From an intrapsychic perspective, emotional maturity would mean that the victim has come to terms with the fact that the abuser in some sense is also a part of her own psychic structure; that is to say, he is not only an outer person, but also a part of herself.

> We must face the truth that we are not merely innocent victims who have suffered at the hands of our families. Instead, we ourselves continue to wound others until we can become conscious of the hurt and anger within us and slowly let go of it. In working with clients who have been abused as children, it is always a sobering moment of truth when the one who was abused can finally see the ways he or she now abuses others. It is a scary but potentially liberating thing to see how the cycle we are trying so hard to escape is repeated with frighteningly unconscious accuracy in our own lives.[33]

What Bennett refers to here as 'a sobering moment of truth,' is that point in the therapeutic process when the victim realizes that she too is caught in the same web of sin which already caught the parent who abused her. She, herself, is subject to the same powerful forces of hatred and rage, of defensiveness, self-righteousness and self-deception that all flesh is heir to. But what makes the recognition of her own sin uncanny is its particular manifestation which has this 'frighteningly unconscious accuracy.' Eventually she comes to see that the abuser also represents an internalized aspect of herself. Even if she has not perpetrated the kind of abuse which was done to her, she recognizes a dark thread of connection between herself and the parent who harmed her. She cannot absolutely dissociate herself from him. She acknowledges, instead, that she, herself, is also a culpable sinner, unable by her own power to extract herself from the web in which she, too, is caught.

If human beings are in truth knit together in sin and in grace, as the gospel attests ('But God shows his love for us in that while we were yet sinners Christ died for us.' Rom. 5:8), it would seem that the only way out of the dilemma is somehow through the narrow gate of repentance and the

---

[33] Bennett, 'Family Complexes,'12.

renewal of life. This narrow gate is approached when a victim of abuse begins to catch glimpses of her own failings and sinfulness before God. But such glimpses would come only after the person has gone through a process of profound grief over the multiple losses involved in the abusive situation.

> Adult reparations and adult mourning are possible when the objects within (both good and bad internalized identifications) are accepted; then others who act evilly (external bad objects) can be seen with empathy and compassion.[34]

Abused persons who begin to mature emotionally in the ways described do so only by virtue of another relationship, a relationship in which they are listened to, believed and understood, cared for and respected. In the context of a loving relationship with another who respects and safeguards proper human boundaries, they can begin to explore the pain and terror of what they have undergone.

The work of psychotherapy has long been conceptualized as a unique kind of 'reparenting' process. Through the offering of new relationship which symbolically recapitulates the relationship between parent and child, the therapist is internalized as a beneficent other, which eventually has a marked impact on the originally internalized parental representations.[35] The 'good-enough' therapist restores trust by respecting the person's inviolable personal boundaries and by providing a safe space in which she can grieve the immense losses of her childhood years. For if therapy is to bring healing, it will involve remembering the abuse, recalling concrete events and connecting them with the feelings she would have had, had she not dissociated herself from them. These feelings inevitably are emotions inherent to the grieving process: shock, horror, fear, rage, outrage, sorrow and despair, interspersed with recurring bouts of denial, minimization, bargaining and numbness, when the intensity of raw feeling seems too overwhelming.[36] Sometimes improvement comes by allowing the emotions to emerge, even if no conscious memories can be attached to them. Put in its simplest form, emotional healing *is* grieving.

Once Gizelle broke through to her memories of the abuse, she was flooded with feelings that needed some kind of containment. Therapy by itself was no longer enough. She needed a whole community of persons to support and

---

[34] Augsburger, *Helping People Forgive*, 166.

[35] Martyn, 'A Child and Adam,' 275–287.

[36] Elisabeth Kübler-Ross first described the emotional stages of the grieving process in her celebrated book, *On Death and Dying,* as denial, anger, bargaining, depression and acceptance. Since its publication, a general consensus has evolved that these are not so much stages that one follows in strict time sequence, as fluid steps that one can cycle through numerous times as one grieves a loss. Elisabeth Kübler-Ross, *On Death and Dying* (New York 1969).

uphold her while she poured out the torrent of formerly repressed feelings that threatened to overwhelm her.

> By that time, I had made a few good friends who stood by me. I started with a very sparse network of support, which has since spiraled, one person at a time. I felt so blessed with the support I had. I went home and made a list of all my dearest friends, female and male, and I said, 'This is what I'm discovering. And I need someone to listen. I'm calling all my friends. I'm going to structure seven days, and I want you to tell me what day you can come, and if you can give me a commitment to come every Monday between two and four, it'd be great.' And people came through. I talked and I talked. About my feelings. About the molestation. About my health. About my suicides. About my father. Giving it form. Giving it shape. Naming it. Feeling it. I just needed to have someone listen to me.[37]

But what about forgiveness? Was it possible in the context of this grief work for Gizelle to forgive her father? Regrettably, we are not told, for her story was still unfolding even as she related it to the authors of the volume in which it appeared. She had made great strides, however, in accepting the full range of her emotional responses, her rage and outrage toward her father, right alongside her feelings of love and compassion, thus showing that she had achieved the 'depressive position.' In terms of her inner world, she was able to bring together the bad and the good of the self, and to recognize how her own struggles had in turn harmed her daughter, to whom she then sought to make amends. She was able, in other words, not only to attain a unit self but also to begin to make amends for the trauma she had inflicted on her daughter when she had despaired of life itself. At the same time, she was also able to acknowledge both the good and the bad in her father, no longer needing to see him only as evil. She recognized, for instance, something of his own suffering by acknowledging the dehumanizing hell from which he had come.

> It was soon after I was born that my father went away to Burma and spent two years in a MASH unit in the jungle, putting together blown-up bodies. When he came back, he was unable to work. He was in a lot of emotional difficulty. One of his best friends had committed suicide right after the war.[38]

Acknowledging his suffering, however, did not excuse his actions, even if, from a Christian perspective, it set it into the proper context of the

---

[37] Bass & Davis, *Courage to Heal*, 454.
[38] Bass & Davis, *Courage to Heal*, 447.

universality of sin, showing that the father's culpability was not his alone, but belonged in the larger context of the ravages and terrors of war and destruction of which human beings are frighteningly capable. Human sin is a mysterious combination of both guilt and bondage, at once a vast web in which we are caught but also particular actions which we culpably undertake by our choices which keep us even more forcefully caught in sin's grip.

Gizelle was able to stand courageously with the abused child who was once herself (and who thus still lived in her), and tell her father that she remembered the incident in which he had raped her. When he proceeded to deny it with some vehemence, she was not dissuaded from continuing her work, even though she did let go of the fantasy that he might help her or that some kind of reconciliation with him might be possible. She also made the brave decision not to protect her father by keeping the abuse a secret from her daughter. 'And then I thought, "No, that's where this is passed on. This is the denial that allows this to happen. My daughter has a right to know the truth of what's going on."'[39]

Near the end of her story she writes:

Sometimes I sit here and feel such compassion for my father, I weep. Other times I see myself taking a gun and shooting [him]. I am letting it all come right on through. And the more I allow all of it to come up, the more I find myself moving toward love. The more I block the rage, the more I stay stuck. And so for me they're both right there. I reconcile it by saying I trust the process. I trust the validity of my outrage. The outrage is because I honor and value and love life.[40]

Although Gizelle herself did not undergo her therapeutic process as a Christian, it may be instructive for our own purposes to make some observations from an explicitly theological frame of reference. First, it is possible to interpret the work of a secular therapist as a sign of God's grace. The healing compassion and gifted insight of the therapist and the support of Gizelle's caring circle of friends can be seen as a sign of God's mercy which comes to Gizelle as a gift of grace and which can be understood as a kind of 'secular parable of the truth.[41] For God's grace and mercy are not limited to working within the sphere of the Church alone. They can also work in indirect and incognito ways as well. The wind of God's Spirit blows where it will.

---

[39] Bass & Davis, *Courage to Heal*, 456.
[40] Bass & Davis, *Courage to Heal*, 455.
[41] Martyn, 'A Child and Adam,' 285.

Second, there is an important distinction between the vertical and the horizontal dimensions of forgiveness. The so-called vertical dimension of God's forgiveness is based on God's free decision to be for us despite our wickedness toward others and godlessness toward him. 'Because of Jesus Christ, God no longer holds my sins against me. Christ alone is my righteousness and my life; Christ is my only hope. Grace alone, not my merits, is the basis on which God has forgiven me in him.'[42] The actuality of God's grace toward sinners not only assures us of our own forgiveness, but is also finally the condition of our forgiving anyone who has harmed us. When forgiveness is received as God's unimaginable gift, it can then be offered to another in love. As we receive the actuality of God's forgiveness, we receive the ability to forgive another who has harmed us. Question 83 in the New Presbyterian Catechism puts these vertical and horizontal dimensions of forgiveness into proper relationship. 'How can you forgive those who have really hurt you?' it asks.

> I cannot love my enemies, I cannot pray for those who persecute me, I cannot even be ready to forgive those who have really hurt me, without the grace that comes from above. I cannot be conformed to the image of God's Son, apart from the power of God's Word and Spirit. Yet I am promised that I can do all things through Christ who strengthens me.

Third, it is a profound mistake to understand forgiveness as a law or moral demand rather than the Gospel of life which it is. Alice Miller, the Swiss psychologist whose vocation has been to challenge the abusive child-rearing practices of her culture, shows how making forgiveness into demand can itself be a form of moral violence. The demand to forgive another in this sense would function as a way of adding layers of guilt and shame to an already overburdened and traumatized soul. The abused person thus wonders why she is unable to forgive and further injures herself by heaping guilt upon herself for being selfish and unforgiving. Miller rejects reconciliation as a goal of the therapeutic process. She writes:

> Since, to me, therapy *means* a sensory, emotional and mental discovery of the long-repressed truth, I regard the moral demand for reconciliation with parents as an inevitable blocking and paralyzing of the therapeutic process.[43]

How would the 'moral demand for reconciliation' block and paralyze the work of healing? It would do so essentially by preventing the person from

---

[42] *The Study Catechism* (Louisville KY 1998), Question 80, 46.
[43] Alice Miller, *Banished Knowledge* (New York 1990), 154.

recalling her own experiences and feeling her own emotions. By putting an overlay of a 'should' over her feelings, it would effectively alienate her from herself. And that is the thing that very likely happened to her as a child. A child with abusive parents is typically instructed as to how she 'should' act, how she 'should' feel, indeed, how she 'should' completely forgo her own true feelings and put forth an acceptable, but false front. Telling her in the context of therapeutic work that she 'should' forgive her parents would only perpetuate this destructive pattern.

The authors of the book in which Gizelle's story appears do not wish to jeopardize the healing process of survivors of abuse by any such moral demands for forgiveness or reconciliation. In their chapter on forgiveness they write:

> The only necessity as far as healing is concerned is forgiving *yourself*. Developing compassion and forgiveness for your abuser, or for the members of your family who did not protect you, is *not* a required part of the healing process. It is not something to hope for or shoot for. It is not the final goal ... You may never reach an attitude of forgiveness, and that's perfectly all right ... 'Why should you [forgive]? First they steal everything else from you and then they want forgiveness too? Let them get their own. You've given enough.'[44]

While the bitterness of such an attitude is an understandable human reaction, can we say from a Christian perspective that it is even possible to grant ourselves such forgiveness? As mere creatures and not God, are we able to grant ourselves forgiveness any more than we can create ourselves or grant ourselves eternal life? Are we not dependent upon our fellow human beings and on God himself to grant us the forgiveness of our sins? There is nothing in the New Testament about forgiving ourselves, although there is much there to indicate a close connection between our forgiveness of another and God's forgiveness of us. ('Forgive us our debts, as we forgive our debtors.' 'What you bind on earth is bound in heaven and what you loose on earth is loosed in heaven.')[45] If forgiveness is not law, but rather gospel, then it is not properly understood as a therapeutic goal, nor even as something which we should strive willfully to attain, but only as something we can pray for. While we cannot forgive another as an act of the

---

[44] Bass & Davis, *Courage to Heal,* 149–150.

[45] L. Gregory Jones also addresses this problem in what he calls 'therapeutic forgiveness.' He says that 'forgiveness, at least as Christians ought to understand and embody it, is not about "healing ourselves"; it is about being healed *by God and by others* in and through specific practices of forgiveness.' L. Gregory Jones, *Embodying Forgiveness* (Grand Rapids MI 1995), 50.

will, we can by grace pray for the willing capacity to forgive one who has harmed us.

But this perspective also raises the question of our fourth point: the relationship between healing and forgiveness. The authors here seem to indicate that forgiveness of the abuser is not a necessary element for emotional healing to occur. While it may be helpful to forgive oneself, so they seem to say, there is no necessity to forgive one's abuser in order to heal. One can heal without taking him into consideration at all. Others have argued that forgiveness of the perpetrator should be pursued precisely because of the benefits, which come to the forgiver. Forgiveness in either case is seen for its instrumental value to the victim. Such a line of thought has recently been advanced by certain social scientists and theologians whose primary aim is to demonstrate the personal benefits and societal advantages of forgiving.[46] In fact, the social utility of forgiveness has recently become big business among academicians. Not only has a $10 million 'Campaign for Forgiveness Research' been launched, but the John Templeton Foundation has dispersed grants to twenty-nine researchers to investigate the effects of forgiveness in ways which 'promote personal, interrelational, and social well-being.'[47] Forgiveness, in this view,

> not only heightens the potential for reconciliation ... but also releases the offender [sic] from prolonged anger, rage, and stress that have been linked to physiological problems, such as cardiovascular diseases, high blood pressure, hypertension, cancer and other psychosomatic illness.[48]

The underlying assumption seems to be that forgiveness is motivated solely by self-interest. If it helps you not to hate, then it is in your best interest to forgive, for it has been scientifically proven that hatred wreaks havoc on our bodies and psyches.

Gregory Jones has maintained that such arguments for the therapeutic effect of forgiveness provide

> an illuminating example of how and why practices and conceptions of Christian forgiveness are radically transmuted and distorted in a

---

[46] Among the social scientists the work of Robert Enright is notable. Robert D. Enright and Joanna North (eds.), *Exploring Forgiveness* (Madison WI 1998). Among theologians such a position is found in the work of Louis Smedes, *Forgive and Forget: Healing the Hurts We Don't Deserve* (New York 1984).

[47] Gary Thomas, 'The Forgiveness Factor,' *Christianity Today* 44/1 (January 10, 2000), 38.

[48] Thomas, 'Forgiveness Factor,' 38. Though the quotation says 'offender,' from the context it seems actually to mean 'offended,' for it is the victim of harm who is filled with the rage and stress that she seeks to overcome by forgiving the offender.

therapeutic context – even when well-meaning Christians are doing the transmuting and distorting.[49]

From a Christian perspective, forgiveness is not merely a means to a psychotherapeutic end. Emotional healing is obviously a good in itself. Theologically, however, it needs to be understood within the context of forgiveness rather than the other way around. It needs to be understood as a sign of God's mercy and grace. It points beyond itself to the salvation accomplished for the world in Jesus Christ. It functions as parable of the Kingdom, a little light reflecting the great light of salvation as the promised end of all things. The theological place of healing is its function as a sign of eschatological hope. Theologically, healing and forgiveness thus stand in an ordered relation of significance.

> They occur on two different levels and indicate two different contexts of meaning. Whereas the significance of the one is temporal, the signifi-cance of the other is eternal; whereas the one is penultimate, the other is ultimate ...The significance of [forgiveness] as the ultimate term is thus independent of that of healing as the penultimate term, but the relationship is irreversible, for the significance of the penultimate depends on that of the ultimate.[50]

As a good in itself, healing is significant in its own right. For Christians, however, it also bears a larger significance. It points beyond itself as a joyful sign of God's coming Kingdom when God will be all in all.

Fifth, what is the relationship between forgiveness and repentance? Some have argued that in situations of abuse, Christians should not forgive the perpetrator unless and until there is evidence of genuine repentance. Thus, Marie Fortune argues that confession, repentance and restitution are all necessary actions to be taken by the perpetrator before a victim of abuse should forgive. 'Prior to justice,' she writes, 'forgiveness is an empty exer-cise.' She goes on to say:

> Forgiveness before justice is 'cheap grace' and cannot contribute to authentic healing and restoration to wholeness for the victim or for the offender. It cuts the healing process short and may well perpetuate the

---

[49] In this quotation, Jones is criticizing Smedes' book, *Forgive and Forget*. See Jones, *Embodying Forgiveness*, 49.

[50] Deborah van Deusen Hunsinger, *Theology and Pastoral Counseling: A New Inter-disciplinary Approach* (Grand Rapids MI 1995), 74–75.

cycle of abuse. It also undercuts the redemption of abusers by preventing them from being accountable for their abusive behavior.[51]

Perpetrators of abuse typically have little awareness of the costliness of the forgiveness they ask for and they ask for it merely as a way to escape the consequences of their violent acting out. Offenders might seem remorseful after battering their partners and terrifying their children, and might offer what seems like a sincere apology. Yet within days or weeks, the cycle begins again with a buildup of tension leading to another explosion of anger and family members being badly hurt. The battered wife who sees it as her Christian duty to forgive her husband 'seventy times seven' when he asks for it, can thus unwittingly continue the cycle of abuse. Cruelly, her very forgiveness begins to function as a form of enabling because it does not take the difficult stand of insisting that the violence cease and that real steps of repentance take place. No mere good intentions are needed, but rather actions which show genuine remorse and a commitment to change. Fortune recommends that persons in such circumstances (and those who minister to them) withhold forgiveness. Repentance on the part of the perpetrator must be genuine and convincing, showing real motivation to come to terms with his violence and not simply to avoid the consequences of his actions. One group of incest offenders who were in a treatment program actually spoke out *against* forgiveness because it gave them the message that they were not going to be held accountable for their actions.

> A group of incest offenders in a treatment program made a powerful plea: 'Don't forgive so easily.' All were Christians and had gone to their pastors as soon as they were arrested, asking to be forgiven. Each had been prayed over, forgiven and sent home. They said that this pastoral response had been the least helpful to them because it enabled them to continue to avoid accountability for their offenses.[52]

It is troubling to think of someone continuing in sin because a Christian minister or priest had forgiven him. For somewhere the preaching of the Church would have utterly failed. What kind of distortions of the gospel are perpetrated when we do not know how to hold people accountable, because we have eliminated all forms of church discipline? 'What shall we say then? Are we to continue in sin that grace may abound? By no means! How can we who have died to sin still live in it?' (Rom. 6:1–2). Forgiveness can

---

[51] Marie M. Fortune, *Violence in the Family: A Workshop Curriculum for Clergy and Other Helpers,* (rev. ed. Cleveland OH 1991), 174.

[52] Fortune, *Violence in the Family,* 178.

never properly mean license for further abuse. Sin may be forgiven but never condoned.

One might ask further whether there are situations where victims of abuse are called to forgive the perpetrator even if the perpetrator never repents, situations, for example, like the one in which Gizelle finds herself? The obligation to forgive would seem to be inescapable in the Christian life. Forgiveness, both God's forgiveness of us and our forgiveness of our neighbor, is at the very heart of the gospel. 'Therapeutic' approaches to forgiveness look only at its healing potential, its psychological functionality so to speak, and have no conception of any other possible norms (such as those intrinsic to a specifically theological perspective) that might bear on the subject.[53] But if forgiveness is first of all God's gift, freely offered to all persons, if 'Christ died for us while we were yet sinners,' then the forgiveness that has been extended to us is costly but it is not conditional. It is precisely the free offering of this unconditional grace that enables us to see the depth of our own sin against God. In the light of God's gracious forgiveness, in other words, our sin is most fully revealed. In the light of our knowledge of God's forgiveness of all, the need to forgive each other is not the necessity of a moral demand, but rather, the freedom of the gospel. Because God has forgiven sinful humanity, and myself along with the rest, so am I called upon to forgive those who have harmed me. But this calling, like all matters of our vocation before God, is a matter of prayer, asking God for the power to do that which is humanly impossible.

Forgiveness needs to be distinguished from reconciliation. Forgiveness means relinquishing all retributive emotions and all desires to retaliate. It does not depend upon the contrition and repentance of the wrongdoer. Reconciliation, however, is another matter. It is hard to see how we can be truly reconciled to those who have harmed us grievously without their acknowledging and repenting of their wrong. While it is possible that Gizelle's forgiveness of her father might one day help him to repent of his violence and brutality toward her, he could also remain in denial and never acknowledge the truth of what actually occurred between them. In such a case, reconciliation would seem to be impossible. For reconciliation to occur, Gizelle's father would need to acknowledge the truth, take genuine responsibility for his actions, express sincere sorrow, and take concrete steps that would communicate how seriously and earnestly he desires his daughter's renewed trust. Even these steps would not be any guarantee of reconciliation, but would at least set forth minimum conditions under which reconciliation could begin to take place. True reconciliation would not mean

---

[53] For a discussion of the different normative frameworks between psychology and theology, and the drawing of distinctions between 'psychological functionality,' on the one hand, and 'theological adequacy,' on the other, see my book, *Theology and Pastoral Counseling*, Ch. 4, 105–150.

a return to the status quo, but would set the relationship on an entirely new basis.

Finally, how might Gizelle's therapeutic process have been different if the Church and its practices had been the overarching context for her work of healing? Might it have made a difference if Gizelle had sought out a Christian pastoral counselor for her therapeutic work, that is, if she herself had sought healing in a Christian spiritual context? If it made a difference, what sort of difference would that be? Pastoral counseling, at least as it is practiced in the United States today would, perhaps, not look very different from the kind of therapy Gizelle received. Notoriously, the pastoral counseling movement has in large part forsaken the traditions and doctrinal riches of the Church in its work. But if pastoral counseling were more truly Christian, it would not only avail itself of modern psychoanalytic insight, but would also attest the ultimate reality of divine love as known through Scripture, prayer, doctrine, preaching and worship. While such an exploration would involve beginning anew, three brief observations might be in order.

First, the work of healing would not be the work of an isolated individual, nor even of an individual with her therapist and her friends. While it is impressive to see Gizelle's creativity at work as she sought to gather a group of friends to help her heal from the trauma of her past, there is nevertheless some pathos in pondering how hard Gizelle had to work to create a community of care for herself. How meager and threadbare it seems by comparison to the Church as a living community given as a gift from God. There is something poignant about Gizelle calling friends and asking for individual commitments of two-hour time slots. Each friend is connected to Gizelle like spokes on a wheel with Gizelle at the center, but none is intrinsically connected to any other spoke. They may not even know each other. The Monday afternoon listener has likely never met the Monday evening friend. So many of our contemporary efforts to create 'communities of care' strike me as just such patchwork affairs pieced together by huge expenditures of individual initiative, rather than a rich interwoven tapestry where everyone is connected to everyone else by virtue of each person's connection to Jesus Christ. Gizelle's crying need, as her actions so vividly demonstrate, is for a whole community to surround her with love and care. That need is not Gizelle's alone, but every person's in our atomized and rootless society.

Second, how might the Church become a real agent of reconciliation, where it could actually provide safe and structured settings for parents and their adult children to meet face to face? How can forgiveness actually take place under the conditions of (post)modern life if parents and children never come together to talk about their common painful history? Estranged families sustained by the daily bread of Scripture would be able to develop an imagination for human forgiveness (as in the story of Joseph and his brothers), could take heed from cautionary tales of warning (like Tamar and Amnon and Absalom), and could visualize anew goals worth striving for (like 'speaking the truth in love'). The intercessory prayers of the community could uphold all those who cannot bring themselves even to ask for the willingness to forgive.

Finally, when faced with the magnitude of the hurt, it seems obvious that a psychotherapist or pastoral counselor, no matter how gifted, would simply be incapable of providing the level of care needed to restore a single individual to renewed life. Yet that is precisely what we have been trying to do in so many of our contemporary therapeutic practices. It seems significant that Anna Freud saw the clear limits of psychotherapy more than fifty years ago. Robert Coles recounts a conversation he once had with Miss Freud, in which she described the painful psychiatric history of an elderly woman. Then she wondered aloud what they (as psychotherapists, as human beings) would really desire for her. 'Oh, I don't mean psychotherapy!' she exclaimed.

> She's had lots of that. It would take more years, I suspect, of psycho-analysis than the good Lord has given her ... I will confess to you: when I was listening to all of this, I thought to myself that this poor old lady doesn't need us at all. No she's had her fill of 'us,' even if she doesn't know it ... What she needs ... is forgiveness. She needs to make peace with her soul, not talk about her mind. There must be a God, somewhere, to help her, to hear her, to heal her ... But I fear she'll not find him! And we certainly aren't the ones who will be of assistance to her in that regard.[54]

But who *are* the ones who will be of assistance in that regard if not Christian pastors and pastoral counselors? Can Christian pastoral counselors once again claim the full power of the gospel as intrinsic to the vocation to which they are called?

---

[54] Robert Coles, *Harvard Diary: Reflections on the Sacred and the Secular* (New York 1990), 177–180, cited in: Johann Christoph Arnold, *Seventy Times Seven* (Farmington, PA 1997), 133–134.

6. The Merciful Economy

Peter Selby

1. Introduction

The entry of the animals into the ark Noah had built before the onset of the deluge is accompanied in Benjamin Britten's setting of the mystery play *Noye's Fludde* by the repeated singing of *Kyrie, Kyrie, Kyrie eleison.* In this great entry the species of the animal creation capture centuries of liturgical introit processions in which the faithful and their ministers enter the sacred space, approaching the sanctuary with a plea for, and therefore a recognition of, the divine mercy. The music of the procession is confident: the divine mercy is not so much implored as it is celebrated, the utterly reliable characteristic of God which even as judgement looms will hold the universe in life.

The animals, with Noah's family, represent in themselves that firm divine commitment to continuity, held alongside an equally firm commitment to justice. God has seen that 'the wickedness of humankind was great in the earth, and that every inclination of the thoughts of their hearts was only evil continually.'[1] Yet God resolves nonetheless to provide *both* for the elimination of the humanity whose creation had become a source of divine grief, *and* for the continuity of the species, including the righteous Noah and his descendants.

The divine vengeance on human unrighteousness requires, it seems, little detailed planning: the waters of the deluge will take care of it, the violence and corruption of the earth engulfed in the chaos which is their inevitable outcome in a universe created by a moral God. What cannot be left simply to chaos and chance, however, is the merciful provision for continuity.

Make yourself an ark of cypress wood; make rooms in the ark, and cover it inside and out with pitch. This is how you are to make it: the length of the ark three hundred cubits, its width fifty cubits, and its height thirty

---

[1] Genesis 6:5; all biblical quotations are from the *New Revised Standard Version.*

cubits. Make a roof for the ark, and finish it to a cubit above; and put the door of the ark in its side; make it with lower, second, and third decks.[2]

Mercy has, that is to say, an architecture, in this case a naval architecture with plans and a bill of quantities in conformity to building regulations. There can be no mercy without carpentry. That detailed instruction prefigures, after all, the art and architecture, the musical composition and execution, the liturgical structure and order that are necessary for Noah's successors to continue to celebrate God's utterly reliable mercy. Moreover, when the ark is ready it is specified, even in an account which avoids unnecessary detail, that survival rations require to be planned: 'Also, take with you every kind of food that is eaten, and store it up, and it shall serve as food for you and for them.'[3]

Thus a deluge that is itself grounded not in the arbitrary outcomes of conflicts or love affairs between heavenly beings but in God's righteous demands is also the occasion of a mercy that is deliberate and detailed. So after the flood had abated the order of an abundant creation can be restored:

God said to Noah, 'Go out of the ark ... take with you every living thing that is with you of all flesh – birds and animals and every creeping thing that creeps on the earth – so that they may abound on the earth, and be fruitful and multiply on the earth.'[4]

More than that, the event which has cost so much destruction concludes with a commitment to the continuation of that mercy:

And when the Lord smelled the pleasing odour [of Noah's sacrifice], the Lord said in his heart, 'I will never again curse the ground because of humankind, for the inclination of the human heart is evil from youth; nor will I ever again destroy every living creature as I have done. As long as the earth endures, seedtime and harvest, cold and heat, summer and winter, day and night, shall not cease.'[5]

The morally ambiguous character of humanity is acknowledged; nonetheless there is established an abundant economy; the created order is redeemed from the arbitrariness of conflicts among deities and settled in God's commitment to a humankind acknowledged to have a 'heart that is evil from youth.' The mercy that saves a few in the ark is prelude to an all-embracing mercy that is God's universal and ultimately victorious purpose of

---

[2] Genesis 6:14–16.
[3] Genesis 6:21.
[4] Genesis 8:16f.
[5] Genesis 8:21f.

salvation. The universal promise expressed in the rainbow set in the clouds is confirmed in Christ, his particular history establishing the sovereignty of mercy for the whole of creation.

> God waited patiently in the days of Noah for the building of the ark in which a few ... were saved through water. And baptism which this prefigured now saves you ... through the resurrection of Jesus Christ, who has gone into heaven and is at the right hand of God, with angels, authorities, and powers subject to him.[6]

Thus from their beginning to their end the scriptures declare the pattern of the merciful economy. Yet to speak of 'economy,' rather than use the gentler and theologically more fashionable term 'ecology' raises an unavoidable issue, one that constitutes the agenda of this chapter. What happens when this vision of the merciful purpose of God is brought into relation with the harsher realm of what we are accustomed to call 'the economy'? The vision of lions lying down with lambs is immediately attractive. But ultimately the beauty of this vision has to include much more difficult practical matters: the establishment of community between bosses and workers or between bankers and the poor of the earth. Even if the Bible sets out such a vision, the evidence of our time is that if all humankind has to proceed according to the ways of the governing economics there is little hope for comity among lambs and lions, or even grass and trees. What has an *economics* of mercy to contend with, and what might it look like?

2. Unpayable Debt and the *Jubilee 2000* Campaign

> When that year was ended they came to Joseph the following year and said to him, 'We cannot hide from my lord that our money is all spent and the herds of cattle are my lord's. There is nothing left in the sight of my lord but our bodies and our lands ... We with our lands will become slaves to Pharaoh; just give us seed so that we may live not die.[7]

The choice of theme for the present volume owes much to the successful use of the Jubilee theme by the *Jubilee 2000* campaign for the cancellation of the unpayable debts of the two-thirds world. That campaign captured the imagination of tens of thousands and became a political force in the councils of the world's most prosperous nations for a range of reasons. Not the least of these was the fact that the injustice and impoverishment that are the

---

[6] 1 Peter 3:20–22.
[7] Genesis 47:13, 15–16, 18–20.

consequences of enforcing the servicing and repayment of the debts in question was easy to grasp. How effective the political and commercial responses that have been made to that campaign in terms of the actual relief of poverty, and whether the campaign can therefore be described as a 'success' is much debated. Certainly it leaves unanswered some radical questions about the operation of the world's economy, and how such a crisis can be avoided in the future. To that we shall need to return.

What makes the campaign particularly germane to a theological enquiry is the evidence that it collected to itself a profoundly religious agenda, which accounts, perhaps, for the weight it came to carry in the churches. The campaign for a material, indeed financial, acting out of the jubilee traditions captured the imagination of believers to the extent that the character of Christ has been appropriated by more and more of them as the one who proclaimed jubilee. The Nazareth synagogue statement[8] has attained a liturgical prominence that I cannot recall in previous times, and that in turn reflects its increasing appearance as the badge of a Christian commitment to liberation.

The recovery of an essential and critical relationship between the language of faith and the realities of the human economy is a significant development, not least because of the role of economic issues in the emergence of Christian faith in the first place. It was naturally gratifying to discover that a theme of my own research was deemed a significant issue by all the provinces of the Anglican Communion. Since I convened the subsection that produced the report and resolution on the subject of international debt, it would be churlish to complain about their virtually unanimous acceptance by the bishops of the Communion.[9] On the other hand it would be important to raise the question whether such widespread public acceptance arises in part from the failure of campaigners, politicians and bishops to examine either the economic or theological significance of the topic radically enough. As often happens, those who were aware that significant questions were being allowed to go by default restrained themselves from articulating them for fear of blunting the edge of a campaign that promised considerable humanitarian benefits. The principal progenitor of the campaign, Martin Dent, set the tone in insisting that the benefit of cancelling unpayable debt incurred in the aftermath of the oil price rises was that it would enable the normal mechanisms of world trade, including lending and investment, to function properly again.

---

[8] Luke 4:16–21.

[9] See *The Official Report of the Lambeth Conference 1998* (Harrisburg, PA 1998), Resolution 1.15 (384ff.) and Report (107–119). The prominence of the theme within the Lambeth conference can also be seen in the report of the plenary presentation (345–361), and the fact that it was the major theme of Prime Minister Tony Blair's address (441–446).

We seek to remit the inert debt which has been built up from the exceptional years of the oil decade ... We are thus attacking not all debt, but inert debt up to the moment of remission. To take the analogy of the human stomach, we are not seeking to remove the food which goes through it day by day for digestion or expulsion, but rather things that have remained and festered in the stomach for many days and can only be removed by a special purge or an operation.[10]

Yet there are grounds for believing that simply seeking to re-establish an economic system that is believed to have been functioning adequately and which we continue to need fails to examine the depth of the crisis. I seek in this chapter to focus on two distinct areas in which a rather deeper examination is needed. First is the *monetary* nature of the debts that were the subject of the campaign. So strong is the assumption that debts are to be measured in money that the point is hardly even noticed. I was about two thirds of the way through the research that led to the writing of *Grace and Mortgage*[11] before it was really borne in on me that the writing of a book about debt would be seriously incomplete if the subject of money itself was not examined. We take it for granted that it would not be open for a debtor nation to 'return' the items purchased with a loan, and that it is rational to insist that what it repays is the money. It is not sufficient to make the point that the goods will (for example through use, or the arrival on the scene of new technology) have reduced in value since the loan was taken out. The same is true of money; it was precisely the interest rate fluctuations and their effect on the 'price' of money, which created the debt crisis that *Jubilee 2000* sought to address.

The second area requiring examination is the character of forgiveness itself. It was not long into the discussion of debt cancellation in the Lambeth Conference, for example, before a strong protest was mounted by members from the two-thirds world at any use of the word 'forgiveness' in this connection. Debtor nations certainly did not want to be *forgiven*; it was creditor nations and their bankers who needed that.[12] 'Forgive us our debts,' the Church of Scotland's preferred translation of the petition in the Lord's Prayer, might appear on the face of it more accurate, at least to the Matthaean version, and more economically radical. But it appears to leave

---

[10] M.J. Dent, 'Theological Help in an Urgent Economic Crisis,' *Crucible* 33/1 (Jan.– March 1994), 25.

[11] Peter Selby, *Grace and Mortgage: The Language of Faith and the Debt of the World* (London 1997).

[12] The issue of the inappropriateness of 'forgiveness' in such cases parallels a similar objection to 'charity' voiced increasingly strongly by churches in the two-thirds world. '... some churches from the south ... cannot accept something granted out of charity when in fact they are already entitled to it for reasons of justice.' See Renier Koegelenberg (ed.), *Transition and Transformation* (Bellville, South Africa 1993).

out of account the essentially *moral* quality that a need for forgiveness has come to connote.[13] Any suggestion that debtor nations required to be forgiven amounted to a suggestion that their debts were their fault, something the campaign was not in general willing to accept. I intend therefore to enter into some examination of the character of forgiveness. These two discussions, of the nature of money and the nature of forgiveness, are to lead in the concluding section of the chapter to a discussion of their implications for our understanding of the place of the atonement in the Christian theological system. It is this area of doctrine that addresses the questions, could there be a 'merciful economy,' and what would be the cost of bringing it into being.

3. Money: The Merciless Economy

Oscar Wilde's snatch of dialogue is well known, though different parts of it have come to the fore at different times:

Lord Darlington:	What cynics you fellows are!
Cecil Graham:	What is a cynic? [sitting on the back of the sofa]
Lord Darlington:	A man who knows the price of everything and the value of nothing.
Cecil Graham:	And a sentimentalist, my dear Darlington, is a man who sees an absurd value in everything, and doesn't know the market price of any single thing.[14]

Since the literature about money spans the ages, and in every age the ambivalence about it is evident, we might well suppose that we are dealing with an unchanging feature of our environment, and that human beings' attitudes to it have remained fairly constant throughout history.

But money itself has a history. For example, a huge variety of objects have served as money in various societies at various times (wampum shells among the native North Americans, woodpecker scalps on the Santa Cruz Islands, reindeer in northern Siberia or dead rats on Easter Island[15]), with

---

[13] Simon Taylor examines the question whether 'forgiveness' is an appropriate word to use for the aim of the international debt crisis in 'Forgiving Debts: A Theological Contribution,' *Modern Believing* 41 (2000), 3–12, an article which I received after this paper was written. He believes precisely the communal and moral aspect of forgiveness makes it an important word to use in connection with the debt crisis, but does so by avoiding the issue that the need for forgiveness arises because of wrong on one side of a relationship. See the section 'Forgiveness: The Benefit of Mercy' below.

[14] Oscar Wilde, *Lady Windermere's Fan* (London 1892), Act III. A host of literary references to money have been collected in: Kevin Jackson (ed.), *The Oxford Book of Money* (Oxford 1995).

[15] See for instance Charles Pinwill, *Democratising Money* (Adelaide 1990).

precious metals the best known. These various objects served as money because there was agreement to allow them to be so, and trust that they would be so accepted. However, they also have in common that they are not in principle unlimited, and could only be increased in quantity at the cost of some labour – by hunting, or mining or collecting.

It was a significant change when similar trust, or legality of tender, came then to be given to paper and coins the value of which was 'inscribed' rather than simply related to their weight in metal. The ultimate dependence of money on trust has been further accentuated by what has happened during the period since the Second World War and particularly over the last three decades, the time of the most rapid change of all. With that change in the character of money have come enormous changes in our response to it.

Such trust was originally conferred by authority, and thus currency was trusted only within nation states. Even that, however, was the product of historical development. For a long time after Thomas Jefferson invented the American dollar, based on the Spanish piece-of-eight though divided into one hundred cents, it was still not a fully national currency. The relationship between money and government was a controversial matter, and so money remained for a long time a private enterprise matter, and notes and coins reflected the different communities that produced them.

> In the days of the private bank note, you had a very direct reflection on where people were ethnically in terms of settlements and silver. For example you have French language notes in New Orleans and Louisiana ..., German notes in Northampton Pennsylvania ... and even bilingual Spanish and English notes in Texas.[16]

The emergence of a truly national dollar was therefore intimately connected with the emergence of a national identity. The 'greenback' has, especially since the Second World War, become the symbol of American power and security. For that reason the United States' departure from the gold standard during the presidency of Richard Nixon, a move resulting from the inflation generated by the Vietnam War, was a moment of considerable significance to the national psyche. No longer was the greenback itself 'backed' by precious metal hidden in solid rock vaults in Manhattan. That had to be explained by the American president to his voters, asserting disingenuously that it was not a devaluation. But much later an anxious post-Communist Russian public which was hoarding dollars as the sign of security had to have a careful explanation of the production of the redesigned $100 bill, so

---

[16] Richard Doty, of the Smithsonian Institution, in 'In the Greenback We Trust,' one of a series of BBC Radio 4 programmes on *Patriotic Money* (BBC radio 4, August/September 1996).

much had they too come to rely on the American currency as a sign of security. The British pound, by contrast, was clearly less reliable, and so during the Gulf War British soldiers wore sovereigns taped to their chests, in case they should need to impress the Kuwaiti population.[17]

The severing of the link between currencies and external standards of value – the gold standard – was the major financial development that made Keynesian economics possible. For it meant that the amount of money in circulation could be adjusted in order to stimulate a higher level of economic activity (and by the same token to reduce it). Yet it is that very development which has combined with other developments in the post-Second World War period to produce some of the major economic crises and uncertainties of our time.

Much has been written in the cause of obtaining relief for two-thirds world countries from the effect of the oil price rises of the early 1970s and 1980s. It was these rises that produced a vast increase in the money lodged within the banking system, money which was then 'sold' in the form of loans to developing countries. As a result of the *Jubilee 2000* campaign it is now widely known that some of the loans were for nefarious purposes, and that in many cases they fuelled militarism and corruption. We also know that many of the loans have already been effectively repaid many times over because of the increases in interest rates. These points are highly relevant to the debt remission campaign, but are not the significant issue here. What is more important for the purpose of this chapter is the fact that this enlargement in the amount of money in the banking system combined with two other features to produce huge changes in the world economy.

First, this expansion in the world supply of money resulting from the oil price rises was compounded by the fact of 'fractional reserve banking.'[18] Because we not only trust money but also trust that not all of us will wish to withdraw our deposits at the same time, banks are enabled to lend out a large multiple of the money that is deposited by account holders. Secondly, it is not only the sheer *quantity* of money in circulation which gives rise to its effect on the total economy, but also the *speed* with which it circulates, and this has accelerated vastly in recent decades. The technological developments which mean that most money is no longer coins or notes in circulation but effectively electronic impulses transmitted virtually

---

[17] From 'The Sovereign in Your Pocket' from the same series of radio programmes.

[18] John C. Turmel has written about this in two generally available e-mail messages, 'Everything about Banking and Debt,' an essay in plumbing and algebra applied to the banking system, and 'All about Banking,' a 670-verse ballad exposing the same deception at the heart of banking. He makes use of the concept of the 'piggy bank' too, but is rather less patronising about it. The material can be obtained from him at <bc726@ca.carleton.freenet>. See also Geoffrey Gardiner, *Towards True Monetarism* (London 1993). This issue of the major agenda of the Christian Council for Monetary Justice, whose secretary, Mike Rowbotham, is the author of a major case for monetary reform, *The Grip of Death* (London 1999).

instantaneously across the world's banking system dramatically increases both the speed of its circulation and the difficulty of its regulation.

These two aspects of money's recent history have been celebrated, unsurprisingly, in the ideology of the New Right. Since it is economically beneficial for there to be competition, and since a 'free market' is the most efficient way of allocating resources and giving choice, why should this be any different in the matter of money?

> Among the things for which human beings compete, money is neutral and may be used in wise stewardship or foolish. Since it is impersonal and instrumental, its possessors may accept it with an infinite range of human attitudes and use it for a vast range of choices. More to the point, those who have money are obliged by it to become careful stewards, under pain of losing it or cutting foolishly into their capital. Their natural interest lies in investing it soundly and well. This interest leads them to produce more of it than there was in the first place. Thus a money economy is inherently dynamic.[19]

Those who do not feel they can enter into an unqualified celebration of the new money economy nevertheless may seek to commend it by declaring themselves, and therefore humanity as a whole, helpless in the face of it. In what simply reflects the statements of his political opponents after their bruising experience of defeat by the currency speculators, the present head of the British Government can say, 'It would be totally dishonest of me or anyone to pretend that we can change conditions in a world market which alter the circumstances in which companies can operate and trade. We cannot do that.'[20]

The emergence of an ideology to justify economic developments in which technological advance (in particular electronic money transmission) work with the reserve banking system to enhance the power of money and those who possess it should not surprise us. The message is that what we cannot change is in any case in the best interests of us all, and the market in money, like any other market, remains the best and most beneficent way of channelling resources. Yet there is an emergent movement of criticism: the facts of experience do not bear out the theory.

> Ingenious minds are always devising new types of financial instruments which they can bet on, or deal in, to provide hedges against the way things turn out ... without this capital ever being involved in any 'real' wealth creating activities at all. There is nothing productive about these

---

[19] Michael Novak, *The Spirit of Democratic Capitalism* (London 1991), 348.
[20] Tony Blair, clip in *Mayfair Set* (BBC TV series 1999).

activities which directly adds to the goods and services which are available to human beings across the globe for the enhancement of their day-to-day affairs and for the provision of employment to more and more people.[21]

David Jenkins' critique of the way in which the world financial markets operate is the stronger for its being derived largely from the pages of the financial press and the lips of its most successful operators, not least George Soros, the legendary financial operator credited with a major role in the ejection of sterling from the European Currency Mechanism. Jenkins' book intentionally avoids an explicitly theological agenda, even if at times his own background shows in the way in which he expresses himself. What he does make clear constantly, however, is the way in which the mechanisms of the financial markets are credited with both the power and beneficence of a deity.

Such critiques of the operation of the money markets and therefore of what has happened to the character of money in our time are becoming increasingly widespread and the number of pressure groups for change and regulation is growing. My concern here, however, is to contrast what we have seen in the development of money with the specifically Christian claim that the world is in the hands of a God whose character has been made known as *merciful*.

For what is the exponential growth in money generated by the acceleration of the fractional reserve banking system other than the creation of an ever-enlarging burden of *indebtedness*? The fact that more than nine tenths of the value of money transactions are speculative and therefore not related to 'real' trade at all should not surprise us. For money that has not been pegged to the value of any external standard and which then acquires the capacity both to grow ever more plentiful and to move faster and faster must take on a life of its own.

Neither on the other hand should we comfort ourselves with the thought that if most money transactions are not in any sense 'backed' in the real economy the real economy is unaffected. As Soros himself points out, when a market is characterised by disequilibrium, the constant creation of price movement by those who bank on a future which will be determined by their own future decisions, this has serious consequences for the proper allocation of capital resources where they are actually needed.

In the absence of equilibrium the contention that free markets lead to the optimum allocation of resources loses its justification. The supposedly

---

[21] David E. Jenkins, *Market Whys and Human Wherefores: Thinking again about Markets, Politics and People* (London 1999), 157.

scientific theory that has been used to validate it turns out to be an axiomatic structure whose conclusions are contained in its assumptions and are not necessarily supported by the empirical evidence. The resemblance to Marxism, which also claimed scientific status for its tenets, is too close for comfort.[22]

A money supply growing and racing out of control and not tied to any external standard of value will impact on the markets in goods and services, and in totally unregulated ways. For money represents *claims* on the resources of goods and services; it is essentially *credit*, a growing weight of claims held in the hands of those who possess and manipulate money which they will exercise in the service of acquiring more money, that is to say yet more claims. Real goods and services, the raw materials of the world, the ingenuity and productivity of human beings, the diversity, beauty and abundance of their fellow-creatures, become literally hostages to the claims which money represents and which may be exercised at any time.

The freedom which money promises, as the most fast-moving of assets, turns out to be an illusion. As Georg Simmel, the classic philosopher of money, observes, 'In itself, freedom is an empty form which becomes effective, alive and valuable only through the development of other life-contents.'[23] The subjection of such 'life contents' to the power of money itself is what in turn the sociologist of money, Nigel Dodd, observes happens when money is set up as arbiter:

> In the mature money economy, money's empowering features have compromised that very freedom which money itself promises to embrace. Monetary freedom has in this sense been alienating. It is a freedom which is empty of content, having only negative connotations linked to the removal of constraint … These life-contents will be stunted whenever money is treated as an end in itself. This is exactly what has happened in modern society. Money, as the ultimate economic instrument, has been turned into the ultimate economic goal. It has imploded in on itself as mammon.[24]

This account has been necessarily brief and could profitably be further developed and nuanced. This essay is not a plea to a return to barter or simply a repetition of grumbles about filthy lucre. It is intended to draw attention to the radical quality of the developments in the nature, quantity

---

[22] George Soros, 'Capital Crimes,' *Atlantic Monthly*, January 1997, quoted in: Jenkins, *Market Whys and Human Wherefores*, 172.

[23] Georg Simmel, *The Philosophy of Money* (London 1978), 401.

[24] Nigel Dodd, *The Sociology of Money: Economics, Reason and Contemporary Society* (New York 1994), 49.

and speed of circulation of money, and what happens when that which was a measure used in the market of goods and services becomes a market of its own. It is not an exaggeration to say that this unrestrained process has submitted our society, and indeed the creation itself, as debtor to arbitrariness.

The character of the mercy promised to Noah and subsequently to the whole created order is first that it is founded upon the moral demand of God. The deluge itself is not the result of arbitrariness but of God's moral requirement on humanity. Any social ordering that substitutes for that moral demand some other measure, be it numbers on currency notes or figures on monitor screens, is returning the universe to the arbitrariness from which the Hebrew people understood God to have saved them. The crisis of unrepayable debt which the *Jubilee 2000* campaign sought to address is not after all a unique occurrence attributable to a particular historical cause, but a symptom of a built-in arbitrariness contained in the development of the nature of money. The lesson of that campaign, however, is that replacing the moral demand of God with such arbitrariness at the centre of power will first of all destroy the lives of the weakest and poorest of the earth.

Secondly, that mercy represents a divine commitment to the survival of the work God had begun, notwithstanding the constant possibility that in the face of human neglect of that demand a deluge of chaos might ensue. The unrestrained power of monetary growth manifests no such commitment. It creates claims today with no regard for how those claims will be exercised in the real world of goods and services tomorrow, let alone for future generations. The economy controlled by the unrestrained power of money is merciless, and if extinction results, so be it.

Thirdly, the divine mercy issues in a commitment to an abundant and sufficient environment, a reliable framework for the created order in general and human flourishing in particular.[25] The connection between the abundance and the sufficiency is crucial to a perception of the mercy of God. The money-directed economy, and the exponential growth in claims upon the world's resources and the ingenuity of humankind that it requires, is in that sense totally merciless. Its demands for constant growth, for an insatiable pushing at the boundaries of sufficiency, and most of all for its insistence on its own right, as money, to claim the debt written on its face render its claim to offer freedom fundamentally deceptive.[26] It is for that very reason that an examination of the developments in the money economy can provide a

---

[25] See John B. Cobb, *The Earthist Challenge to Economism: A Theological Critique of the World Bank* (Basingstoke 1999), especially 168–184.

[26] For an account of the way in which the money economy works itself out in the life of persons, see John M. Hull, 'Spiritual Education, Religion and the Money Culture,' in: James C. Conroy (ed.), *Catholic Education Inside Out/Outside In* (Dublin 1998).

major source of theological reflection about areas of living that appear at first sight not to have to do with money at all.

4. Forgiveness: The Benefit of Mercy

A recent programme in the *Analysis* series,[27] devoted to the subject of 'Forgiveness,' began with an apology that a programme normally devoted to political and economic subjects should examine a matter normally associated with interpersonal relationships. Yet as the programme proceeded the range of issues in which forgiveness is the key to any possibility of human flourishing grew to cover most significant aspects of the life of the human community.

The mother with whose searing personal story the programme began reached the point of deciding she must seek to forgive her daughter's murderer because she knew that if she did not her anger would destroy her. The larger historical tableaux with which the programme engaged – South Africa and the work of the Truth and Reconciliation Commission, Northern Ireland and its peace process, a ruthless or a lenient attitude to debt within the commercial world – all revealed the same point.

In the matter of personal wrong, there comes a point in the nursing of a grudge, in holding on to a grievance, when the question arises, 'Is this doing any good?' Coming to the point of forgiveness is frequently about reaching the point of recognition that being in the right is not in fact sufficient. A failure to move into the mode of forgiveness simply means that the grievance, however legitimate, possesses the aggrieved person more than it brings any repentance or recompense from the guilty one. Whole nations and parts of nations manifest this very point; unfortunately the apprehension of this element of self-interest in forgiving and of the advantage in surrendering a grievance can take a great deal of time and suffering.

Yet there is a precise parallel with the economics of debt reduction and cancellation. To the extent that the need for it has been understood (and that is still a limited extent) it is due to a recognition of the economic harm done by the continued economic paralysis imposed on nations by unpayable debt. The merciless economy dominated by the power of money is paralleled by the merciless economy of retained grievance. The illusion of the money economy is that of 'financial discipline,' of figures in ledgers, of keeping accounts.[28] The economy of grievance presents the same illusion: 'scores'

---

[27] BBC Radio 4, 17 December 1999.

[28] The illusion created by the fact that money expresses value in *numerical* terms, with the appearance of 'objectivity' is well captured by Theodor Bovet, the pastoral theologian. See Theodor Bovet, *That They May Have Life: A Handbook on Pastoral Care for Christian Ministers and Laymen* (ET London 1964), 81.

of wrongs are kept – and settled. Crimes are allocated 'tariffs'; and criminals therefore accounted to have a 'debt to society.'

Held in place by a larger vision of human community, the disciplines of accounting have their place. Within such a vision, due rewards and due punishments, proper charges and repayments, can all give stability and security to relationships, upholding fairness in commercial transactions and encouraging a measure of responsibility. Such is true in the economy of all social relations, not only, but not least, those described as 'economic.' Unregulated and unchecked, however, detached from accountability to a wider vision of the human community and thus themselves accountable to nothing and nobody, the ledger accounts whether of money or of wrongs serve only themselves and feed on themselves.

As became very clear in the previous section, in the realm of the money economy the allegedly fixed standard of monetary value emerges as self-determining and self-serving. The outcome is far removed from the accepted discipline of debt and repayment and becomes instead paralysing for the poor and the master of the rich. It turns out not to be very different in the matter of wrongs and their hoarding. The appearance is all of accurate memory of the past, of preparing a day of reckoning, of the search for justice. The reality is tragically different in national as well as more local or personal affairs: grievances are amassed, and then 'invested,' that is to say cherished and nurtured, so as to produce a return of mounting anger and bitterness.

Yet the assertion that forgiveness confers a *mutual* benefit must not obscure a further analogy between the money economy and the 'economy' of relationships generally. The disciplines of financial accounting are not to be dismissed simply because the unrestrained growth in the supply and power of money renders them impotent. During most periods the under-standing that debts are to be paid and that money is a useful medium of exchange represents an entirely appropriate economic framework. Similarly the terrible consequences of the nourishing of grievances and the failure to forgive provides no justification for abandoning our general perception of the demands of justice. We generally accept that justice demands recompense for wrongs done and that forgiveness is not a burden to be laid upon those whose suffering at the hands of others has not been adequately recognised. As the President of the International Forgiveness Institute in Wisconsin observed: 'When I forgive I can still ask that my rights be respected. I can still ask that I as a person be respected ... To forgive never has meant that we simply exchange mercy and justice.'[29]

---

[29] Bob Enwright, *Analysis* radio programme on 'Forgiveness,' BBC Radio 4, 17 December 1999.

Our brief survey of the development of the money economy into a merciless and disordered one revealed the distortions that occur when monetary disciplines continue to be asserted in a context where money itself has been subject to no discipline at all. The language of owing and repayment, of fiscal responsibility, of 'living within one's means' or financial accountability becomes highly deceptive. That which was invented to facilitate the exchange of goods and services becomes destructive of the lives of people and nations if money itself, the *measure* of accountability and fairness, has been allowed to cease to be a stable measure and become in itself an instrument of domination.

Such is what also occurs, in non-financial matters, when our usual sense of what is fair and just becomes a disguise for dominating feelings of injury and revenge which hold sway in the lives of individuals and communities. Then the demand for the measured imposition of penalties and expectation of recompense becomes a camouflage for unresolved hatreds and bitterness that no recompense could possibly assuage.

Yet the analogy fails at one key point, one of immense theological significance. So far as one can tell in both theory and practice, there is always a strategy that would deal with financial indebtedness: the debt can be cancelled, or cleared by a third party, or simply defaulted on. But in the score of wrongs there may indeed be ones for which no recompense is possible and forgiveness beyond the bounds of even theoretical possibility. The holocaust is such an example: in Simon Wiesenthal's *The Sunflower* he describes an encounter with a former Nazi officer near the point of death. When the officer asks for forgiveness Wiesenthal walks away, and for two reasons: first, he has no mandate to forgive from those who were the officer's victims; and secondly because the crimes seemed beyond forgiveness. The holocaust may be the example that serves as an icon of a situation which stretches the economy of mercy beyond human limits, but it is not the only example, where the level of injury and wrong simply is such that no remedy seems possible. The entail of such situations in a continuing spiral of paralysing resentment or chronic violence simply sharpens the issue. It is at that point when the human possibilities of a merciful economy seem exhausted that the *theological* issue becomes most sharply focused: how is what we earlier described as God's commitment to an economy of mercy sustained? If no change is possible within the human economy, is there currency in the divine economy that will fill up the empty human well of mercy? What is God's response to the reality of unrepayable human indebtedness? What compensation could there be for such injuries beyond valuation?

4. Atoning Mercy

> Against the background of the holocaust, and the ongoing holocaust of
> the new world order, perhaps we can look again at the original tale of
> redemption. From it we learn that though we are far from equal as
> victims, yet we are nevertheless all considered slaves to the rule of sin.
> None by their own judgement may claim exemption; but equally, none
> by our judgement may be deemed beyond redemption.[30]

Angela West's critique of the modern, and particularly the feminist, suspicion of the tale of redemption comes after a journey through the supposed
distinctions between oppressor and oppressed. She plumbs the depths not
merely of the distorted relationship between the sexes but also the power of
the military-economic nexus. She has passionately taken sides, in debate
and demonstration, on issues of violence and non-violence. She comes to
the conclusion that the human situation cannot after all be resolved on the
basis of whether you happen to be 'innocent' or 'guilty.' Precisely at the
point where there seem the greatest grounds for pessimism about the
possibility of an economy of mercy, she finds in Augustine a renewal of the
possibility of solidarity. 'Augustine in his rejection of the doctrines of
Pelagianism refused to accept the pessimistic and uncompassionate idealism
which held each individual personally accountable for all their moral
failures.'[31]

Human solidarity is not of course sufficient. In terms derived from our
survey of the character of the money economy, more is at stake than the
writing off, by whatever mechanisms, of this or that unpayable debt, or even
of all unpayable debts. For the 'debts' that need to be paid are the debts
which have been accrued by the exploitative operation of a money-driven
economy out of control; they are debts to the whole human community, and
to the ecosystem – the economy – which we share with all other creatures.
For such debts to be paid requires not the selling of gold in bank vaults in
quantities however vast, but a change involving everything from systemic
reconstruction to mass personal conversion. Fundamentally, the debt is
owed by the economy as a whole to the economy as a whole.

That is the cosmic significance of the parable of the 'unforgiving servant'
in Matthew 18. Enormous though the disparities in indebtedness may be,
and vast though the distinctions between oppressor and oppressed may be,
those differences do in the end only instantiate the fundamental dislocation
of the 'economy' of creation. In the parable of the prodigal son, the elder

---

[30] Angela West, *Deadly Innocence: Feminism and the Mythology of Sin* (London 1995),
160.

[31] West, *Deadly Innocence*, 144.

son's declaration that he has more *claim* on his father's generosity than his wastrel brother is judged irrelevant to the determination of the father to display a mercy that transforms debt into delight. But our question remains, what has to happen to the debts and the claims if the economy of mercy is to be re-established?

The economic analogy has at least made clear that classical debates about the atonement, debates about the way in which the death of Christ was efficacious, all involve people taking partial positions about something which has to have effect at every level. The death of Christ has to convert the heart of the beholder and believer, but it has to do more than that. For the dislocation of the creation is a moral fact, that both involves human responsibility and is too big for human responsibility to discharge. Something has, that is to say, to happen within the history whose dislocation needs to be cured, but altogether larger than can be contained within the categories of that history. As Donald MacKinnon states in describing the theology of the Fourth Gospel:

> In the Word made flesh, we have to reckon not with the disclosure of a principle, but with a human history that, in virtue of its origin, grounds an issue in eternity, is in its concrete particularity decisive for all who went before, who were its contemporaries, and who came after.[32]

That 'human history,' if it is to effect real transformation, has to enter into the reality of the 'indebtedness beyond payment' which is so powerful a metaphor for the human situation. So the cosmic effectiveness of the death of Christ, manifested initially in its transcending the boundaries of the first covenant, lies in its entry into solidarity with the real moral consequences of the human condition:

> Christ redeemed us from the curse of the law by becoming a curse for us – for it is written, 'Cursed is everyone who hangs on a tree' – in order that in Christ Jesus the blessing of Abraham might come to the Gentiles, so that we might receive the promise of the Spirit through faith.[33]

So it is that through God's solidarity in Christ with the consequences of sin debt is transformed into grace, and curse into blessing. 'At the heart [of the narrative] lies the actuality of Jesus' condemnation.'[34] This is the language of transformation of the whole economy, not the discharge or remission of

---

[32] D.M. MacKinnon, 'Subjective and Objective Conceptions of Atonement,' in: F.G. Healey (ed.), *Prospect for Theology: Essays in Honour of H.H. Farmer* (Welwyn Garden City 1966), 173.

[33] Galatians 3:13f.

[34] MacKinnon, 'Subjective and Objective Conceptions,' 180.

individual elements within it. The entry into the full moral consequences does also have the possibility of transforming individual believers from slavery to freedom. 'The independence that the vicarious death of Jesus assures for those who are linked to him is characterised by Christian freedom from the tyranny that sin and death exercise over human life.'[35] In economic terms what this represents is the assumption of the life-situation of the debtor by a creditor with vast claims. In an act far transcending the mere 'generosity' (mere, if admirable) that cancels this or that debt, it is the willed surrender of the ambitions, aspirations and possessions of the creditor in exchange for the deprivation of the debtor. 'Go, sell your possessions, and give the money to the poor, and you will have treasure in heaven; then come, follow me.'

This is 'atoning sacrifice,' in that it refuses to adopt strategies that would accommodate Christ within the merciless economy while making gestures of individual alleviation that ignore the fundamental nature of the problem. 'Why this waste?' is a proper economic question – and an implicit acceptance of the terms on which that economy operates.

The campaign for *Jubilee 2000* has yielded ameliorative strategies, moments of mercy in the merciless economy. Arguably, that is faithful to the origins of Jubilee itself: a pattern of regular interruption enacted by a society aware at the deepest level of the inherent tendency of all human structures to tend towards oppression and injustice, 'for the human heart is corrupt from its youth.' Rightly, for instance, Geiko Müller-Fahrenholz sees the Sabbath and Jubilee traditions as prefiguring what we now vitally need, namely, 'time ceilings for the growth of money.'

> It is the fascinating insight of the sabbatical concept that the flow of activity must be regularly intercepted to keep it from accelerating beyond proportions … and it is the fascinating insight of the Jubilee that even the cumulative potentials of human endeavour must be submitted to radical interruptions.[36]

But he also rightly describes his proposals as 'utopian and fragmentary.' For the reality is that the imposition of 'time ceilings' on the growth of money represents a direct confrontation with the morality of the money economy itself. Those considering how Christians might best engage with the economy have always to weigh the relative merits of utopian vision and readiness to compromise for the sake of attainable, but penultimate, goals.[37] It

---

[35] W. Pannenberg, *Systematic Theology* II (Edinburgh 1994), 436.

[36] Geiko Müller-Fahrenholz, 'The Jubilee: Time Ceilings for the Growth of Money?', contribution to the WCC-ICCJ Colloquium on the Jubilee (Bossey, WCC, 1996).

[37] For a nuanced discussion of this dilemma, see Malcolm Brown & Robin Morrison, *Challenging Mammon* (Manchester 1999), 91–94.

is certainly encouraging to observe that there is more and more recognition that the monetary orthodoxy that declares money to be beyond control or regulation will eventually have disastrous consequence, and not just for the poor. If we are to concern ourselves with the *transformation* of the economy at a fundamental level we have to engage with more costly questions than are raised by this or that particular debt, or even the whole range of unrepayable debts burdening the two-thirds world. The argument will be about whether all are willing – and especially those who have been taught that their salvation lies in the power of money – to pay the much larger costs that transformation involves.

Yet even so there might be more things to do with the economy than engage with it, important as that is. Jesus, it seems, was very ready to learn from it, taking the morally dubious actions of its most successful participants as models of the 'enterprise' required of those who seek first the Kingdom of God and its righteousness. Above all, however, the economy became in his hands a medium for learning about the character of God, and his merciful intentions towards his creation.

It would appear that God's dealing with the fundamental problem of a universe locked in unrepayable indebtedness, out of control in an economy perpetually feeding on its own illusions, has all the marks of the dispersed generosity of an enterprising sower or grasping businessman, the opportunism of a steward about to be sacked, and the wastefulness of a woman declining to do the obvious with an expensive box of ointment. But it has these marks alongside one other: a determined solidarity with the guilty participants *and* the innocent victims of the cosmos he longs to save, one that avoids neither the sins of the guilty nor the sufferings of the victim. Such is the morally serious, utterly gracious, character of God's merciful economy.

Afterword: Response to the Discussion of the Paper at the Conference

Of the many points raised in an interesting and testing discussion of the conference paper, three stand out in my mind as occasions for further reflection.

1. Surprise was expressed at the absence of reflection on *idolatry* in the paper.
2. There was some important discussion on the need for stability in the *political* economy of the world, a stability undermined by the essential volatility of money.

3. The global, money-drive economy is characterised by a lack of face-to-face contact with those affected by decisions. (The conference took place in the immediate aftermath of the Rover crisis, one in which decisions were taken at a considerable distance from those immediately affected.)

With regard to the omission of the first, I plead only that I have written and spoken on this aspect elsewhere. However it is important to name the connections that exist among these three points. The issue is well focussed by Psalm 82, where the gods are portrayed as contributing to the total instability of things ('The foundations of the earth are shaken') precisely by their failure to attend to the most vulnerable of human persons. The point is made in this essay about the essential chaos of a money-driven economy. The dominance of money represents a submission of the world to arbitrariness (the 'salvation' promised by the lottery is a parable of that), in contrast to the essential humanity of the God of Israel, the Father of Jesus Christ. It is in the name of that essential humanity, the face-to-face encounter with God in Christ, that the restoration of the power of human decision-making and the regulation of the market in money has to be promoted. Our salvation is essentially the rescue of the world from the chaotic power of the idols.

7. Forgiveness and Our Awareness of Truth

Conference Response

1. Introduction

One of the most difficult topics for theology is to understand how the knowledge of truth is to be found in the diversity of its subject matter. This is especially the case when contributions come from disciplines so distinct as systematic theology, psychology, pastoral theology and social ethics. The cross, for example, stands for more than the unchanging truth that God is love, 'whose property is always to have mercy.' The truth of the atonement is interwoven with the contingent facts of history, and the truth about these facts. What sort of 'truth' do we refer to here? When we move on to the nature of pastoral theology, there is a proper emphasis on listening to experience and the reality of that experience as heard and interpreted by the therapist. Feelings, hopes, fears make up human consciousness. As such they may vary in intensity but not in falsity. The question of truth arises in two ways: first, it arises when these experiences are used to make assertions about the past or the present. These assertions are about something beyond the self, and they are experiences of something. False memory, and the ability conversely to recover buried encounters which may be deeply painful, all show the fragility of human cognition when experiences subject the human person to an experience which they cannot bear. Secondly, there are insights into the nature of human personality, and its capacity for good or evil. A novel such as Golding's *Darkness Visible*[1] picks up Milton's description of

---

[1] William Golding, *Darkness Visible* (London 1979), 260–261: 'the real hardship is that there's no end.... all the time to know with a kind of ghastly astonishment.' Golding explores the awareness of morality and the powerlessness of this knowledge in the face of unbridled desire. The definition of evil given by Marilyn McCord Adams in *The Problem of Evil* (Oxford 1990) cited by Wilko van Holten in his article 'Eschatology with a Vengeance' in D. Fergusson

hell in the same words, and attempts to portray evil in contemporary relationships. How 'true' is this attempt, and in what way is the veracity of this novel related to the truth of the atonement which systematic theology expresses? Contingency, the finality of the action of the cross, and truths about human personality meet with the assertions about past or present events in speaking about the claim that a person who has been abused is speaking the truth about their experience; has revealed deep wickedness in what has happened between them and another; can be healed by therapy; and in the power of the atonement wrought by Christ can also experience salvation, and offer forgiveness to the abuser because of what Christ has done for them. In what sense is all this spoken of as true, or do we move to a claim that truth (while ultimately controlled by the discipline of the Triune God in creation and redemption) is analogical?

2. The Encounter with Sin and Evil

Sin is clearly at the root of the need to be forgiven. In the encounter with fallen humanity God forgives through the action of the cross. The forgiveness that Christians should show to one another is based on the forgiveness that has been made real in the death of Christ, and his resurrection. It may, however, be asked whether there is an intentional passing beyond sin, to the direct and intentional pursuit of evil for its own sake. Such a theme seems to be developed in Haddon Willmer's chapter, when he writes that 'evil becomes our good: when sin, because it shapes our life, ceases to be sin for us.'[2] In my own experience I would contrast brutality in a prison (intentional, and enjoyed by its perpetrators) as an experience of evil, with the daily fallen nature of custody, where sinful humanity rubs shoulders in many different ways. Other examples would be the experience of institutional racism in a police force (see the description in the Lawrence Inquiry[3]) which is an example of corporate sin. This can be put alongside direct experiences of the canteen culture, where deliberate racism still flourishes and can be said to be evil. If there is any merit in categorising evil as a subset of sin, as in the conscious corruption of a relationship by sexual abuse which may lead in the fullness of time to the suicide of the person corrupted because of what was done to them, then we are faced with how we might know what is evil?

& M. Sarot (eds.), *The Future as God's Gift* (Edinburgh, 2000), 184 is one which gives reason to doubt whether one's own life is a good to one. Adams cites examples of torture and the abuse of children. I suggest that intentional participation in moral wickedness without being able to restrain from this is also an example of a 'horrendous evil.'

[2] See Ch. 2, p.23 above.

[3] *The Inquiry into the Death of Stephen Lawrence*: A Report by Sir William MacPherson of Cluny (London 1999).

3. The Knowledge of Evil in Christ

To be brief: all evil is sin but not all sin is called evil. Luther's revival of the ancient symbolism of Christ's defeat of the powers of evil in the theme of the Christus Victor is not a philosophical explanation of evil but rather a dual affirmation that Christ has defeated sin and evil, and that in Christ we too can overcome the forces of sin and death. This is a dualistic account of evil, turning on its enmity to the good, but also giving an explanation of evil in the act of defeating it. The reality of forgiveness is predicated, as George Hunsinger shows,[4] on the action of Christ in his victory, which is not an act in which we participate except *post hoc* (writing as I do in the Anglican tradition) in the Eucharistic sacrifice. The only explanation of evil, and therefore the only attempt at giving a truthful account of it, is found in the action of defeating it. If we speak of the veiling of God on the cross, in the action of defeating evil, we are both plunged into silence before the *Deus Absconditus* and yet we both make an affirmation and at the same time we use a metaphor. Literal and metaphorical terms interpenetrate, and the discussion of liturgy must have (as the late Donald MacKinnon once put it) 'a deeply interrogative nature' which holds the participant to the dialectical relationship between the sacred and humanity. Even so the stranger spoke on the road to Emmaus explaining the nature of the defeat of evil in the past few days, and the darkness was illuminated by his speech.

Evil is central to both Luther and Bonhoeffer. The *theologia crucis* looks at the evil of doubt and terror and yet sees God there. The criterion of the Christian faith is to find forgiveness in the midst of hell because of the cross of Christ. 'Having entered into darkness and blackness I see nothing; I live by faith, hope and love alone.'[5] It is interesting that one of the constant themes of Bonhoeffer's *Ethics* is the inability to see evil for what it is. Here I develop my central point. It seems that in the *Ethics* some sinful actions become demonic, and pass beyond the moral categories of ethics. If that is so, then the task at some moments in history is to see clearly what might be not merely sinful but demonic, or perhaps evil, and to know this reality in truth. My point then is to suggest that the forgiveness of evil is a sub-set of the forgiveness of sins which raises profound problems. Certainly Bonhoeffer was clear in the *Ethics*[6] that the problem of reasonable people is to perceive the depths of evil, which often appears in the form of light and renewal. The moral theorist is often blinded by the nature of evil and he suggests that being evil is worse than doing evil. Liars who tell truths are worse than

---

[4] In a paper not included in this volume, but published in *International Journal of Systematic Theology* 2 (2000), 247–269.

[5] Luther, *Operationes in Psalmos*, vol. 5 176.16.

[6] Dietrich Bonhoeffer, *Ethics*, edited by Eberhard Bethge (London 1978), 47.

those committed to truth who sometimes lie. What matters is to discern when we encounter evil, and here we are in danger in Bonhoeffer's words of the danger of being burdened by the ethical. This recalls Christopher Jones' warning in Chapter 3 about the danger of idealising the churches and the failure to recognise where false peace is promoted. Jones cites the remarkable study by William Cavanaugh *Torture and Eucharist*[7] in order to argue that the Eucharist must always create a confrontation in the presence of Jesus with the ambivalence of judgment and forgiveness. The question of how the encounter with Jesus Christ in the liturgy can be known truthfully raises the issue of how far the temporal world is taken seriously. The concern must be that a liturgical enactment of forgiveness enacts the divine drama of reconciliation in such a way that the kenosis of the earthly life of Jesus is generalised into a necessary moment in the eternal dialectic of sin and redemption. Jones is alive to this danger at the end of his chapter, citing Edwin Muir's description of ideology as the danger into which signs of mediation fall. My concern is rather that there is a danger of mythologising the enterprise, so that the limits of truth are stretched as the liturgy is 'mapped' on to the Gospels themselves.[8]

4. Emotions and Theology

In Chapter 4 Fraser Watts raised the possibility of exploring the theme of forgiveness through the emotions. Emotions are a means of indicating how we might respond to a situation, but the description of the situation will be by beliefs. They are a response, which must be grounded in whatever it is that they respond to. The logical status of emotions requires careful consideration. The recent study by Richard Wollheim distinguishes between beliefs, which map the world; desires, which target the world with things we aim at; and emotions, which colour the world by lightening or darkening it. It is interesting that Wollheim wishes to link a philosophical study of the emotions with psychology in a way that has not been typical of twentieth-century moral philosophy, since Watts in many ways as a psychologist is making a similar journey in connecting psychology to theology and philosophy. The descriptive power of Watts' account avoids the fault of depersonalising emotion, which is a criticism that has been made recently of

---

[7] William T. Cavanaugh, *Torture and Eucharist* (Oxford 1998).

[8] See for a fine discussion of this problem Rowan Williams' essay in the festschrift for Donald MacKinnon on the criticisms made by MacKinnon about Moltmann for doing exactly this: Rowan Williams, 'Trinity and Ontology,' in: Rowan Williams (ed.), *On Christian Theology* (Oxford 2000), 160–162.

Wollheim.[9] Shame in Wollheim's account seems to be estranged from the person whose state it is, so that shame develops independently of a person's beliefs, and the issue of truth is lost in the power of fantasy. While there may be some merit in this analysis, Wollheim abandons a belief in a Kantian reason or the divine presence (through the work of the Spirit in conscience) in humanity, and is left with a moral internal battlefield. Watts' careful discussion relates shame to the beliefs which we hold, and relates divine grace (as a truth about the activity of God) to our feelings of shame, so that we can live forgiven lives in the truth. It is valuable that such attention should be given to the attitudes that should be found in a Christian disciple, especially when they are held alongside the objects that render them appropriate. As Peter Baelz pointed out there is no future in adopting certain characteristics of discipleship without saying what they are a response to. 'Christian faith is more than the free exercise of human subjectivity. It has a determinate content ... It is, rather, the acknowledgement that what is true for me is ultimately dependent on what is true in itself.'[10]

5. Corporate Truth

Peter Baelz in the same volume argued that the idea of integrity is mediately transitive: sincerity refers to the intention of the agent and the moral worth of the individual, or corporate body, but integrity refers us beyond the agent to that to which they are faithful. It is clearly the burden of Peter Selby's contribution (Chapter 6) that the economic system in which he is placed as a Bishop at the end of the twentieth century both lacks all integrity and also corrupts human relationships. In a similar vein the sociologist Richard Sennett has argued that the work ethic has been so corrupted by contemporary capitalism that it corrodes human character.[11] There are some suggestions from Peter Selby that wish to put in place an alternative to the monetary system, which will create an 'abundant and sufficient environment, a reliable framework for the created order in general and human flourishing in particular.'[12] The issue of transformation remains central to this debate, even if some of us would wish to resist the condemnation of the global economic system that is given by Peter Selby. Transformation involves 'solidarity with the real moral consequences of the human condition.' What remains open for debate is in what way global economics can regain integrity. Harking back to the discussion by Deborah van Deusen

---

[9] Richard Wollheim, *On the Emotions* (Yale 1999) and the appreciative review by Elizabeth Spelman in the *London Review of Books* 30 March 2000, 9–11.

[10] Peter Baelz, *Christian Theology and Metaphysics* (London 1968), 64.

[11] Richard Sennett, *The Corrosion of Character* (London 1999).

[12] See Ch. 6 above, 110.

Hunsinger there is a similar issue of how a church can allow repentant sex offenders to be accepted back into a worshipping congregation: what is the integrity of forgiveness in a corporate body?

6. Truth, Forgiveness and the Knowledge of Good and Evil

What I wish to press is whether the way we know sin becomes more intractable as sin deepens into evil. I would need time to come up with a working distinction between the two, and my response feels fragmentary. It is striking that Bonhoeffer did not offer a definition either, but any attempt to do so would have to turn on the conscious pursuit of wrong actions that are delighted in for their own sake: *corruptio optima pessima*, and the perversion of relationships for harmful purposes. I am intrigued by Christopher Jones' reference to the way some people have used the language of impurity to demean others who are different from them as suggestive of some of the roots of evil speech. I realise of course that Fraser Watts and Deborah Hunsinger are not only referring to speech but to actions and inner states of being. I would have wished to press Deborah Hunsinger here on the theological account of the abuser: in what sense not only sinful, but evil, whatever the causation? Again Fraser Watts' very helpful discussion enables me to see in his correlation between atonement theory and psychology how we might use modern scientific knowledge to understand what we are about in knowing the truth. I end by repeating my main point. Does our response to evil, rather than simply sin, demand a harder task of knowing and understanding from the Christian? If so, does that make the conception of truth in relation to evil more dialectical, as MacKinnon would certainly have argued? In other words, do we know evil fully only when we see the way, by our allegiance to Christ *pro nobis*, to pass through evil? And what does that imply for the oft-discussed question of whether evil can be forgiven? The central task of theology is to illuminate the beliefs that the Christian Church holds about the nature of God, and the truth claims that Jesus made about his living in the truth. On this basis he acted to forgive sins and the reaction to him was to bring a charge of blasphemy.

The question of truth is then raised in many ways in these chapters: in the relation of emotions to beliefs; in the accuracy of the memories of those in therapy; in the relation of historical actuality of the Gospels to accounts of the presence of Jesus in the liturgy; in the issue of what the global economy lacks integrity to; and in the question of whether the life and death of Jesus can be known except through a dialectic of veiling and unveiling. The discussions reveal again the intractability of epistemological issues in the question of forgiveness and reconciliation, which Christian theology encounters at every turn.

8. Forgiveness in Context

Conference Response

Jane Craske

1. Introduction

My response to the contributions collected in this volume is coloured by three situations that formed the context within which I engaged with the original papers and the ensuing debates. The first 'situation' was my question as to the meaning and effectiveness of the many words and actions with which Christian churches had expressed their repentance, and asked for forgiveness for the sins, mistakes, and atrocities perpetrated by Christians over two millennia. Forgiveness was one of the central planks of the 'Millennium Prayer' suggested for use by Churches Together in Britain and Ireland.

The second situation was focused in the British Methodist Church's handling of a concern for all Christian churches. For the last eighteen months or so there has been a debate in the church precisely about the meaning of forgiveness. A decision was made by the Methodist Conference of 1998 that anyone who has been convicted of or cautioned for a sexual offence against children shall not hold office in the church *for life*. That decision suggested for some an apparent limit to forgiveness, or at least to restoration and reconciliation, and there the debate in many ways begins.

The third situation consists of a multitude of conversations with people who are struggling with the recent death of a loved one, or with the longer-term process of bereavement. Issues about forgiveness *and truth* become particularly pertinent for me here, as also in the practice of conducting funerals. For there is the question of what truth is told about a person at their funeral, and how it is related to the various truths of others' lives. There is further the question of how it is possible to speak of God's judgement on sin, in order to put God's forgiveness in a proper context. Beyond that, the process of grieving, and the part played in it by regret, blame, and forgiveness, especially where there can be no reconciliation with the person who is dead, may have something to teach us about the theology of forgiveness.

These situations, then, formed the space within which I listened to the deliberations on 'Forgiveness and Truth.' I draw out from the process of listening three main threads.

2. Context

The notion of forgiveness cannot be adequately discussed if it is addressed as an abstract concept. The subject is treated in a truthful manner when it is contextualised. There was a particular keenness, a particular attentiveness in the conference atmosphere when stories of people struggling with forgiveness were told. David Self's contribution, 'Enfolding the Dark' (Chapter 12 below) recounted the story of a woman whose sister disappeared, and who then discovered some fifteen or so years later that her sister had been murdered by Fred and Rosemary West. Stories have a power in giving us a context for our theology, and they emphasise the *messiness* involved in the process of forgiving which we are often reluctant to introduce into our theology.

It is narrative that highlights the temporal dimension of forgiveness. It has become almost axiomatic to describe forgiveness as a process, though this was at its clearest in Deborah van Deusen Hunsinger's contribution (Chapter 5 above). But it is a process that involves other elements also. These various elements are further seen as a process through which we move, and that process is usually seen as linear and one-directional. It runs, I think, implicitly, as follows:

sin ... judgement ... repentance ... forgiveness/release/healing ... reconciliation.

Some of these elements were clearly delineated from each other in the papers, and some of them were implicitly linked. For instance, it was not always clear in our discussions whether repentance was seen as necessary to forgiveness, or whether reconciliation was somehow a part of forgiveness or an entirely different concept. Narrative shows up how often the process of forgiveness, or progress through the various elements linked to forgiveness (if seen as linear) may seem to go backwards, or stall. Perhaps the elements may not actually appear in that order at all. The process may be better described as cyclical, or as even more random. There is scope, even at a relatively simple level, for systematising what the relationships of these elements might be. But it is also this insistence on seeing forgiveness as a process that makes the noun 'forgiveness' (with static overtones) seem less adequate than the verb participle 'forgiving' (with the notion of 'continuing to forgive' implicit within it).

The idea of forgiveness as a process raises questions about the liturgical mediation of forgiveness, particularly the relationship with the 'once-for-all' rite of baptism (in the papers by Christopher Jones and George Hunsinger[1]). Discussions of liturgy and how forgiveness is expressed in it (whether referring to baptism, or to worship as a whole) seem to set up forgiveness as a completed act within the liturgical context. The *repetitions* of the liturgy might mirror a better notion of forgiveness as a process. But perhaps these concepts might yet question each other more creatively.

If we give attention to the contexts in which forgiving takes place, we must ask questions about the standpoints of others and ourselves, and the ways in which those standpoints affect the theology that we create. Some contributions have concentrated on our need to be forgiven, either by God or by other people. Christopher Jones, George Hunsinger and Fraser Watts concentrated chiefly on the forgiving activity of God, and therefore on the place of human beings as sinners. Deborah van Deusen Hunsinger offered reflection first and foremost on the situations in which human beings need to forgive, as those who are sinned against. (The relationship between this standpoint and that of the sinner was, however, examined as her paper progressed.) It became clear that the position of 'being in need of forgiveness' is seen by many as having only a horizontal aspect – being applicable only to human beings. Some, however, in discussion (with more explicit engagement in Haddon Willmer's contribution in Chapter 2 above), have asked whether there is meaning in language about forgiving God.

Whether we stand in the place of sinner/perpetrator or victim/sinned against may determine much about the shape of forgiveness for us. It is at this point that we need to consider whether it is possible (or desirable) to develop a notion of forgiveness which straddles all these perspectives.

But then, the lines between being sinner and victim of sin may be blurred. This is most clearly so where we recognise that people may be trapped in situations that leave them few choices in life, and in places where they are both sinned against and sinning, therefore in need of forgiveness in a number of ways. Situations of abuse make this particularly plain as we increasingly see the patterns in relationships by which people echo abuses perpetrated on themselves, in similar or very different forms.

One further reflection does not follow directly from the notion of context, but does follow from language about the 'victims' of sin. Fraser Watts' paper on a shame-oriented theology of sin (Chapter 4 above) was fruitful in many ways, but its perspective allowed us to ignore the victims of sin. George Hunsinger specifically argues that sin is primarily against God

---

[1] For Jones's paper, see Ch. 3 above; George Hunsinger's paper is not included in this volume but has been published in *International Journal of Systematic Theology* 2 (2000), 247–269.

and sometimes exclusively so. Thus we might posit God as the ultimate victim of sin. The danger of such a theology is that it might turn our attention away from human victims of sin, and lead to our minimising the suffering of others. A re-positioning suggests that we only pay proper attention to God as the victim of sin if we truly pay attention to the victimisation of those God created.

3. Metaphorical Language of Forgiveness

Whether in linguistics or in theology, we have become accustomed to registering that metaphorical language conveys both similarity and dissimilarity. Theologically we have nothing better than human language to point to the divine (assuming of course a realist framework to begin with). We are dependent on an analogical relationship between human activities (including human words in the Bible) and God's activities for our understanding of God's ways and purposes, even as we recognise the inadequacy of such analogies, and know that they must break down at some point. But the place at which they may or may not be breaking down could be a fruitful, if difficult, place theologically. So I push some of the analogies that seemed, at least at first, unhelpful.

In the discussion of George Hunsinger's paper, it was pointed out that an apparent analogy between salvation/sinner and liberation/victim had most of its impact in the meaning-creation between the two terms 'salvation' and 'liberation.' However, the concurrent analogy between 'sinner' and 'victim' looked much more problematic, leaving considerable space for the blaming of the victim. In Peter Selby's paper (Chapter 6 above), an interesting analogy is developed on the model of the relationship between debtors and creditors, to expound the notion that God transforms the human situation (brings about atonement) by, God being our creditor, becoming the debtor on the cross. If that, however, is put alongside the comment of bishops of debtor nations at the Lambeth Conference, that it is the creditor nations which need forgiveness rather than the debtor nations in the current global debt situation, we are left with questions about God's responsibility, which also need to be worked through in the course of a theology of atonement. Here again is a tentative question about God's need for forgiveness, which might be taken by some to be creative, or by others to be blasphemous.

Fraser Watts was explicit about using human experiences of shame as a way of learning something about God's forgiveness. He explored both 'negative' and 'positive' aspects of shame, and related some elements of experiences of shame to our need for God's forgiveness. For me, however, the 'negative' side of shame, its ability to damage, as well as a tendency for shame to be understood in gender-specific ways within human societies, is insufficiently explored to make it clear whether such experiences detracted seriously from the analogy that is being drawn.

One final example: the *process* of forgiving was well-explored in human terms. We are left with the question as to whether we would want to use that as a metaphor for God's activity. Would it make any sense to as whether God finds forgiving a more easily completed (or a less temporal) activity than we do?

There are two ways of developing this theme. Either I am pushing analogies beyond their breaking point and showing up the areas where human forgiveness and divine forgiveness are completely different, even alien, activities, which would lead us to very different descriptions of God's forgiving and human forgiving. Or there is interesting space opening up for further exploration. In brief, there is more work to be done on the relation between the so-called 'horizontal' and 'vertical' aspects of forgiveness.

4. Forgiveness and Healing

The title of this section might be more problematically expressed as 'forgiveness and self-interest.' We tread on the most delicate and difficult ground where we recognise that it is impossible to *demand* that others forgive those who have harmed them (particularly within an externally imposed time frame). Yet we know also that there is a canker, destructiveness in the lives of those who cannot forgive. For the Christian Church this is complicated by the practice of pronouncing the forgiveness of God over the offender in a context that is not always *seen* to take the victim of the offence into account.

So the question here is, for whose sake do we forgive? And for whose sake do some church ministers pronounce forgiveness? Secular therapeutic practitioners are divided about whether forgiveness is necessary to a person's health, but they would not take the effect of forgiveness beyond the realm of the one 'sinned against.' Christians often look first to the effect of forgiveness in the life of the sinner/perpetrator. Could we ever add that forgiveness is somehow for God's sake also?

In speaking of the health (or self-interest) of the one who needs to forgive, there often comes into play a language of distinction, even opposition, between a person's *choice* to forgive, and an *obligation* to forgive. The 'choice' is usually conceived as an internal matter, with the 'obligation' seen as imposed from outside. Perhaps we could re-configure the language by abandoning the 'either/or' aspect, using the word 'necessity' instead. It makes the situation no less challenging, but acknowledges the rightful place of a therapeutic understanding within a theology of forgiveness. Still the words we choose are dangerous: Deborah van Deusen Hunsinger uses a language of 'maturity' to describe the person who comes to the point of being able to forgive great harm perpetrated against them. Such language is in danger of carrying overtones of blame for the victim who can't forgive, at least for now (being less mature). Perhaps any language of 'necessity' does the same. It is at this point that we acknowledge how much our words need testing against pastoral experience, much as we need to use our theological concepts to test pastoral experience also.

From the bland phrase 'forgive and forget,' which is both unhelpful and untrue, we move to a phrase like 'remember and forgive.' This is where 'forgiveness' and 'truth' clearly feed each other. Still in a therapeutic framework (one which understands healing to be part of what God desires for people), it is critical that the person offended against acknowledges the unacceptability of what has been done to them, if forgiving the offence is to be distinguished from excusing or condoning. 'Remember and forgive' might better describe the necessary stand for a self-respecting person. In that framework we can understand judgement as 'truthful remembering' (a phrase used in the original title of Deborah van Deusen Hunsinger's paper), and remember that the concept of 'justice' in languages other than English can include the word 'mercy,' rather than being construed in opposition to it.

5. Conclusions

I have traced three main threads where questions might elicit more detailed working through of notions of forgiveness and truth, especially in the relationship (or lack of it) between the forgiving activity of God and the forgiving activity of human beings. One final line of enquiry came for me in a short paper given by Ken Hart.[2] He reported on research work with recovering alcoholics in the framework of the Alcoholics Anonymous 12-step Programme. That programme involves participants acknowledging the harm they have done to others by their addictive behaviour, and acknowledging the resentments they hold against other people: i.e., recognising their needs to be forgiven and to forgive. For very many participants the 'others' in the two categories coincided. Here is a way to acknowledge the intimate links between forgiving and being forgiven within our human experience. It still leaves us with as many questions as ever about how that human experience reveals to us the ways and purposes of God in Jesus Christ.

---

[2] Not included in this volume.

9. Truth and Reconciliation

Is Radical Openness a Condition for Reconciliation?

Nico Schreurs

1. Introduction

In an interview printed in the April 1995 issue of the communication journal of Pax Christi, the Belgian Primate, Cardinal Godfried Danneels, summed up three conditions that have to be met by true reconciliation: truth, justice, and creativity. What, in Danneels' view, was apparently the most important condition – the formulation returns in the heading of the article – is that reconciliation must ultimately be based on truth. Reconciliation is part of a sequence, which starts with the search for the truth. This is confirmed by the name given to the commission that in South Africa had to supervise the transition from the Apartheid regime to the present multiracial society. Unlike similar commissions in, especially, South America,[1] this commission was not just named a truth commission, but the Truth and Reconciliation Commission. The emphasis on the combination of the search for truth about the violent past and the pursuit of reconciliation was quite clearly and protractedly shown in the TV reports of the interrogations held by the Commission, in which the camera repeatedly zoomed in on the slogan: 'Truth is the road to reconciliation.'

The question I will address in this chapter is that of the relationship between truth and reconciliation. Is that relationship quite as clear as it was made out to be by the South-African Truth and Reconciliation Commission? In order to give a more concrete idea of the things one might think of here, I sum up three possible options. First: without truth, no reconciliation. In this case, truth is a necessary but not a sufficient condition for reconciliation. Second: truth leads straight to reconciliation. In this case, truth is a necessary and sufficient condition for reconciliation. Third: truth is far from

---

[1] Cf. P.B. Hayner, 'Fifteen Truth Commissions – 1974 to 1994: A Comparative Study,' in: N.J. Kritz (ed.), *Transitional Justice*, vol. 1 (Washington 1995), 225–261.

conducive to reconciliation; rather, radical openness stirs up hatred and irreconcilability. My starting-point is the Truth and Reconciliation Commission in South Africa.

2. The South African Truth and Reconciliation Commission

On July 31, 1998, the South African Truth and Reconciliation Commission finished its activities, its mandate having been prolonged several times. In the more than three years during which it was active, it heard 21,298 witnesses and received 7,127 requests for amnesty.[2] The Truth and Reconciliation Commission was in fact the alternative to a blanket amnesty, but also to a strictly judicial trial. The search for the truth caused the Commission to resemble a court of law, but the other aim pursued by the Commission, i.e., reconciliation, reached further than the imposition of rightful punishment and the satisfaction of a violated sense of justice.

The commission's special position aroused very mixed feelings. It could invite people to assist in bringing the truth to light, and then grant them amnesty, but it did not have the authority, for example, to test that truth by cross-examination. Moreover, inequality of justice arose for those who had previously been convicted and for whom the possibility of discharge by the Commission did not exist. All these are consequences of truth-finding having been made subservient not to criminal law but to improving the chance of reconciliation. Having established the conciliatory character of the Truth and Reconciliation Commission and its consequent quasi-judicial status, we come to the core of the question we started out with: does reconciliation benefit from the complete revelation of the truth, even if this is at the expense of judicial claims and of careful judicial procedures?

To begin with, reconciliation is not a judicial term. Nor is it the outcome of a judicial process. Where justice is administered, a judgement is passed and a verdict pronounced. The verdict can either allocate blame and impose a penalty, or entail acquittal. Neither of these is the same as reconciliation. Punishment conceived of as retaliation, as in a philosophy that equates criminal law with retribution, is no guarantee for reconciliation between perpetrator and victim. More modern views equating punishment with re-education do not automatically result in reconciliation either. As already mentioned, even acquittal does not mean reconciliation. Reconciliation requires more. On the other hand, reconciliation cannot come in the place of justice. There are situations that demand that justice be meted out to victims and perpetrators. The victims have a right to clarification of the

---

[2] Truth and Reconciliation Commission of South Africa, *Report* (Cape Town 1998), Vol. I, 166, 276.

circumstances under which an injustice was done to them and to a disclosure of the perpetrators' identity. That is the task of the judicial process. The Truth and Reconciliation Commission in South Africa recognised not only that right, but also the value of quick and efficient truth finding. The Commission therefore summoned the perpetrators to appear before it, but accepted the fact that it could not offer the same guarantee of the truth and nothing but the truth as the regular procedures of a court of law. Once more, this proves the supra-judicial character of reconciliation. Reconciliation is not a component part of a legal process in which an impartial judge passes judgement, but a process that takes place between the perpetrators and victims themselves. At this juncture, we can repeat our question: what is the function of the truth finding in this process?

3. The Role of the Truth in the Process of Reconciliation

Apparently, the role of truth is crucial, judging from the quasi-judicial procedure followed by the Truth and Reconciliation Commission in its attempts to find it. Reconciliation builds on truth, one might very generally put it, regardless of whether that truth is established in a judicial, a quasi-judicial, or a non-judicial context. Reconciliation is a relationship between people, a relationship that presupposes trust. Trust has its roots in the past. The sincerity of the present and future relationship must not be blocked by the burden of an unclarified and undigested past. Clarity about the facts of the matter is a *sine qua non*. If one turns a blind eye to the past because of the pragmatic necessity to co-operate, or from an attitude of forgiving and forgetting, of letting bygones be bygones, one will ultimately regret it.

Let us linger over the situation of the South African Truth and Reconciliation Commission, whose research into the truth took the form of a judicial investigation of facts, motives, and perpetrators. However, the Commission did not go through with the procedure to the very end, i.e., until legal and conclusive proof had been obtained. It contented itself with hearing declarations by witnesses who sincerely intended to tell the truth, to the best of their knowledge, about the atrocities of the past.

The risk of subjectivity and distortion was consciously taken; time-consuming safeguards of legal and historical research were dispensed with. It was, after all, not the full facts and finesses of what had exactly happened, but the existential knowledge of the truth which was deemed important for a possible reconciliation. What, according to the Commission, was even more important than incontrovertible proof of what in its report was called 'factual or forensic truth,'[3] was the willingness of perpetrators to gain in-

---

[3] Truth and Reconciliation Commission, *Report* I, 110.

sight into their actions and, on the basis of this, to confess their guilt and apologise. This means that other aspects of the truth come into play, such as 'personal or narrative truth,' 'social or dialogue truth,' and finally 'healing and restorative truth.'[4] The real character of the relationship between truth and reconciliation can only be made clear by closer scrutiny, once again, of what reconciliation means, a term that is familiar to everybody, but the ramifications of which apparently reach further than is often assumed.

4. Reconciliation: A Free Process

One of the reasons why there are people who look askance at the South African Truth and Reconciliation Commission is that they are baffled by the idea of reconciliation. They *are* capable of imagining a commission that, in reaction to a transitional situation from repression to liberation, goes in search of the historical or judicial truth behind alleged crimes and mis-demeanours, but not a commission that attempts to bring about reconciliation via a judicial route. There is, these people say, no right to reconciliation, nor is there any action that can legally thwart reconciliation. Others feel that reconciliation is not even a philosophical term, since it is only discussed in religious and theological contexts. Although this is not entirely fair – even in profane language, we talk of enemies who are reconciled, of being recon-ciled to a loss, etc. – it is not illogical to seek the origin of reconciliation in religious attitudes.

If we try to get to the core of what reconciliation means in a Christian religious context, there is no getting away from the fact that reconciliation, no matter what model is applied, rests on the belief that God's mercy appeared in Jesus. Jesus proclaimed that God reconciles himself uncondi-tionally with mankind, preferably with the poor and the meek, with those who were least entitled to it. St Paul lived on the apocalyptic experience that he no longer needed to worry about God's judgement, since he had already been justified. For Paul, the revelation (apocalypse) of the reality of that salvation was just as true as the irrefutable truth 'that all men have sinned and all are bereft of divine bliss' (Rom. 3:23). Paul devoted the first chapters of his letter to the Romans to proving this shattering truth, which was the foundation of his message of reconciliation. Only when it is no longer possible for anyone to take pride in their own merits (Rom. 3:27; 1 Cor. 1:29) and sin is rampant, is the grace of reconciliation without end (Rom. 5:20). Paul did not keep this truth from his audience; nor has Christian preaching ever failed to inculcate the fact of our human inability to bring about a reconciled reality ourselves, even though, fortunately, this has not

---

[4] Truth and Reconciliation Commission, *Report* I, 110–114.

always taken the form of doom-mongering but more often that of the joyous proclamation of undeserved reconciliation.

Seen in this way, reconciliation is indeed a theological notion *par excellence*. The revelation of the truth of human guilt serves only to throw into relief the fact that reconciliation is a matter of grace. The insight into, or, to use a theologically more correct formulation, the belief in that truth is a necessary condition for our certainty about the undeserved divine forgiveness and reconciliation, as is the truth, also revealed, of the ransom Jesus paid for it.

By referring to Jesus' death on the cross, however, we have again established a connection with the sphere of justice. The closeness of the link between the theology of reconciliation and justice is evident from the fact that, ever since the days of St Augustine, theologians have been engaged in a bitter struggle over the question whether reconciliation is primarily the work of God's justice or of God's mercy.[5] At bottom this is the question whether the core of the evangelical message, the message of salvation and reconciliation, should be uttered, discussed, and described in the metaphor of justice or in that of love. In a recent study, Timothy Gorringe has described the parallel development in the thinking along the lines of criminal justice and the theology of reconciliation from the time of Anselm of Canterbury. In this study, he notes that the representations of the divine bestowal of salvation and the application of criminal justice influence one another. The common denominator is thinking along the lines of retaliation. Retribution theory, which is the technical term for retaliatory thought, is the philosophy or, as one might prefer to call it, the ideology governing the mechanism of divine forgiveness and reconciliation as well as the fight against crime.[6]

We may conclude that it is not at all impossible to establish a connection between the seemingly elusive, theological term 'reconciliation' and the judicial and political-pragmatic questions around the South African Truth and Reconciliation Commission. It is especially the question about the function of truth finding which becomes relevant when it turns out that there is more at stake than a broad confirmation of the general sinfulness of man and the undeserved forgiveness by God.

---

[5] T. Talbott, 'Punishment, Forgiveness, and Divine Justice,' *Religious Studies* 29 (1993) 151–168.

[6] T. Gorringe, *God's Just Vengeance: Crime, Violence and the Rhetoric of Salvation* (Cambridge 1996).

5. Retribution Theories and the Increased Importance of Truth Finding

In the wake of Norbert Elias' research into processes of civilisation, and as a correction of Michel Foucault's historical reconstruction of disciplining, punishment, and the prison system, Pieter Spierenburg and David Garland have shown that thought about punishment is to a very large extent shaped by socially accepted sensitivities and differences in mentality.[7] The core of retribution theories consists in the subtle balance that ought to exist between the seriousness of the offence committed and the punishment imposed. In a strict retribution theory, there must be an exact balance between crime and punishment, or, since the principle also holds elsewhere, between merit and reward. The punishment or the reward must not be greater than deserved. In a mild form of retribution theory, the punishment must not be heavier, and the reward not smaller, than deserved.[8] It is obvious that for determining the penalty, a clear picture of the offence is essential. Not only the fact that a crime has been committed, but also the circumstances under which it was committed, should be matters of scrupulous investigation. The true facts of the case must be established beyond a shadow of doubt. Only then can justice be done.

Since the twelfth century (Anselm) a similar balanced way of thinking has become dominant in the theology of reconciliation. While the penance books from the eighth century onward served for the classification of sins and the matching atonements, the later *Beichtspiegel* ('confession guides') made it possible for the confessants in good conscience to reconstruct the truth about the sins committed. For forgiveness of sins and reconciliation with God, conditions are laid down that link up perfectly with retribution thinking. It boils down to reconciliation following the atonement achieved by the penance imposed. In this way, the doctrine of reconciliation fits perfectly into thinking in terms of criminal law; indeed, it justifies the retaliatory practice in criminal law. Consequently, radical openness also forms part of the conditions for forgiveness and reconciliation. Thomas Aquinas named these conditions as follows: expression of regret (*contritio cordis*), confession of guilt (*confessio oris*), repair of damage done, or atonement (*satisfactio operis*), and penance (*poenitentia*).[9]

---

[7] P. Spierenburg, *The Spectacle of Suffering: Executions and the Evolution of Repression* (Cambridge 1984); D. Garland, *Punishment and Modern Society* (Oxford 1990). Cf. Gorringe, *God's Just Vegeance,* 9–10.

[8] R. Purtill, 'Justice, Mercy, Supererogation,' in: Th. P. Flint (ed.), *Christian Philosophy* (Notre Dame 1990), 37–50, here: 40–41.

[9] Thomas Aquinas, *Postilla super Ps. L.*

6. Truth, Sincerity and Radical and Complete Openness

The investigation of the South African Truth and Reconciliation Commission fitted in well with the hard-line approach of what is often called the 'objective' reconciliation doctrine, in which truth-finding is looked upon as an integral part of the process. The initiative was given to the party that had caused the damage, helped by the mitigated procedure of testimonies and interrogations. Reconciliation did not follow automatically, since the victims had to consent as well, but was clearly in line with the investigation.

Besides legitimisation from 'objective' reconciliation theology, however, there is one more justification, which could be given for the procedure followed by the commission. Along with Anselmian atonement theory, an alternative view of reconciliation has maintained itself throughout history. On this view, the reconciliation that God offers to sinful people is not the fruit of divine justice, but exclusively the result of divine love. Here, no conditions are stipulated at all. God reconciles people from an overflowing love or for the sake of the free self-sacrifice of the Son, Jesus Christ. God's conciliatory action is entirely directed at the restoration of the relationship of trust.

Although I take this so called 'subjective' reconciliation theory completely seriously as a theologically important testimony of God's unconditional love, I can understand that, in everyday life, it is realistic to impose some conditions. I agree with the Dutch psychiatrist Andries van Dantzig, who claims that if the perpetrator fails to realise that he has misbehaved and does not express remorse, or if the victim is not convinced that under similar circumstances he might have done the same, forgiveness and reconciliation are merely a 'nice gesture.'[10] People are not God, who can forgive and reconcile unconditionally and beyond any judicial safeguard. It is appropriate that truthfulness and sincerity are required as integral parts of the reconciliation process. It is a different question, however, whether it is also right to demand *radical* openness, and the revelation of the *entire* truth, on pain of reconciliation not being brought about. Radical openness and absolute truth often can only, if at all, be achieved after prolonged research. Seeking to achieve them, as the Truth and Reconciliation Commission realised, would interfere with the reconciliation process. In addition, radical openness and final truth may open up so many old wounds or arouse new uncertainties and misunderstandings that the reconciliation process would not be served at all.

---

[10] A. van Dantzig in an interview in the Dutch magazine: *De Bazuin* (20 February 1998).

7. Conclusion

The situation in which the much-criticised Truth and Reconciliation Commission in South Africa found itself raises the question of the relationship between truth and reconciliation. It stands to reason that, given the framework, i.e., a quasi-judicial investigation, within which the commission operated, the factual reconstruction of the events was given high priority. From the Commission's perspective, truth was an indispensable first step in the direction of, and a necessary condition for, reconciliation. However, in the concrete political setting with which it was confronted, the Commission decided to dispense with an exhaustive investigation of the facts and the testimonies. That would have been counterproductive. This applies even more emphatically to reconciliation pursued in a pre- or supra-judicial context, since it is even clearer that a different truth than the revelation of facts is required. What is required is not an exact reconstruction and conclusive historical proof, but an existentially convincing testimony of the truth, both on the side of the perpetrator and on that of the victim. But even this truth can only be a necessary condition for reconciliation; it does not automatically lead to reconciliation. Reconciliation cannot be enforced. It is an act of, or on behalf of, the victims, who in freedom extend a conciliatory hand to their former enemies or oppressors.

10. Forgiveness and the Political Process in Northern Ireland

Alwyn Thompson

1. Introduction

This chapter deals with the wearisome and apparently never ending subject of Northern Ireland's conflict. It is not written from the perspective of a theologian or an academic but from that of – for want of a better word – a practitioner. I want, in a few sentences, to give you some background to that practice so that you can better comprehend my argument.

I work for an organisation called ECONI – Evangelical Contribution On Northern Ireland. Our staff, board and members are drawn from the broad evangelical Protestant tradition. We work primarily – but not exclusively – with churches in that tradition. Our goal is to enable that community, and the wider Christian community, to become instruments of peace, justice and reconciliation. We do, after all, believe in a God who works miracles.

In relation to the theme of this volume, I want to make three points that arise from our experience of working with conservative Protestant churches in Northern Ireland. These are:

1. The theology of forgiveness held among conservative Protestants in Northern Ireland impinges directly on political processes at all levels, including the current political process.

2. Other church traditions were unable to offer credible alternative models of a theology of forgiveness in relation to the political process.

3. Churches in Northern Ireland need to develop credible theological models of forgiveness – and embody them in teaching and practice – for the well-being of both church and community in the future.

2. The Theology of Forgiveness and the Political Process

Northern Ireland is one of the few communities left in the Western world where religious belief still has the power to shape attitudes towards society and politics. Christianity in Northern Ireland is not merely a set of private beliefs held by discrete individuals. Rather, it contributes significantly to the way a great many people interpret and respond to the world.

This is true for many in the conservative Protestant community that ECONI works with. This, in turn, is significant because that community remains numerically strong in Northern Ireland. Extrapolating from different sources[1] we estimate that one in three of active churchgoing Protestants could be defined as evangelical. This evangelical constituency is spread across all the main Protestant denominations as well as smaller groupings.

It may be, however, that conservative Protestantism is more significant still. While the role of religion in the Northern Ireland conflict remains disputed, there are a number of social scientist and historians who argue that conservative Protestant religion has a significance and influence within the wider Protestant community – including those Protestants who could best be described as secular.[2] Thus conservative Protestantism, argues one social scientist, has 'by virtue of its place in the history of the Protestant people ... become the core of ethnic identity, the guarantor of the ethnic group, and that, from that position, it impinges strongly, albeit subtly, on the responses of large numbers of apparently secular Protestants.'[3]

So, what does this conservative Protestant community believe about forgiveness? On 8 November 1987 a bomb exploded near the Cenotaph in Enniskillen, County Fermanagh, on Remembrance Sunday. Eleven people died. One of them was Marie Wilson. Her father, Gordon, was interviewed that evening. Having recounted the events of that day he continued, 'We see this as part of God's plan, even though we might not understand it. I shall pray for those people tonight and every night. God forgive them for they know not what they do.'[4] Gordon Wilson's comments were, perhaps inevitably, reported as his forgiving of his daughter's killers.

Alberta Clinton also died. Her daughter, Aileen, interviewed at a later date said, '[Gordon Wilson] never said he forgave. Has everybody else started saying that? To me it is morally indefensible to forgive people who

---

[1] In the 1991 census of population 89% recorded their religious identity – 38% Catholic and 51% Protestant. Denominational statistics gathered in the Irish Christian Handbook of 1992 indicate that 63% of Protestants are actively involved in their denominations.

[2] Steve Bruce, *God Save Ulster: The Religion and Politics of Paisleyism* (Oxford 1986); Bruce, *The Red Hand: Protestant Paramilitaries in Northern Ireland* (Oxford 1992); Bruce, *The Edge of the Union: The Ulster Loyalist Political Vision* (Oxford 1994).

[3] Bruce, *Edge of the Union* 29–30.

[4] *Irish News* 9 November 1987 'Eleven Killed by Cenotaph Bombers.'

aren't sorry.'[5] So, while it is possible to pray that God will forgive the killers, it is inappropriate for people themselves to forgive in the absence of repentance.

This conviction came up repeatedly in interviews with the relatives of victims. Gladys Gault, whose husband Sammy was killed, said, 'I don't think it is up to us. In time God will deal with these people. I wouldn't want vengeance or retaliation, but I don't think it is up to me to judge on forgiveness.'[6] Joe Kennedy, whose mother and father-in-law, Kit and Jessie Johnson, both died said, 'Don't ask me about forgiveness – it's not relevant. I believe there is no forgiveness without repentance. If you brought some person along who said, "We did it. We are sorry. Will you forgive us?" we might start to think about it.'[7] The strongest assertion of this conviction came from Jim Dixon, seriously injured by the bomb. He said, 'It annoyed me badly to hear that [Gordon Wilson] forgave the IRA. What right had he? It was obnoxious. They had committed a sin against humanity, not against him. They had committed a sin against God. Forgiveness has a criterion built into it. God never forgives an evil man, God only forgives a repentant man.'[8]

This is the understanding of forgiveness that has been most common among the Protestant community in Northern Ireland over the years of violence: no forgiveness without repentance.[9] This very strong sense that repentance is required before forgiveness is possible derives in part, I think, from the prior emphasis within this conservative Protestant tradition on justice. Forgiveness is possible only because of the death of Jesus Christ. But Jesus' death, in this tradition, is interpreted primarily in judicial terms. Jesus dies in order to satisfy God's just demand.

In a universe ordered by justice, the demands of justice cannot be taken lightly. Forgiveness is possible, and forgiveness can and does happen, but it does not and cannot happen in a way that threatens disorder. So God may choose to forgive human beings, but in doing so he must act in a way that is

---

[5] Denzil McDaniels, *Enniskillen: The Remembrance Sunday Bombing* (Dublin 1997), 124.

[6] McDaniels, *Enniskillen*, 124.

[7] McDaniels, *Enniskillen*, 124.

[8] McDaniels, *Enniskillen*, 131.

[9] I should point out that, while this is the most common understanding of the nature of forgiveness, it is not the only one to be found among this conservative Protestant tradition. So Bertie Armstrong, a Methodist minister whose brother Wesley was killed at Enniskillen, said, 'Those of us who tried to keep the message of repentance, forgiveness and reconciliation at the centre of our suffering have been greatly encouraged.' (McDaniels, *Enniskillen*, 121). David Cupples, minister of Enniskillen Presbyterian Church of which six of the dead were members preached a sermon on forgiveness five weeks after the bombing: 'The debate also rages in the Christian Church about whether you can forgive people before they repent. I believe if we are to follow the example of Jesus, we must offer forgiveness unconditionally. But the person who has committed the injury cannot actually have an experience of forgiveness unless they admit they have done something wrong.' (McDaniels, *Enniskillen*, 124–125).

consistent with justice. Hence alienation, broken relationships and conflict cannot be overcome by forgiveness alone but only by a choreographed dance – or, better, an ordered procession – of repentance and forgiveness.

How does this translate into the political sphere? Conservative Protestants look to the current political process in Northern Ireland and see a process that disorders. Justice – which in this tradition privileges the retributive function of justice, justice as being primarily in terms of crime and punishment – is set aside for political reasons: the unjust are not punished but appeased. Without repenting, they are accommodated and accepted – forgiven politically, if you will.

So a brief trawl through the website of the Democratic Unionist Party[10] – a Party that strongly opposes the current political process – turns up a great many references to 'the representatives of unrepentant terrorists.' The same phrasing can be found on the website of the ostensibly secular United Kingdom Unionist Party.[11]   Many of those in the more mainstream Ulster Unionist Party who oppose the process are themselves practising Christians of a conservative Protestant kind.

At the time of the Referendum a group calling itself *Christians Against the Agreement* put advertisements in newspapers and published materials condemning the process as violating Christian principles. One such advertisement was entitled 'The Sin of Voting Yes.'[12] Another, discussing the release of prisoners, was headed, 'Christ or Barabbas?'[13] The Orange Order, an organisation heavily influence by conservative Protestantism, formally declared itself against the process during the referendum campaign.

The support for the Belfast Agreement in the referendum of May 21 1998 was significant at 71.8% in favour. However, this result obscured the fact that among Protestant voters, attitudes to the process were much more evenly balanced. The subsequent election to the Assembly demonstrated the strength of Protestant opposition to the process. Of the fifty-six members elected as unionist of one stripe or another, twenty-eight were elected as anti-Agreement unionists. Clearly, there remains strong opposition among unionists to the political process.

While I am not arguing that Protestant opposition to the political process is driven solely by theological considerations of forgiveness, repentance and justice, I am arguing that they carry considerable weight in the thinking of a considerable number of Protestant people as they interpret and respond to the political process.

---

[10] Http: www.dup.org.uk.
[11] Http: www.ukup.org/home.htm.
[12] *News Letter* 24 April 1998.
[13] *News Letter* 21 May 1998.

3. The Failure to Offer Alternative Theological Models

Not all conservative Protestants have been as hostile to the political process. Some have enthusiastically endorsed it, while others have been prepared to consider what is on offer. And many in other streams of Christian tradition have actively endorsed and supported the process. However, these groups have failed to offer any credible theological response to the theological objections held by the opponents of the process.

Instead, those willing to support the process have simply offered a church endorsement of the general arguments in favour of the process. So, at the time of the referendum 151 ministers and 112 other church members put their names to an advertisement in a local newspaper under the title 'We're saying Yes!'[14] Their rationale for saying 'yes' was that 'the agreement offers an opportunity for a new beginning for our society and that it is clearly worthy of the support of Christian people.' This may or may not be true. The problem is that it does not engage with the serious theological and moral reservations held by a great many people in the conservative Protestant tradition.

Throughout the subsequent developments of the political process – particularly at moments of crisis – this has repeatedly been the line that has been taken: support the process, it offers us a new opportunity. The result is that there has been little serious work – at any stage – on shaping or promulgating theological models or theological visions that might reshape how the conservative Protestant community view the relationship between their Christian faith and the political process. This is a double tragedy. On the one hand, it leaves the field wide open for those who wish to sustain opposition to the process theologically, while on the other it implies that support for – or even openness to – certain kinds of political process cannot be justified or sustained theologically.

4. The Necessity of a Theology of Forgiveness for Church and Community

If theology, and Christian faith in general, is to be saved from social and political irrelevance in Northern Ireland then it is necessary for the Church to shape a theology of forgiveness – necessary both for the Church and for the wider community.

Consider the future on offer to us. We are told that the current political process is the only game in town, it is the only way forward, there is no

---

[14] *News Letter* 13 May 1998.

plan B, the best opportunity for a generation. Again, this may all be true but it is important to note that there no moral argument is being offered to us.

The other line of argument we hear most often is that governments and businesses are ready to back political resolution with their chequebooks. Peace will bring investment; investment will bring jobs; jobs will bring personal wealth then we can all become modern Western people – consumers. Don't fight, shop.

Northern Ireland is, of course, already part of the capitalist culture of the West. However, what is happening here is not just an argument about the increasing opportunities and possibilities offered by a capitalist economy in conditions of peace and stability. Rather, people in Northern Ireland are being encouraged to set aside political arguments in order to share in the common goal of wealth. While political ideologies may have bound communities in Northern Ireland to forms of idolatry, we are just as surely being encouraged to bind ourselves to a new idolatry – the idolatry that sees human life, human aspirations and human relationships in terms of patterns of consumption. I have no doubt that the promises of consumerism are powerful incentives to the pursuit of political stability and peace. Equally, I have no doubt that they are also powerful incentives to us becoming morally shallow people.

The end result of these processes for the Church is clear: marginalisation, in terms of levels of attendance, influence in society and the inability to shape how remaining churchgoers interpret the world. So the development of a theology of forgiveness – and, more generally, of a theology that helps us make connections with society – is necessary for three reasons.

1. It is necessary to help us deal with the past in moral ways – we are not doing this very well. At the moment we either bury the past or exploit it. Modern secular societies do not appear to have any effective means of dealing with the past.

2. It is necessary to help us manage ongoing political conflict which derives its energy from the past. The attempt to redefine competing political aspirations as two traditions to be celebrated and accommodated simply illustrates the intellectual poverty of liberal society when confronted with a political order it cannot understand.

3. It is necessary to help us envision the future. The ideology of consumerism offers no moral resource for embodying or envisioning a society of shared values, a shared sense of the common good, or a society permeated by virtues of forgiveness, reconciliation, mercy and the like.

To the extent the Church can, through its theological reflection, understand how to embody these things in its own life, to that extent it functions as a witness and a reproach to a society that is struggling to come to terms with past, present and future.

11. A Feminist Ethics of Forgiveness

Pamela Sue Anderson

'Forgiveness gives memory a future.'[1]

1. Introduction

In this chapter I propose to impose a hermeneutics of suspicion upon (or simply, bracket) a traditional Western, very loosely speaking 'Christian' notion of forgiveness. This notion is often implicit in the command, 'Love your enemy,' in particular. I will be concerned mainly with the persons who forgive their enemy or oppressor; and not with the transgressor. My aim is to see if we can discover a less pernicious notion than has been employed, whether implicitly or explicitly, in relation to women and marginalised others (i.e., those from whom forgiveness of massive wrongdoing is expected) in various social contexts and periods of history. By pernicious I mean that 'forgiveness' has been used, perhaps unwittingly, to reinforce the lack or loss of self-respect suffered by oppressed persons. I will also employ a strategy from feminist standpoint epistemology, 'to think from the lives of others' in order to attempt to reinvent the self-conception which has been at play, often uncritically, in the dominant accounts of forgiveness in Western ethics and politics. The new conception would be characterised by a robust sense of self-respect as a rational good for individuals and societies. To give a focus, I will apply my feminist epistemological strategy to the history of slavery and works by African-American philosophers[2] who provide ample material for examples of difficulties in affirming, let alone developing, self-respect.

Self-respect in the context of contemporary philosophy is one of the rational goods which Anglo-American philosophers, especially those ethical

---

[1] Paul Ricoeur, 'Memory-Forgetfulness-History,' *ZIF* (Universität Bielefeld 1995), 13, quoted by Richard Kearney, 'Narrative and the Ethics of Remembrance,' in: Richard Kearney & Mark Dooley (eds.), *Questioning Ethics: Contemporary Debates in Philosophy* (London 1999), 27.

[2] For argument that supports the insight to be gained from African philosophy for feminine moral philosophy, see Sandra Harding, 'The Curious Coincidence of Feminine and African Moralities,' in: Emmanuel Chukwudi Eze (ed.), *African Philosophy* (Oxford 1998), 360–372.

and political philosophers who follow John Rawls, maintain is necessary for every fully fledged person (i.e., a person's own sense of self-worth).[3] However, my feminist standpoint argument begins by thinking from the following definition of self-respect from African-American philosopher Michele Moody-Adams:

> Self-respect, or due respect for one's own worth, has two fundamental components. The first, more fundamental, component involves the conviction that one best affirms one's own value by using one's abilities and talents to contribute to one's survival. One who fails to act on this conviction fails to affirm self-respect, while one who lacks the conviction fails to have self-respect ... The second component of self-respect is a willingness to do whatever is within one's power to enhance or develop one's abilities and talents ... The relation between the two aspects of self-respect is typically unproblematic ... [Yet a] complication arises when a person is consistently thwarted in her efforts to develop or exercise her talents and abilities. Such a person may begin to mistrust her abilities ... [A] robust sense of self-respect must comfortably combine the two components (to some degree) over a lifetime. [Moreover] a robust sense of self-respect generally makes one better able, and more willing, to engage in the social cooperation that makes possible the rational pursuit of life plans.[4] Since it is in general rational to want to encourage such cooperation, it is also rational to want every member of one's society to be given the fullest possible chance to develop a robust sense of self-respect.[5]

The first component may appear to have instrumental value only; but the second component ensures that self-respect is a duty to oneself (we might say, 'oneself inasmuch as other'); this latter is reminiscent of Kant's formula of the universal law as end-in-itself which requires that every

---

[3] Michelle Moody-Adams, 'Race, Class and the Social Construction of Self-Respect,' in: John Pitman (ed.), 'African-American Perspectives and Philosophical Traditions,' Special Issue of *The Philosophical Forum* (1992–1993), 251–266; Howard McGary, 'Forgiveness and Slavery,' in: Howard McGary & Bill E. Lawson (eds.), *Between Slavery and Freedom: Philosophy and American Slavery* (Indianapolis 1992), 90–112; Bernard Boxill, *Blacks and Social Justice* (Totowa NJ 1984), 189; cf. John Rawls, *A Theory of Justice* (Cambridge MA 1971), 440–442.

[4] But the latter (i.e., life plans) is a matter of self-esteem, not self-respect; so a person could lose self-esteem without necessarily losing self-respect.

[5] Moody-Adams, 'Race, Class and Social Construction,' 252–254. Here she also disagrees with Rawls' notion of self-respect: what he calls self-respect she calls self-esteem; and she argues that (her notion of) self-respect is more fundamental than self-esteem, since I might lose faith in my life-plan which gives self-esteem (what Rawls calls self-respect) without ceasing to value myself as a person.

subject is treated with intrinsic value; so each person should have intrinsic value as a subject. The third point (above) recalls Kant's ideal of a kingdom of ends whereby it is rational to ensure self-respect for every subject.

I would like you to keep the above, complex account of robust self-respect in mind. We can, next, turn to a line of questions relevant for a feminist ethics of forgiveness. Do we need a secular, non-Christian notion of forgiveness which can release us from the past without sacrificing the rational/emotional self-respect of those who lack the conviction necessary for recognising themselves as fully fledged persons? Another way of tackling this issue might be to ask, How can we allow for the righteous hatred, or rightful resentment, in proper measure which necessarily follows certain sorts of wrongdoing (e.g., racial or sexual abuse), if forgiveness is also necessary? With the qualification of 'proper measure,' I acknowledge that righteous hatred could easily get out of control. As a passion, even if rational in some sense, it might be inherently unstable. Yet without allowing at least rightful resentment the person wronged is likely to lack either some or all of her self-respect. I will return to this.

Other relevant questions would include: Is forgiveness a Western concept? Do religions other than Christianity and Judaism (possibly, Islam as well) have a different way to deal with the past and its injustices than by forgiving …? I might suggest that Eastern rituals of lament or Ancient rites of mourning offer insight for answers to this question. For different conceptions of the struggle with justice involved in dealing with death, I have elsewhere considered the writings of Gillian Rose and more briefly Parita Mukta.[6] Here I am building upon both Rose's conception of 'a transcendent, mournable justice'[7] and Mukta's critical question: 'The incapacity to feel grief cedes more power to violent formations [which, for example, undermine social cooperation. So] … how can lives be sustained without their passing being mourned?'[8]

2. Forgiveness: An Ethical Virtue?

Now to develop a hermeneutics of suspicion let us consider forgiveness in a secular, ethical sense – and not, at least in the first instance, in the sense of forgiveness as a gift from God. The secular sense which I have in mind would treat forgiveness as a virtue like courage. Yet as a virtue it is not meant in the same sense as honesty, since the latter can be treated as an ethical duty,

---

[6] Gillian Rose, *Mourning Becomes the Law: Philosophy and Representation* (Cambridge 1997), 14, 104. Also see Parita Mukta, 'Lament and Power: The Subversion and Appropriation of Grief,' *Studies in History* 13/ 2 (1997), 209–246.

[7] Rose, *Mourning Becomes the Law*, 14, 104. Also see Mukta, 'Lament and Power.'

[8] Mukta, 'Lament and Power,' 246.

following Kant, or possibly as an '*intellectual* virtue,' following Aristotle. Instead forgiveness as a certain sort of *ethical virtue* would have to be cultivated rationally *and* emotionally. This ethical reading of forgiveness as a virtue is derived from Howard McGary's philosophical reflections on the history of slavery. On the basis of his reflections McGary has delineated four necessary conditions for forgiveness. These are: (1) a wrongdoing, or breach of trust, has been committed and the wronged person genuinely believes she has been wronged; (2) the wronged person intentionally ceases to resent; (3) the (ethical) reasons for forgiving are not purely selfish; here non-selfish reasons can still be, in McGary's words, 'self-pertaining'; (4) an emotional stransformation occurs whereby the person wronged no longer feels resentment (but this occurrence, or change of emotions, is not fully voluntary).

Although not the same as forgiveness, the following may occur with or without this ethical sense of forgiveness: forgetting a wrong; ceasing to hold someone culpable for wrongdoing; showing compassion (which may, however, motivate forgiveness); pardoning (an equation of forgiveness and pardon may be Christian); signifying forgivenesss in action; bestowing a gift on the transgressor and the transgressed (here forgiveness is not primarily about the transgressor).[9] These distinctions are worth considering for a feminist ethics and more generally for a feminist philosophy of religion.

A critical challenge for a feminist account of the history of women's oppression is the issue of self-respect. As already noted Moody-Adams distinguishes different degrees of self-respect.[10] (Other terms might be employed to cover similar issues including integrity or qualitative personal identity). In addition to African-American philosophers such as McGary and Moody-Adams, Black women writers of fiction and nonfiction such as Toni Morrison and bell hooks supply further material for recognising the ways in which the history of slavery renders difficult the creation of stories recounting forgiveness that do not involve the lack or loss of rational self-respect. Morrison ends *Beloved* suggesting that the story of slavery and acts in its aftermath should not be told.[11]

It was not a story to pass on.
They forgot her like a bad dream. After they made up their tales, shaped and decorated them, those that saw her that day on the porch quickly and deliberately forgot her. It took longer for those who had spoken to her, lived with her, fallen in love with her, to forget, until they realized they couldn't remember or repeat a single thing she said, and began to believe

---

[9] Howard McGary, 'Forgiveness and Slavery,' 90–112.
[10] Moody-Adams, 'Race, Class and the Social Construction of Self-Respect,' 251–266.
[11] Toni Morrison, *Beloved* (New York 1987).

that, other than what they themselves were thinking, she hadn't said anything at all. So, in the end, they forgot her too. Remembering seemed unwise.[12]

Nevertheless, I submit that a feminist ethics of forgiveness must persist beyond the postmodern inability to remember and tell stories, in order to recognise the inevitable struggle of oppressors and oppressed persons to create new narratives of forgiveness and promise.

The complex nature of slavery supports the supposition that forgiveness is neither fully voluntary nor strictly passive. Instead forgiveness can be described as an emotion with an intentional content and a phenomenal character. It would be naïve and presumptuous to think that the slave can simply forget or cease to resent without foregoing full-fledged personhood (and so self-respect). The act of thinking from the lives which shaped the history of slavery further supports the need to confront the past as a psycho-social reality which continues to shape the experiences of slaves, former slaves and their descendants. The attitudes and stereotypes of not only the latter, but also the views of the oppressors (e.g., as mistress/slave or master/slave) about black women and men which dominated the history of slavery – and which continue today in however new forms – are not easily or quickly overcome.[13]

3. Rational and Emotional Transformation (of the Soul)

In the light of my consideration of McGary I would like to single out the *emotional transformation* of the person wronged as a decisive condition for forgiveness.[14] The narrative account developed by bell hooks in her autobiographical writings supports the decisive role of emotional transformation. From her *Bone Black: Memories of Girlhood* we learn of hooks' struggle with the stereotypes which restricted the real possibilities for black women's identities in African-American contexts; particular restrictive images (stereotypes) were created by her upbringing in a segregated, black community in Kentucky in the 1950s–60s; later in her *Wounds of Passion: A Writing Life* and *Remembered Rapture*, we read about her struggle with this past, but we also find that the gradual release from these stereotypes becomes part of a redemptive process of 'a writing life.'[15] One could argue

---

[12] Morrison, *Beloved*, 274–275.

[13] See bell hooks, *Ain't I a Woman: Black Women and Feminism* (Boston 1981); McGary, 'Forgiveness and Slavery.'

[14] McGary, 'Forgiveness and Slavery,' 104.

[15] bell hooks, *Bone Black: Memories of Girlhood* (New York 1996); bell hooks, *Wounds of Passion: A Writing Life* (New York 1997), v.

that hooks refigures her own past to achieve an emotional transformation, but at the very same time she plays a crucial role in theorising, more generally, about the endeavour of black women, including Morrison in *Beloved,* to create literature which refigures the dominant myths of gender identity. Perhaps we have not yet understood Morrisons refigured myth of the mother who kills her child in order to preserve her from the self-denigration and other suffering of slavery.

> So they forgot her. Like an unpleasant dream during a troubling sleep. Occasionally, however, the rustle of a skirt hushes when they wake, and the knuckles brushing a cheek in sleep seem to belong to the sleeper. Sometimes the photograph of a close friend or relative – looked at too long – shifts, and something more familiar than the face itself moves there. They can touch it if they like, but don't, because they know things will never be the same if they do.
> This is not a story to be passed on.
> … Beloved.[16]

Nevertheless, forgetting is not, as already noted, the same as forgiveness. So in the light of the above we might still say that the more general endeavour of black women writers (such as Morrison) is to transform the attitudes which dominated the history of slavery and have continued in its aftermath. I submit that the African-American context provides a test case of an adequate conception of forgiveness – and truth.

To support this further I direct you to a closer look at bell hooks' non-fiction writings. hooks presents a positive, social form of making narrative sense of the past (what I have called elsewhere, 'an ethics of memory'); this involves a form of passionate rationality. Admittedly danger rests with the ease of distorting this form of rationality. Yet hooks insists upon the importance of truth-telling in the light of the recognition that lies and distortions destroy community and individual souls. Forgiveness must not blind us to truth; lies undermine self-respect in particular.[17] To understand the struggle for self-respect reflected in hooks I have advocated, as stated at the outset of this chapter, applying not only a hermeneutics of suspicion to dominant conceptions of forgiveness, but a strategy of feminist standpoint epistemology to think from the lives of others. With the latter, my aim has been to reinvent the self-conception, or lack thereof, in oppressive accounts of mistress and slave, or master and slave – with a robust sense of self-respect as a rational good for each individual making up a society. To repeat, the material for this strategy and for my hermeneutics comes from African-

---

[16] Morrison, *Beloved*, 275.
[17] bell hooks, *Remembered Rapture: The Writer at Work* (London 1999), 120–121.

American writers who provide ample material for examples of difficulties in affirming, or developing, self-respect. To quote hooks:

> All too often, individuals think of community in terms of being with folks like themselves – same class, race, ethnicity, social standing, and the like. It is when we are able to empathize, feel with and for experiences that are not our own and may never be, that we come to know 'how good and pleasant it is for brethren to come together in unity.' To make community, we need to be able to know truth, to speak openly and honestly.
>
> Truth-telling has to be a spiritual practice for many of us because we live and work in settings where falseness is rewarded, where lies are the norm. Deceit and betrayal destroy the possibility of community. In challenging the separation of public and private in feminist activism, or any struggle of the exploited to move from the object being to subject being, we act to restore the idea that meaningful ties, bonds of love and affinity, are fruitful in a world beyond domestic reality.[18]

At this stage, I propose that the case of African-American history becomes highly relevant to the more general history of women's struggles for freedom. Not only have privileged white feminists had to think from the lives of others in order to see the social reality of their racism, but they have found (like women of other social situations) that the freedom to explore their own selfhood in terms of gender, race, class, ethnicity and sexual orientation, must involve a personal struggle with a psycho-social reality. Drucilla Cornell, for instance, has argued for reconceiving the (mimetic) space of freedom as 'an imaginary domain' in which persons can recover and relocate themselves in relation to a past of pain and oppression.[19] Implicit in Cornell's work is the fact that memory raises ethical questions. My own work in progress on memory informs my response to the question of 'a feminist ethics of forgiveness'.

My response is that whether a person *ultimately* forgives another involves *the assessment of reasons they have for forgiving, as well as overcoming certain potentially destructive emotions* like resentment. One (Kantian sort of) problem for oppressed and powerless people who are inclined to be forgiving in their nature is whether acting on their inclinations signals that they do not hold themselves in proper regard as human beings. We are each subject to exaggeration, distortion and self-deception. But a dilemma of self-respect is especially acute in situations of oppression:

---

[18] hooks, *Remembered Rapture*, 120–121.
[19] Drucilla Cornell, *At the Heart of Freedom: Feminism, Sex and Equality* (Princeton NJ 1998), 8–11, 14–17, 174, 182–186.

[Oppressed persons] want to be able to get rid of their resentment because of the toll it takes on them, but to do so would be to ignore or underestimate the nature of the injustice they are being forced to endure. There is a conflict between holding on to their self-respect as persons who do not condone or capitulate to injustice and, at the same time, letting go of the rightful resentment they feel because of this injustice.[20]

This intractable dilemma becomes an additional wrong of oppression. Following the commandment 'Love Your Enemy' is not a sufficient explanation for the forgiveness of some slaves, former slaves and their descendants who may not be able to respect their own worth (e.g., if it is a duty to love their enemy).[21] Yet the pressing question about the past for a feminist ethics of forgiveness is, why were some slaves able to exemplify the virtue of forgiveness in the most adverse circumstances? Personally I do not see how a mere reference to Christianity, as if there was a single unproblematic notion of Christian forgiveness or grace, could be a sufficient explanation let alone a justification for this.

4. Ethics, Politics and Narratives of Transformation

It is necessary to turn to possible political and ethical factors to explain how the soul and its emotions can be transformed to achieve forgiveness without a loss of self worth in the face of massive wrongdoing. For example, Gillian Rose seeks to hold together the tensions of the political and the spiritual, philosophy and theology, in a 'tale of three cities.' Rose presents a narrative reading of Nicholas Poussin's painting *Gathering the Ashes of Phocion* (1648) which is reminiscent of Greek mythology. According to Plutarch, Phocion was an Athenian general and statesman who lived virtuously in his public and private life. However, Phocion was wrongly accused of treason by his enemies, and similar to Socrates' fate, was sentenced to death. Furthermore, his burial within Athens was forbidden; his body was taken outside the city walls and burnt by a paid alien. In order that his soul does not wander forever, his wife gathers her husband's ashes to her home, buries them, dedicating them to the household gods. According to Rose:

---

[20] McGary, 'Forgiveness and Slavery,' 110.

[21] A difference between continental philosophers Jean-Luc Marion and Jacques Derrida on their understandings of the duty or debt/gift of forgiveness has been recognised; the former sees forgiveness as a duty, the latter rejects any connection of duty and gift; see John Caputo, 'Apostles of the Impossible: On God and the Gift in Derrida and Marion,' in: John Caputo & Michael Scanlon (eds.), *God, The Gift and Postmodernism* (Bloomington, IN 1999), 185–222.

Phocion's condemnation and manner of dying were the result of tryanny temporarily usurping good rule in the city.[22] The tension of political defiance appears here in the figure of the woman servant, whose contorted posture expresses the fear of being discovered. The bearing of the servant displays the political risk; her visible apprehension protects the complete vulnerability of her mourning mistress as she devotes her whole body to retrieving the ashes. This act is *not* therefore solely one of *infinite love*: it is a *finite act of political* justice.

The magnificent, gleaming, classical buildings, which frame and focus this political act, convey no malignant foreboding, but are perfect displays of the architectural orders: they do not and cannot in themselves stand for the unjust city or for intrinsically unjust law. On the contrary, they present the rational order which throws into relief the specific act of injustice perpetuated by the current representatives of the city – an act which takes place outside the boundary wall of the built city.[23]

So, for Rose, in the gathering of her husband's ashes the wife of Phocion, accompanied by her servant, does not protest against power and the law as such. Nor is the woman's act one of infinite love – not only grounded in religious sensibility but in political justice.[24] According to Rose, Poussin's painting configures 'a transcendent but mournable justice'; the absence of justice is given presence in 'the architectural perspective which frames and focuses the enacted justice of two women.'[25] Rose compares the wife of Phocion with Antigone. Both women insist on the right and rites of mourning: '[they] carry out that intense work of the soul, that gradual rearrangement of its boundaries, which must occur when a loved one is lost – so as to let go, to allow the other fully to depart, and hence fully to be regained beyond sorrow.'[26] Forgiveness would seem to involve a similar process of emotional and rational transformation of the soul. So release from resentment occurs as the transgressed or grieving person recognises justice not in the transgression but beyond in representations (and new acts) of justice. Narratives representing what Rose calls 'mournable justice' render suffering of experience visible and speakable: 'Mourning draws on transcendent but representable justice.'[27]

---

[22] Phocion is a figure in the ancient Greek writer Plutarch's work *Parallel Lives*.

[23] Rose, *Mourning Becomes the Law*, 25–26; italics added.

[24] Also see Pamela Sue Anderson, 'Rereading Myth in Philosophy: Hegel, Ricoeur, Irigaray Reading *Antigone*,' in: Morny Joy (ed.), *Paul Ricoeur and Narrative: Context and Contestation* (Calgary, Alberta), 51–68.

[25] Rose, *Mourning Becomes the Law*, 25–26.

[26] Rose, *Mourning Becomes the Law*, 25–26.

[27] Rose, *Mourning Becomes the Law*, 35–36, also 104.

Rose demonstrates that philosophy and its representations remain necessary for theology in creating a just memory. In this she also supports what I seek in a feminist philosophy of religion, even if she does not employ these terms; Rose would also seem to support what I am calling a feminist ethics of forgiveness as an urgent topic for a feminist philosophy of religion. In particular, I agree with Rose that the new ethics of Jerusalem should not be opposed to the old justice of Athens. Instead the architectural perspective framing the enacted justice of two women in Poussin's painting represents the continuing, critical relation to the perspective of order and rationality worked out by philosophers. In this light, philosophy's representations are crucial for an ethics of memory which is perhaps not new, but exists to enact every situation anew in relation to justice, including the postmodern situation of gendered knowledge, truth and justice.

The feminist Chicana poet Gloria Anzaldua provides an image and narrative for the epistemological and ethical struggle needed to move beyond the past in order to forge new links with the future. The struggle is not to interiorize harmful memories, but to create just memories which move us toward a reconciliation with *truth* as imagined in mimetic acts of yearning for justice.[28] Anzaldua employs the image of a snake shedding its skin. She queries, 'Why does she have to go and try to make "sense" of it all? Every time she makes "sense" of something, she has to "cross over," kicking a hole out of the old boundaries of the self and slipping under or over, dragging the old skin along, stumbling over it. It hampers her movement in the new territory, dragging the ghost of the past within her.'[29] The difficulty of making narrative sense of one's life renders action and truth a process, of remembering and moving with a just memory forward into a more ethically and epistemologically informed future. No straight line of progress toward justice exists. In Anzaldua's words:

> It is only when she is on the other side and the shell cracks open and the lid from her eyes lifts that she sees things in a different perspective. It is only then that she makes the connections, formulates the insights. It is only then that her consciousness expands a tiny notch, another rattle appears on the rattlesnake's tail and the added growth slightly alters the sounds she makes.[30]

In struggling to articulate a third-person standpoint – at 'the broken middle' – the woman's, or a 'feminist,' standpoint is constantly deconstructing

---

[28] Gloria Anzaldua, *Borderlands / La Frontera* (San Francisco 1987), 49.

[29] Anzaldua, *Borderlands*, 49.

[30] Anzaldua, *Borderlands*, 49.

itself. A feminist struggle at the broken middle uncovers the role of our social and material positioning in achieving truth and justice. [31]

5. Conclusion

At the mediating site of a feminist standpoint or, in hooks' terms, 'self-reflexive speech,' difference is expressible in narrative forms by which beliefs and convictions are enacted. The re-enactment of narratives can shape or reshape the identity of an individual or a culture because of the discursive nature of a standpoint achieved through struggle with difference. Ricoeur explains this shaping of narrative identity in terms of the 'entanglement' of an individual's stories with the stories of others. This, then, calls us to take responsibility for 'the story of the other through the life narratives which concern that other.'[32] In this light, a feminist ethics of forgiveness would have to take responsibility for the life stories of the other, through the exchange of narratives in imagination and empathy.

Thus I maintain that a feminist ethics should not deny the reality of the past, the repression of female desire and the eclipse of justice and reason. Instead it should seek the interaction of desire and reason in narrative expressions of a particular sort. The struggle for this expression leads to personal and social transformation in so far as the response to the injustice of shattered lives involves forgiveness. Through forgiveness the one transgressed can intentionally cease to resent the other for sometimes massive wrong-doing done to oneself and/or one's community. True forgiveness transforms life's narratives. Rituals of mourning or lament as practiced respectively by, for instance, ancient Greek or traditional Hindu women can also serve the purpose of transforming the emotions of those who grieve. The latter, in so far as they allow us to see from a different perspective, can potentially tell us something about emotional transformation that our own [Christian] perspective on forgiveness cannot. In whatever manner it is achieved, true forgiveness changes our relation with the past and to the future. Enacted stories of emotional and rational transformation represent the reordering of the soul that makes forgiveness possible. Such stories are informed by a just memory. In creating a pregnant present, they aim to give birth to a future with new ethical – emotional and rational – possibilities.

---

[31] Pamela Sue Anderson, '"Standpoint": Its Rightful Place in a Realist Epistemology,' *Journal of Philosophical Research* (forthcoming); and 'Ethics within the Limits of Post-Ricoeurian Kantian Hermeneutics,' in: David Jasper & Jeff Keuss (eds.), *Hermeneutics After Kant: A Consultation on Current Demands in Hermeneutics* (forthcoming); in the latter I stress that the struggle for a feminist standpoint is usefully supported by post-Ricoeurian Kantian hermeneutics.

[32] Ricoeur, 'Reflections on A New Ethos for Europe,' in: Richard Kearney (ed.), *Paul Ricoeur: The Hermeneutics of Action* (London 1996), 6–7.

12. Enfolding the Dark

David Self

In 1999 I was able to interview a number of people on their experience of forgiving, being forgiven, or not being able to forgive. Here is one of the stories, given with permission.

Lucy Partington, my sister, 'disappeared' in December 1973. In March 1994 we learnt that she was one of the young women murdered by Frederick and Rosemary West. I wrote an essay about her life and what it felt like to be in this position as a family and how we found ways of relating to the reality and the enormity of the revelation of what had happened to her. I personally found it increasingly difficult, not knowing what had happened to her. I had a deep anxiety about the reality that life is impermanent and that you can't know what is going to happen from one moment to the next and even people disappear, and the not knowing. I realise in retrospect that it contributed to me becoming quite self-destructive in some ways, not trusting life and making decisions that made my life very difficult and was very hurtful to other people at times. People used to say things like 'God chooses the best, takes them young.' Those sort of things made me feel really angry and I think I had a whole decade of life being really meaningless and not understanding what it was all about. There was this huge confusion that I was in because nothing was resolved, and partly because it became almost taboo to talk about her in the family. We hadn't had the ritual, we hadn't had a funeral, everything was on hold and it was as if part of me was frozen, waiting and I couldn't go on as a whole person.

I couldn't even face the fact that she had probably been murdered until about three years before we found out. It was almost as if we could avoid it if we didn't talk about it but it didn't work. One of the things we always tried to do was to get together on Lucy's birthday. Even then we wouldn't talk about her much but we would be there in this rather numb way. I suggested in December 1993 that we planted a tree in memory of her and we all got together. My daughter, who is incredibly honest and direct, commented afterwards that none of us mentioned her name and she just realised at that moment how painful it was and how stuck we all were. Three months later they started digging up the bodies. We phoned the police up and asked, 'Was it anything to do with Lucy, did they know?' They said at that point they had only dug up three bodies, but they would let us know. Later they revealed there were five more in the sand. One of them was called Lucy. I was very grateful that my life was in a state where I was able to receive this news, because I am in a very stable loving relationship.

The Quakerism, and the Ch'an Buddhism which I explore both have the medium of silence in common. Part of my personal theology that I am working towards relates to a dream that I had shortly after Lucy disappeared but it has become something that is very rooted inside me that has great meaning if I can fathom it. At the time of the dream I had this experience, the profound feeling of peace that I call the peace that passes understanding. I woke up with this feeling and I knew then, it felt like a real communication, it felt as if at that moment whether Lucy was dead or alive, if she was in that state it was all right. So part of me really wants to know: how do you get to that state? Because when you are in it, everything works and forgiveness is a spontaneous authentic permanent act. But I know that it is very difficult to get to that place and the issue of forgiveness we are exploring today is not something that is easily done. In the dream Lucy came back and I said, 'Where have you been?' She said 'I have been sitting in a water meadow near Grantham. If you sit very still you can hear the sun move.' So it seemed to convey the state of profound inner stillness, and to me there are the words, 'Be still and know that I am God' and it's that really.

All of our rituals of laying to rest, including for me the very profound moment of going and actually wrapping Lucy's bones, were healing acts. Several weeks after Lucy's bones were removed from Cromwell Street I had a dream about embracing Lucy's skeleton and her becoming Lucy and putting her head on my shoulder. I woke up feeling that I had to actually go and physically do that. I had to wrap what was left of her and treat it with love and respect because we didn't know how long they would stay in the mortuary because of the whole trial. The whole ritual was profoundly healing. Later we were able to have a Requiem Mass for Lucy with the priest, the dear priest who had prepared her to be received into the Catholic Church five weeks before she was murdered. He is still alive and had been praying for her every day since she disappeared. We were able to rebury her with reverence and love in a place that was important to her which is this little twelfth-century church, Hailes Church next to Hailes Abbey, where there are medieval wall paintings which Lucy had been studying. And to have the gravestone setting ceremony, all these rituals were helpful and needed although one of my children said something like, 'Not another thing, when are we going to stop?' But it was important that they were involved in it too because for them it was very much them learning a process of grieving and the importance of doing that.

I did make a vow at the end of one of my Buddhist retreats, I think it was in 1998, to try and forgive the people who killed Lucy and the first thing I experienced after I had made that vow when I got home was this extremely violent involuntary feeling of rage. It was just a huge eruption beyond logic or words, which was terrifying because I knew at that moment that I was capable of killing. So that connected me immediately to the Wests. At that moment I knew that part of the process of forgiveness was facing within myself my own potential for perpetrating abuse or being a victim.

I think what I have been learning about forgiveness is that it is a long process and that it's rather pretentious and hypocritical of me to think that I can forgive the Wests before I have actually faced up to in my own life people I need to be forgiven by and people I would like to forgive. And in a way I am left with trying to stay true to what is actually happening. Not avoid anything that comes up because I feel the teaching is in that. I know that I can't find that of God in the Wests until I find that of God in myself. And finding that of God in myself involves actually facing my own potential for evil and destructive acts. I am trying to understand an experience, the profound reality of who I am and that is sacred and that life is sacred and what I would like for Rosemary West is for her to know something of that. I have had a dream about trying to forgive her which was very revealing because it was all about the fact that I wasn't ready to do it. But I think I am getting closer to it. What I have been trying to do is find a voice for the light without denying the reality of the darkness and really exploring the relationship between the two. And that's where the crucifixion and the resurrection come in.

Would you say therefore that what you wrote was an affirmation of the light, or an affirmation of Lucy's life, but it was done in the context that the darkness was very strong, because the revelation was emerging in its full blast? It's not that you gave the last word then, because your own journey since has been one of discovery of where you can find darkness and each time you have to affirm that the light is still there.

Yes, that's good, it is and also to affirm, to be true to the fact that the light does seem to go out sometimes. I saw this lovely poster which was of a candle stating about it is better to strengthen the light than rail against the darkness and that's what my journey is really, finding ways to strengthen the light, so that whatever happens now it is not going to destroy me too.

The image I had in my dream of Rosemary West was very much of utter darkness. The first scene was very much about me meeting her and my saying I forgive you and it being meaningless and nothing happening. The second scene was her sitting in a basement with a pile of flesh and putting handfuls of flesh into little polythene bags and throwing them out of this hole in the wall and saying 'I keep throwing them away but the sea keeps bringing them back' and in that dream it was very odd and she looked at me and I don't think she could see me and what I saw was that her eyes looked like two sharp points trying to push themselves out of a black bin liner. It was really as if something awful was going to burst out and it was terrifying. I sometimes use that dream almost like the Ignatian practice. I go back into it and realise that that image, which is monstrous, is me. That is the sort of darkness that is within me. This dream came up within me, it's part of my unconscious. There is something about those words which I come back to, that you can't think that you can just throw these things away. The sea will bring them back and that maybe the message of the dream for me is that one day if I sit with her I can help her understand that meaning.

And does that mean then that you are learning how to forgive yourself and learning to believe that others can forgive you?

Yes, I definitely have in this process explored my rotting pile of mistakes. But I also see that that is my compost. It has a meaning. It doesn't have to remain repulsive and something I can't acknowledge and that I want to edit out. It actually is part of who I am and I have to have another relationship with it. Once I have accepted that and really truly acknowledged it I can then realise, know that I don't have to do that again, I don't have to make those mistakes again because I have more of a sense of who I am, the sacredness of my life and that every moment is an opportunity to go forward in a way towards the light and that we do have a choice. What happened to Lucy is very much something that makes it seem really important and almost urgent for me to find what it is that would possibly give one strength and transcend in some way the reality of human atrocity.

I think the thing that horrifies me a lot was the fact that she was gagged so that she couldn't speak her truth, so the minute she was gagged she became flesh and bones and she had already lost who she was and the thing about her that was so valuable was her love of words and the beauty of life. That's what she wanted to go on and study and she had real refined sensibility. So to find herself in that basement with people who were pursuing the opposite path is most painful to me. And that's why it is important for me to find my truth and speak about it and about the truth that died with Lucy that needed to be reaffirmed.

That really is very important, isn't it? Because what you have struggled with is the need for physical expression, a need for truth, a need for the recognition of the pain and the suffering of the loss imposed by the darkness and yet the capacity of God, the sacred, to be creative with it.

That's great because I feel that the position I feel most true to myself in is one of vulnerability. That involves pain, and it does involve being open to the reality of pain. That's how the creativity comes from the position where you have accepted, faced, experienced the pain. And then you are free to forgive, but you can't forgive until you've done that because anything you do from the position of pain has the potential to have negative emotions that destroy. Hatred, anger, rage, vengeance, all come from that place of pain and to me the actions of the Wests come from that place. In that way I have compassion for them because I know once you are brutalised you lose that sense of who you are in the sense of beauty or that of God within you.

Some reflections on Marion Partington's story

The Importance of Ritual

Marion sought in a whole variety of ways to remember her sister and to say farewell. She described what it is like to be in the frozen period of denial and unknowing, with a deep sense of the instability of life. While the limbo remained, with all the surrounding uncertainty, then the uncertainty could become the describing feature of life, with destructive consequences for those who left behind. During that period she began instinctively to seek for mute, physical expressions of loss through ritual, but recovering the body was essential so that the family and friends could be released from the limbo of unknowing and try to move forward in their grief.

The Importance of Truth – in the Heart as well as the Head

Truth takes a long time to be faced and absorbed, especially when it is difficult. Coming to face not only the fact of Lucy's death but also the way in which she died was a slow process, calling for a lot of courage to look at the implications of being required to absorb a brutality inflicted on the family as well as on Lucy. Much of the struggle with the dark news was to continue to affirm the worth and beauty of Lucy's life in the face of such a devastating death.

Acknowledging the darkness without led Marion to face the darkness within herself, the capacity for huge rage and murder that lies in the heart. Refusing to take that step in the process would have led to denial and the projection of darkness upon others, and therefore to scapegoating. With such a refusal the pain remains inside and can then lead to all sorts of unacknowledged destructive behaviour, such as a life of bitterness or addiction. Marion recognised the need for grace, that she was not capable of looking at the darkness on her own, let alone of trying to articulate it creatively through ritual, words and behaviour. Much of the time we need others we can trust to help us, and we need a faith that can try to make sense of a world in which goodness and wickedness, light and dark have such strength. How do we live enfolding the dark without being taken over by the dark?

The Importance of Forgiveness as a Way of Living

Before embarking on these interviews I had not taken on board just how much of a process can be entailed in the struggle to forgive or to be forgiven. All the people I met displayed considerable courage to sustain integrity in learning how to live with the darkness without and within. 'What can give one strength to transcend in some way the reality of human atrocity?' asked Marion. The more we have the courage to see with the heart something of the atrocities that we as human beings are capable of inflicting on each other, the more we can see the importance of forgiveness as a way of living, an art, a craft, at the heart of the Christian belief. If the cross is seen as a display of the nature of sin, in all its brutality, then the whisper of forgiveness from the cross in the heart of darkness becomes even more important to hear.

To wrestle with the darkness, Marion needed to do at least two things. The first was to refuse to remain in victim mode, that passive stance that says there is nothing to be done, let us shut away the pain and pretend it is not there. The second was the fundamental movement within to recognise her own capacity to inflict harm, her own need to be forgiven and to forgive herself. And an important step was to come to realise that the place of mess, of mistakes in our lives is where God is most creative, the place which has a fundamental role in the emergence of our identity. To discover God there is to be released into forgiveness.

The completion of forgiveness is eschatological. Verses from Psalm 85 are surprisingly apt for describing this completion. *Mercy and truth are met together, righteousness and peace have kissed each other.* Both mercy and truth are needed and we are not very good at holding them both in balance. There are those who emphasise the truth at the cost of mercy. Judgement, meaning condemnation, appears rapidly and there is little release into joyous forgiveness. There are others who emphasise mercy at the expense of truth, so trivialising the reality of evil and the wounds inflicted. Perhaps only in heaven will mercy and truth be met together. In the meantime there continues the struggle to be creative with the deep wounds that others have inflicted, or with the history of sin that we come to recognise we have committed and that others are now carrying the cost. There has been so much atrocity this past century, that without the quiet struggles to enfold the dark creatively with integrity that so many courageous people have undertaken, there would be little hope for us. There are more candles in the dark than we realise.

Jesus tells Peter at one point that forgiveness is a matter of seventy times seven, and I had always read that as forgiving again when the same person continues to commit an offence. But a member of my congregation gave me another insight, in that it could also be applied to the task of forgiving, or being forgiven for, the one sin day after day for a very long time. We grow into forgiveness, and are shaped by it. So Marion still seeks the place of stillness, where the heart has come home to rest and forgiveness can be spontaneous and complete with a sense of release and joy. We get glimpses of it in this life, but we have been cast out of Eden and we are not yet ready for heaven.

13. Probing the Relationship between Divine and Human Forgiveness in Matthew

Hearing a Neglected Voice in the Canon

Todd Pokrifka-Joe

1. Introduction

This chapter will analyze the relationship between divine forgiveness and human forgiveness in Matthew, and show something of its significance for Christian theology. To do so is to attempt to hear a canonical voice that, to a large extent, has been drowned by the voice of Paul. At least this is the case in the history of biblical interpretation in the West since the Reformation. Given that Christian theology ought to be normatively shaped by *all* portions of the Christian canon, contemporary theological reflection on forgiveness therefore needs to hear and recover Matthew's neglected voice. Towards that end, I will undertake a theological exegesis of two significant Matthean passages on forgiveness, considering them both on their own terms and in relation to each other. By 'theological exegesis' I mean simply exegesis of the 'plain sense' of a passage of Scripture with a view to the theological claims it is making.

I will argue that these two Matthean texts yield the following threefold theological understanding of the relationship between divine and human forgiveness. First, human acts of forgiveness of others are an appropriate and necessary response to a prior act of divine forgiveness. Second, acts of human forgiveness arc nonetheless the usual prerequisite for the continued human experience and appropriation of divine forgiveness, both in the present and in the future eschaton.[1] Third, and in summary, human acts of forgiveness

---

[1] In Matthew, 'the fulfillment of the human imperative' is 'a prerequisite for the ultimate, full and final expression of the indicative.' Robert Mohrlang, *Matthew and Paul: A Comparison of Ethical Perspectives* (Cambridge 1984), 80.

are both an essential expression of divine forgiveness already received and an essential condition of the continued and ultimate reception of that divine forgiveness.[2]

2. Theological Exegesis of Matthew 6:12–15

The first crucial text for discerning Matthew's understanding of the relationship between divine and human forgiveness is found in the Lord's Prayer and the comments that immediately follow it. Matthew places this prayer (6:9a–13) at the structural centre of the Sermon on the Mount (Mat. 5–7), a placement which points to an interconnection between prayer and ethics.[3] Nowhere is this interconnection more evident than in the fifth petition of the Lord's Prayer, the petition on forgiveness. In the NRSV, it is rightly translated as follows: 'And forgive our debts, as we also have forgiven our debtors' (v. 12). The reader may have noticed that the verb in the second clause is in the past tense ('as we have forgiven') instead of the present tense ('as we forgive') found in the traditional liturgical renderings of the prayer. The reason is that, according to the better Greek texts, the verb in the second clause is an aorist past tense (ἀφήκαμεν). Therefore, the usual versions of the Lord's prayer are based upon an inferior, later text marked by a present tense verb (the ἀφίεμεν of the *Textus Receptus*).

With this clarification in mind, the key question for our purposes is how this second clause about past human forgiveness is connected with the first clause requesting God's forgiveness. Specifically, how should we take the comparative terms 'as also' (ὡς καί)? A straightforward reading of these words would suggest that the people praying are asking God to forgive *in the way that* they have forgiven others.

There is no good exegetical reason to reject this straightforward reading, and this has important theological implications. Especially with the past tense in the second clause, the petition would place significant responsibility on those praying to make sure they have already forgiven others if they desire to be forgiven by God. This would mean that Jesus here teaches that

---

[2] I risk using 'synergistic' terms like 'prerequisite' and 'condition' in this paragraph and below because I have not been able to find any alternatives that can more faithfully render what Matthew is saying. It may be that such terms would prove inappropriate for a dogmatic soteriology that takes into account all the relevant biblical material on forgiveness, but that is not my concern. Also, it may be possible to read Matthew's 'conditions' in non-synergistic way. I thank George Hunsinger for his helpful comments regarding these matters in the discussion following my presentation of this chapter at the SST conference in Oxford, 2000.

[3] Ulrich Luz, *The Theology of the Gospel of Matthew* (Minneapolis 1995), 49f.

'human forgiving is a condition for divine forgiving.'[4] By implication, Christians should be hesitant to pray the Lord's prayer if they have not truly forgiven their fellows beforehand.[5]

This conditional reading is decisively corroborated by the explanatory comments that Matthew places immediately after the prayer: 'For if you forgive others their trespasses, your heavenly Father will also forgive you; but if you do not forgive others, neither will your Father forgive your trespasses' (vv. 14f.). By this combination of conditional statements, Matthew could hardly put it more emphatically that human forgiveness is a necessary condition for divine forgiveness.

This 'conditional' interpretation of the passage is accepted by a large majority of interpreters in both biblical and theological circles, despite the lack of emphasis on this 'conditional' theme in Western theology.[6] Even so, non-conditional readings of the fifth petition have been put forward. Such readings tend to hold to a present tense rendering of the second clause, in which that clause refers to the *present intention* of those praying to forgive others, rather than to a *past action* of forgiveness. These readings, however, are not adequate. Even the best of them rest either on a poor Greek text (above), or on speculative conjectures about the text's pre-history.[7] Therefore, some version of the broadly 'conditional' understanding of the relation of human to divine forgiveness must be maintained. The key question is, 'What is the nature of this condition?'

3. Theological Exegesis of Matthew 18:23–35

To begin to answer this question we will need to consider a second key Matthean text on forgiveness, namely, Matthew 18. Although much of the

---

[4] E.g., Ulrich Luz, *Matthew 1–7: A Commentary* (Cambridge 1989), 389 (referring to Mat. 6:14f.); cf. C.F.D. Moule '"As we forgive..."': A Note on the Distinction between Deserts and Capacity in the Understanding of Forgiveness,' in: Ernst Bammel a.o. (eds.), *Donum Gentilicium* (Oxford 1978), 69; Mohrlang, *Matthew and Paul*, 80.

[5] Bastiaan Van Elderen, 'When do we forgive?', *Calvin Theological Journal* 33 (1998).

[6] Besides being held by most modern biblical scholars (note 5 above), a conditional view of the passage (although with present tense textual reading) is held by important representatives of all three major divisions of orthodox Christianity. (1) Eastern Orthodoxy: Maximus the Confessor, 'Commentary on the Our Father,' in: George C. Berthold (tr.), *Maximus Confessor: Selected Writings* (New York 1985). (2) Protestantism: Martin Luther, Sermons on 'The Sermon on the Mount' in: *Luther's Works*, Vol. 21 (St Louis 1956). (3) Roman Catholic: *Catechism of the Catholic Church* (Liguori, MO 1994).

[7] Joachim Jeremias, *The Prayers of Jesus* (ET London 1967), 92 gives a 'non-textual' defense of the present tense based on a supposed Aramaic original: '[T]here lies behind Matthew's past tense form what is called in Semitic grammar a *perfectum praesens* ... which refers to an action occurring here and now.'

chapter relates either directly or indirectly to forgiveness,[8] we will concentrate only on the most directly relevant section, the parable of the unmerciful servant in verses 23–35. This parable can be summarised as follows:

- Servant A owes an unpayable debt to a king, and pleads for mercy.
- The king graciously forgives the debt of Servant A completely.
- Servant B owes servant A a small payable debt, and pleads for mercy.
- Servant A refuses to forgive it.
- The king punishes servant A and effectively takes back his initial forgiveness.

In comparison with Matthew 6, the salient new feature in this story is the king's extraordinarily gracious act of forgiveness. The king's forgiveness comes before any mention is made of that servant's response of unforgiveness. In this way, the parable teaches that God's forgiveness is *unconditional*, at least initially. God does not *wait* to see whether sinners will forgive others before God forgives them.[9] Accordingly, the comparative 'as'-relation between divine and human forgiveness goes in the opposite direction than it did in chapter 6, from God to humans (18:33), rather than from humans to God (6:12, 14f.). The servant is now expected to forgive others *as* God first forgave him.

Is Matthew 18 incompatible with Matthew 6, then? I think not. Rather, the full narrative context of chapter 18 shows that the relationship between divine and human forgiveness can go in *both* directions, depending on which part of the story of divine and human forgiveness one is talking about. Matthew 18 shows that there are three key moments in the story of divine-human forgiveness:

(1) The moment of God's gracious initiative: the king's initial act of forgiveness.
(2) The moment of human response: the wicked servant's outrageous refusal to forgive his fellow servant.
(3) The moment of 'God's response to the human response': the king's final act of punishing the unforgiving servant.

In terms of this three-step narrative sequence, the conditional statements in Matthew 6 describe the relationship of the *last two* moments to each other. As such, the scope of the conditions in 6:14f. do not include the first moment of unconditioned divine forgiveness. Thus, chapter 6 does *not* make the

---

[8] E.g., 18:15–20, a crucial passage for understanding forgiveness 'ecclessially' or even 'liturgically' (see Christopher Jones' discussion; Ch. 3 above).

[9] Richard Bauckham, 'Forgiveness,' an unpublished Sermon on Mat. 18:21–35 (2000), 4.

theological claim that human acts of forgiveness condition the initial divine act of forgiveness. In the perspective of the parable in 18, such a claim would violate the rules of the parable's narrative logic. It is precisely the fact that the servant's act of unforgiveness *follows* the king's prior act of lavish forgiveness that makes the servant's act so morally outrageous.[10]

4. Inter-Textual and Theological Synthesis

We have already begun to see how the theological contributions of Matthew 6 and 18 can be brought together in a mutually illuminating fashion. We now take up this synthesis explicitly.

To begin, how might we read Matthew 6 in light of Matthew 18? If we give Matthew the 'benefit of the doubt' regarding theological consistency, then the conditional statements in and around the Lord's Prayer in Matthew 6 should be regarded as *presupposing* the prior divine act of forgiveness that was explicit in Matthew 18. There are several features in the wider context of Matthew that confirm this suggestion. First, Jesus' teaching on prayer in Matthew emphasises the merciful and trustworthy nature of the Heavenly Father (7:7–11). Second, Jesus gives this teaching to disciples, and disciples those who have been chosen by Jesus in an initial transformative act of grace. (Matthew himself is a paradigm of this: a tax collector turned disciple.) Third, Matthew's central teaching that 'the kingdom of heaven is at hand' points to God's prior unconditioned grace and forgiveness. Fourth, specific passages speak of God's gracious initiative quite directly. For example, Jesus tells his disciples, 'You have received without payment; give without payment' (Mat. 10:9). In Matthew 26:28, Christ speaks of his life being 'given for many for the forgiveness of sins' (cf.1:21ff. and 20:28), and clearly he does not refer here to forgiveness that depends on prior human forgiveness. These four strands of evidence confirm that Matthew 18, rather than contradicting Matthew 6, helps to deter the reader from a misreading of Matthew 6 that excludes God's gracious initiative.

And how might Matthew 18 be read in light of Matthew 6? Matthew 6, especially vv. 14f., can be seen as a clear, universal statement of the human 'conditions' of divine forgiveness aimed to motivate the disciples of Jesus to forgive. As such, Matthew 6 clarifies a specific aspect (the conditioning relation of 'moments' 2 and 3) of the larger plot of divine-human forgiveness unfolded in Matthew 18. What might appear as an isolated incident in the parable, is seen in Matthew 6 to be an expression of a consistent pattern in which God responds to the human forgiveness and unforgiveness.

---

[10] Bauckham, 'Forgiveness,' 3.

5. Clarifying How Human Forgiveness is a Condition of Divine Forgiveness

One point that arises from the preceding inter-textual dialogue between Matthew 6 and 18 is that, despite differences in form and content, the two passages are united in the disturbing conviction that divine forgiveness is in some respects conditioned by human forgiveness. God's forgiveness is not conditioned initially, but it is conditioned in so far as God responds to the human response to God's initial forgiveness. Perhaps the best way to describe this condition more precisely is to state what the condition does *not* mean. There are at least three misunderstandings of this condition that need to be excluded.

First, when Matthew 6 says that if we forgive our debtors then God forgives our debts, it does not mean that humans can merit or earn forgiveness. This is true even in respect to the relationship between moments two and three, between our response and God's response to our response. Rather, human forgiveness is best seen as a description of what makes a person *capable* of receiving God's forgiveness and appropriating it rightly.[11] In a sense, we could say that it is the continued appropriation or reception of God's forgiveness that is conditional, rather than the forgiveness itself.

For Matthew, God does not tolerate people who refuse to treat others with the same grace and forgiveness that God first extends to them. God's forgiveness is consistently a *gift* that is given without consideration of human just deserts. But the gift is given 'with strings attached.' The gift of forgiveness is retractable in the event of a human refusal to forgive, even if this is an unexpected 'extreme case' (the servant in Mat. 18). The gift can be forfeited if not handled rightly. In this sense of a necessary capability (perhaps itself God given), human forgiveness is a necessary condition of divine forgiveness.

Second, while human forgiveness might be a necessary condition for the continued appropriation of divine forgiveness, it ought not to be regarded as a *sufficient* condition of this appropriation. This is closely related to the first denial, that the condition is not a condition of merit. Human forgiveness may express human capacity to receive and appropriate God's forgiveness, but God's grace is what moves God to forgive. The sufficiency of God's forgiveness lies in God's grace, even if that grace necessarily includes human response and responsibility. The parable of the vineyard-workers in Matthew 20:1–16 provides evidence that this is Matthew's perspective. The owner of the vineyard, a figure for God, gives the same wage to all workers even though some worked all day and others worked only an hour. So also with forgiveness: some human 'work' in forgiving is a necessary condition

---

[11] Moule, 'As we forgive,' 71ff.

of the appropriation of God's forgiveness, but this work is not at all sufficient to explain God's gracious act of complete forgiveness of all of the disciple's sins.

Third, the human conditioning of divine forgiveness is also not to be taken too rigidly or strictly. Such over-strictness could be expressed in various ways, but one example is sufficient to indicate what I have in mind. A 'strict' interpreter could say that Matthew makes the disciple's final destiny entirely dependent on whether or not she forgives her fellow disciple perfectly on every occasion. Failing to forgive once would mean forever forfeiting God's forgiveness. Such a view misreads Matthew's point in both chapters 6 and 18. In the parable, the unforgiving servant's attitude and action towards the other servant is best seen as expressing a pattern of life that refuses to live within God's mercy, rather than as an isolated one-time event. His act of unforgiveness is a manifestation of a heart that is fundamentally alien to the reception and consequent enactment of God's grace. In such a case, the sinner willfully steps out of the sphere of God's grace and forgiveness into which God initially brought him. Similarly, in the context of Lord's Prayer, one cannot regard the basis of divine forgiveness as a one-time act of human forgiveness, and so it is with a human failure to forgive. Further, the fifth petition is stated in the plural, and thus implies a sharing with others in a praying and forgiving community.[12] Such considerations show that the relationship of human forgiveness and divine forgiveness cannot be construed in terms of a strict account of individual acts and *quid pro quo* justice.

6. Conclusion

In this paper we have begun to delimit the character of the relationship of human and divine forgiveness in two Matthean texts. To state the matter more precisely than we have would risk imposing an artificial precision on Matthew that he was not concerned to have. Therefore, we are left with a measure of vagueness, ambiguity in our conclusions.

Nonetheless, the distinctive theological contribution of Matthew is clear. In the texts we considered, Matthew teaches that, while God takes the initiative in forgiveness, the full and lasting experience of God's forgiveness is conditional on human forgiveness.

The Matthean emphasis on human responsibility to forgive has long been either neglected or misinterpreted in much Christian theological interpretation. And this has affected Christian practice, finding expression in the

---

[12] This corporate dimension could be developed considerably, as the contributions by Jones and Selby to this volume indicate.

standard liturgical version of the Lord's prayer used and in and the nature of the catechesis that interprets it. Such tendencies risk an evacuation of human response and responsibility from forgiveness and a reductive, non-biblical cheapening of grace. Matthew declares that Christians cannot receive the benefits of forgiveness without expressing those benefits in relationship to others. If Christian theology and practice fails to make room for this message, it encourages what Dietrich Bonhoeffer referred to as 'squandering the precious treasure of the Lord's forgiveness.'[13]

---

[13] Dietrich Bonhoeffer, *The Cost of Discipleship* (New York 1963), 324.

14. May God Forgive?

Karin Scheiber

1. Introduction

Consider the following case: Tilda sets Otto's house on fire and it burns to
the ground. May God forgive Tilda for what she did? I will first clarify what
I mean when I ask about God's authority to forgive. Then I will test
different models of God-talk to find out whether they are useful in making
plausible God's authority to forgive. I will conclude by suggesting that the
model of God as a lover offers a possibility for understanding how God is
in a position to forgive what Tilda has done to Otto.

2. The Ethical Question: Who May Forgive Tilda?

When Tilda sets Otto's house on fire, who is in a position to forgive her?
The spontaneous and intuitively convincing answer will be: Otto, of course.
If a bypasser wanted to forgive Tilda, we would reject her offer as
presumptuous. But why do we consider Otto's forgiveness as a possible
appropriate reaction but not the bypasser's 'forgiveness'? Because Otto – in
contrast to the bypasser – is the victim of Tilda's action. So far, so clear.
But what about Otto's friends who have been instrumental in building the
house and now see their work destroyed? What about Otto's aged mother,
who is concerned about her son because she realizes that for him much
more than reparable material damage has occurred? What about all those
who morally condemn Tilda's action and are worried about the foundations
of social life? And what about those who judge Tilda's offence as a
violation of the indispensable rules of social life and a disregard of the
democratically legitimated will of the people? Are they all to be counted as
victims? Or are they to be considered as not affected by Tilda's action at
all?

Most philosophers who consider the question of who is in a position to
grant forgiveness hold that only the victim has the right to forgive. To quote

the American legal philosopher Jeffrie G. Murphy: 'To use a legal term, I do not have *standing* to resent or forgive you unless I have myself been the victim of your wrongdoing. I may forgive you for embezzling my funds; but it would be ludicrous for me, for example, to claim that I had decided to forgive Hitler for what he did to the Jews. I lack the proper standing for this. Thus, I may legitimately resent (and hence consider forgiving) only wrong done *to me.*[1] It is still not clear, however, who is to be considered as the victim: Otto only, or his mother and friends as well?

If the ethical criterion of 'concern' should be used to answer the question of who is in a position to grant forgiveness, then we must be able to determine who is 'concerned' by an action. For that purpose I want to introduce three distinctions: I differentiate between being concerned directly or indirectly, to a higher or lower degree, and personally or morally.

I begin with the last distinction. Personally concerned by Tilda's action are Otto as well as his sympathetic mother and his helpful friends. Morally concerned are all those who as outsiders – watching the spectacle or reading the newspaper – feel indignation about Tilda's action. Maybe they are bewildered that someone can do such a thing to a fellow human or they are worried about the humaneness in our society. They are concerned by Tilda's action but they are morally not personally concerned. To use Peter F. Strawson's distinction, their reaction is 'indignation,' not 'resentment.'[2] It is not necessary to define forgiveness as the overcoming of resentment to hold that one must be personally concerned by an action to be in a position to forgive the wrongdoer.

Those who are personally concerned by Tilda's action can be divided into those who are directly or indirectly concerned as well as those who are concerned to high or low degree. Otto, as the owner of the burnt house, is directly concerned by Tilda's action; Otto's mother, being sympathetic with her son, is concerned indirectly. Otto's friends, too, are directly concerned but to a lower degree. My opinion (which cannot be defended in detail here) is that the appropriate recipient of Tilda's possible plea for forgiveness is the one who is concerned by her action directly and to a high degree, namely, Otto. Those who are concerned indirectly or to a lower degree may forgive as well but only what has been done to *them.*

---

[1] Jeffrie G. Murphy, in: Jeffrie G. Murphy & Jean Hampton, *Forgiveness and Mercy* (Cambridge 1988), 21 (italics in the original).
[2] Peter F. Strawson, 'Freedom and Resentment,' *Proceedings of the British Academy* 48 (1962), 187–211.

3. The Theological Question: May God Forgive Tilda?

The view that only the victim is in a position to forgive the wrongdoer is widely held. Attempts to challenge it are usually not very convincing,[3] nor are attempts to concur with this view but to allow for an exception in the case of God. If one does not want to pursue these attempts there are but two remaining possibilities. Either God is not considered as being concerned personally, directly and to a high degree by interpersonal actions, in which case God does not have the authority to forgive such actions, or it can be shown that God is indeed concerned in the way just mentioned by what Tilda did to Otto. To show this is what I will attempt to demonstrate in this section of the chapter. I want to make plausible how – more precisely: as whom – God is concerned by the harm humans inflict on their fellow humans. For that purpose I examine three models of God: God as the moral lawmaker and cosmic judge, God as the creator, and God as a lover. Each of these models could be qualified in a different way, but that is of no importance for this endeavor. I am just dealing with the question of what kind of relationship between God and humans allows us to view God as a direct victim of human action.

The Model of God as the Moral Lawmaker and Cosmic Judge

Usually the topic of forgiveness is linked with the idea of God as the moral lawmaker and cosmic judge.[4] I maintain that this idea of God is unsuitable for demonstrating God's authority to forgive. When Tilda sets Otto's house on fire, Otto is the victim and not the legislator who has enacted the law against arson. The lawmaker may in some sense be concerned, but like the moral concern discussed above, his concern is not specific enough to meet the ethical criterion. If the lawmaker goes beyond that and feels *personally* concerned, he misunderstands the connection between the law and the action to be judged: arson is not wrong because there is a law against it; it is because arson is wrong that a law has been enacted against it.

Nor if Tilda is brought to court ought she to expect forgiveness from the judge. Why not? The judge is not directly concerned by Tilda's action. He is not even permitted to be, since otherwise he would be a 'biased' and thus a bad judge. He does not represent the victim either (that's the job of the victim's lawyer), but he represents law and justice. His task is to assess the punishment justly, according to the law, with regard to the circumstances

---

[3] E.g., William Neblett, 'Forgiveness and Ideals,' *Mind* 83 (1974), 269–275; Carl Reinhold Bråkenhielm, *Forgiveness* (Philadelphia 1993), 35; Margaret Paton, 'Can God Forgive?', *Modern Theology* 4 (1988), 225–233; Martin Hughes, 'Forgiveness,' *Analysis* 35 (1975), 113–117.

[4] Thus, e.g., Immanuel Kant, *On Religion within the Limits of Reason Alone*; Anne C. Minas, 'God and Forgiveness,' *The Philosophical Quarterly* 25 (1975), 138–150.

surrounding the case. He may mitigate or remit a just punishment when other moral obligations require it (e.g., when the just punishment of the offender would entail intolerable consequences for an innocent third party). This is what is called 'mercy' in legal terminology.[5]

But mercy offered by a judge is not forgiveness. Offering mercy, that is, mitigating a just punishment on moral grounds, requires a certain official authority (such as that of a judge or queen) but not personal concern; with forgiveness it is the other way round.[6] The difference between mercy and forgiveness is also to be seen in that Otto may forgive Tilda no matter what sentence the judge assesses, and the judge assesses his sentence without regard to whether Otto forgives Tilda. This means that God's authority to forgive is not illuminated by talking of God as a judge. This does not mean, however, that one should not talk of God as judge or that the idea of God as a judge should be changed until it no longer is judge-like. Nor does it mean that God is not in a position to forgive. It simply means that in order to understand how it is that God may forgive what Tilda did to Otto the idea of God as a judge is not useful.

The Model of God as the Creator

Can God's authority to forgive be grounded within the scope of a theology of creation? That the creator is concerned when his work is being damaged seems plausible in the first instance. But upon what is this concern founded? Talking of the creator in itself explains hardly anything. It has to be further unfolded in either of two directions: the creator as the 'owner' of his creature, or the creator as the 'father' of his creature. In both cases the anthropological and the theological implications of such an argument must be thought out.

An artist as the creator of his work is at the same time its owner. God, too, is according to the Bible the owner of his creation (Ps. 50:12). Thus, when Tilda causes harm to Otto she is damaging God's property. God is directly concerned and therefore entitled to grant forgiveness. Otto's interests are looked after indirectly *in so far* as they are in accordance with God's interests. God's authority to forgive can be defended this way but Otto's is being abandoned. Such a comprehension of God's authority to forgive is paid for dearly: with the conception of a God who does not care about the well-being of his creatures as such but cares only about maintaining his ownership, and with the conception of humans as an object of their owner. With a mitigated concept of ownership both God *and* Otto might be conceived of as victims. Then Otto would be concerned by Tilda's action as

---

[5] Alwynne Smart, 'Mercy,' *Philosophy* 43 (1968), 345–359.

[6] R.S. Downie, 'Forgiveness,' *The Philosophical Quarterly* 15 (1965), 128–134. Cf. Murphy, in: Murphy & Hampton, *Forgiveness and Mercy*, 167.

the owner of the burnt house; God would be concerned as the owner of the harmed Otto. Tilda's action would produce two different victims, whereby God only becomes a victim by means of Otto's being a victim; and she would need the forgiveness of both in order to be really forgiven. God and Otto could grant or withhold forgiveness independently.

But the idea of God as the owner of the humans is not thought to the end yet. If God as the creator of humans is the owner of Otto in such a way that he (and not Otto) is the victim proper of Tilda's action, then he is the owner of Tilda as well – with the consequence that he (and not Tilda) is responsible for her action. Tilda would indeed have done the action, but it would be God as her owner who would be liable for it. So guilt and forgiveness would be completely – or partly, according to the mitigated version – assigned to God: God becomes guilty to himself and forgives himself. This conception is absurd. The model of God as an owner does not render feasible the evidence of God's authority to forgive but renders impossible any sensible understanding of guilt and forgiveness.

From the perspective of a theology of creation another point is essential. The Bible's talk of God as the creator does indeed include the idea of God as the owner of his creatures, but that is not the point of the Judeo-Christian concept of creation. According to this concept, humans have not been created as mere property of God, at his disposal, but as God's image in responsive freedom. Using the model of God as an owner to defend God's authority to forgive cannot in the end account for either human freedom or human responsibility.

This objection can be met by picturing God not as an owner but as the father of his creatures. This concept, too, is rooted in biblical God-talk.[7] A father does not consider his children merely as his property but treats them with affection and a sense of responsibility. He does not seek his own profit only, in the way that an owner might, but seeks the well-being of his children as well. Additionally, he wants not only their obedience but their affection as well.

In this way the criticism uttered from the perspective of a theology of creation can be met, but God's authority to forgive has not yet been demonstrated. How can it be derived from talk of God as father? God is either seen as the father of mature (capable of guilt and forgiveness) or of minor children. Both cases must be considered separately.

In the view that humans are minor children of God, they are not capable of granting forgiveness themselves. God grants or withholds forgiveness in their place and stead. One consequence of this conception is that God's authority to forgive is demonstrated at the expense of the humans' authority to forgive. Another is that we again have the problem we had with the

---

[7] This can be seen already in the Old Testament, e.g., Isa. 63:16; 64:7; Sir. 51:10.

model of God as an owner: God as the creator is not the father of Otto only but also of Tilda. If Otto is minor and therefore incapable of granting forgiveness, Tilda is minor as well and incapable of guilt. For both of them the responsibility is God's by proxy – again guilt and forgiveness become events within God and for God only.

In the view that humans are mature children of God, they are capable of becoming guilty and bear responsibility for their actions. For what happens to them, they themselves can grant forgiveness. Then the father's view is irrelevant. Were he to refer to his paternal authority to decide upon forgiveness, he would incapacitate his children and behave as a despotic owner. Thus the model of God as father is subject to similar difficulties as the model of God as owner and is of no use for showing God's authority to forgive.

The Model of God as a Lover

How else then may God's authority to forgive be substantiated? We need a model with which – other than with the model of God as a judge – God's direct and personal concern may be shown; and for which – other than for the model of God as an owner or father – God's relationship to both Otto and Tilda does not mean a predicament. As such a model I propose the talk of God as lover.

Oscar and Tilda are a couple united in sincere love. They trust each other and take care of each other's well-being. Oscar is Otto's brother. They have a close relation and share joy and grief with one another. Now, when Tilda sets Otto's house on fire, Oscar is concerned by her action in two ways. First he is indirectly concerned as Otto's brother since he is sympathetic with his brother. At the same time he is concerned as Tilda's partner. Tilda knows how much he cares for Otto's well-being and how much an offence against Otto also must strike him. With her action she takes this into account. The seeming ease with which she does so takes Otto aback, alienates Tilda from him. He doubts whether she really loves him. He tells her: 'Because I love my brother I wish you had not caused any harm to him. But if you didn't want to refrain from your action for his sake, you ought at least to have refrained from it for my sake – if you love me.'

The main injury caused to Oscar lies in Tilda's coldness and neglect towards *him*. By this he is directly concerned even if this attitude of Tilda's is expressed in an action that only concerns him indirectly. It is Oscar's (betrayed) love for Tilda that makes him a direct victim of her offence against Otto.

I suggest that the concern God has for human actions can be understood according to the model of Oscar. God has associated himself with Tilda in a love that is whole and undivided. To express this idea with the picture of matrimony is not alien to the Bible. But God has associated himself in whole and undivided love with Otto as well. Tilda's offence against Otto hurts God since he is sympathetic with Otto. At the same time Tilda's action hurts God since it shows her lack of love not only for Otto but for *him* as well.

But has God's authority to forgive been demonstrated yet? After all it is not Oscar's pain as such but only an illegitimately caused pain that makes him an appropriate recipient of Tilda's possible plea for forgiveness. Oscar's pain is to be understood as caused illegitimately only against the background of his formerly (perhaps only seemingly) intact relationship with Tilda. But such a formerly intact relationship between God and humans is out of the question for theological reasons.

How then can God count as a direct victim of Tilda's action against Otto, since the basic prerequisite for Oscar's being a direct victim – that is, Tilda's and Otto's existing partnership – is not fulfilled? At this point the model of Oscar reaches its limits.

Tilda is not obliged to answer the advances of a persistent admirer, nor is she obliged to continue to love Otto just because she has loved him up to now, nor is she obliged to love God. If love is to be understood as a free and indisposable gift, an obligation to love cannot be claimed without inconsistency. But there is one thing that can be said about Tilda relating to God that cannot be said in the same way about her relating to others. Tilda is 'created' for a relationship with God or 'meant' to be in communion with God. In theology, the terms 'likeness' and 'image of God,' taken from the creation account in Genesis, are used to express this thought. This human 'likeness' with God does not consist in a certain human attribute such as appearance or reason; instead, 'likeness' expresses the basis upon which humans can enter a relationship with God. The human being as God's image was created as the vis-à-vis of God. Humans can fail to fulfill this purpose but they cannot escape it for the reason that it remains nonetheless their purpose. Humans can make a desperate attempt to live their life without God but still they cannot help but lose thereby what they wanted to gain, namely a true and fulfilled life.

Talking of 'meaning,' 'purpose' or 'human nature' always entails a descriptive and a normative dimension. On the one hand, it is to be understood as a 'descriptive' statement about how humans factually are: They *are* created in God's image. At the same time it is 'normative' as it implies that humans *should* be or become who they (according to their nature) are. Humans can fail to fulfill this, but the term 'fail' already includes a judgment; it qualifies the miss of one's nature negatively.

While for human relations, which are not rooted in a specific destiny, only a factually entered partnership sets the scope within which Otto becomes the direct victim of Tilda's coldness, in the relationship between God and humans the scope is set by the creaturely destiny involved in bearing the 'likeness' of God. When Tilda refuses to enter into communion with God she does not neglect a moral obligation but fails to fulfill both her nature and the self-determination of God. Her failure is not guilt in the ethical sense. Rather it is, in relation to God, what theology calls 'sin,' specifically 'original sin.'

The model of Oscar elucidates not only the difference between sin and guilt but also the difference between original sin and actual sin. Tilda's failure to fulfill her destiny (communion with God) is traditionally called 'original sin.' It is not primarily an action or a deed of Tilda's but a situation, in which Tilda finds herself 'since ever.' Therefore – and not because of any biological process of transfer – it may be called 'inherited sin' as well. Tilda's refusal of love for God is not primarily an action but is expressed again and again in actions. In so far as Tilda's arson is an expression of her coldness toward God – and not because it is moral guilt – her action can be qualified as 'actual sin.'

So we have two direct victims of Tilda's action: God (Oscar) and Otto. Both are concerned by the same action but not in the same respect. (That's the difference between this case and a case where Tilda burns a house with several owners.) Otto is directly concerned by Tilda's arson; God (Oscar) is directly concerned by what is expressed through Tilda's action. Tilda becomes morally guilty relating to Otto. In relation to God she does not become morally guilty but her action is an actual sin, an expression of her failure to fulfill her purpose (communion with God).

As direct victims, both Otto and God are in the position to grant forgiveness. But what is the relation of these two 'sources of forgiveness' to each other? Can God and Otto each forgive only a part of Tilda's offence? Or can they each forgive the whole? Does Tilda need the forgiveness of both to be forgiven? Or is the forgiveness of one party sufficient? These questions need further inquiry. Here it is sufficient to conclude that the models of God as a lawmaker and judge and of God as an owner or father (qua creator) are not suitable to make plausible God's authority to forgive what humans do to each other. The model of the relation of God and humans as a loving communion is more successful in elucidating God's authority to forgive.

4. Conclusion

My initial question was: May God forgive Tilda for what she did to Otto? My answer to this question is: When we think of God as turned towards humans in whole and undivided love, and think of humans as meant to be in a loving communion with God, then God is directly concerned by Tilda's offence against Otto and thus in the position to grant forgiveness.

15. Forgiveness in the Twentieth Century

A Review of the Literature, 1901–2001

Nigel Biggar

1. Introduction

Our subject is the concept of forgiveness. Although some theological thought on this matter has been developed in the course of work on the doctrine of the Atonement, that is not our focus. While any account of the Atonement is bound to concern itself with the means of reconciliation, and every description of those means will accord the grace of God a decisive role, not every such description has proceeded primarily in terms of forgiveness. Sometimes God's grace is seen as manifesting itself in the gracious provision of the means of satisfaction or of a substitute for punishment. It is true that both of these presuppose forbearance from vengeance, the expression of compassion, and the desire for reconciliation, all of which are the germs of forgiveness. They are not, however, its fulfilment. That comes, not in giving to satisfaction the recognition that it merits, nor in accepting the punishment of the innocent instead of the guilty, but rather in volunteering to the guilty something that they can never strictly deserve: the restoration of broken trust. The paradigmatic context of forgiveness is neither feudal nor forensic, but friendship.

Our subject is forgiveness in the twentieth century. This chronological limitation has not been adopted just to make possible a review of the relevant literature within the confines of a single essay. Most of the significant writing on forgiveness has taken place within that period, certainly in philosophy (excepting Joseph Butler), politics, and psychology, but also in theology.

The structure of the survey that follows is basically chronological. Since the material is complex, involving several different disciplines and touching on a wide range of topics, a thematic structure would have been more complicated than helpful. Besides, a chronological ordering has the advantage of laying bare such actual conversation as has occurred between subsequent writers and their predecessors. Nevertheless, what follows is not ordered simply by chronology. In my necessarily selective accounts of what particular authors have to say, I have focussed on especially significant themes. Further, I have supplemented actual discussion of these themes either by creating conversation between authors who did not refer to each other's work, or by developing conversation between those who did. Occasionally, I have allowed my own voice to come to the fore.

2. Theology, 1901–1941

R.C. Moberly opens his modern classic of Atonement theology, *Atonement and Personality* (1901), with a discussion of three 'fundamental' concepts: punishment, penitence, and forgiveness. His begins his treatment of the last of these by distinguishing it ideally – and therefore as it pertains to God – both from the mere remission of penalty and from a decision on the part of the wronged party simply to ignore the injury and *regard* the wrongdoer *as if* they were innocent; for these could amount to a condoning of wrong-doing.[1] 'Forgiveness,' he says, 'is no mere transaction outside of the self, … which leaves the self unchanged.'[2] On the contrary, true – divine – forgiveness is never unconditional; it is correlative to the forgivableness of the wrongdoer.[3]

This correlation of forgiveness with forgivableness means that 'earthly forgiveness' is provisional and conditional upon the (eschatological) per-fection of the penitent's righteousness; and that if this is not achieved, then forgiveness is forfeited and turns into condemnation.[4] It does not mean, however, that forgiveness is simply earned or deserved, reduced to the acknowledgement of 'the goodness of the good; or, at all events, the imperfect goodness of the incompletely good,' rendered indistinguishable from justice, and made redundant.[5] It does not mean this, because the forgivableness of the wrongdoer consists in 'the germinal possibilities of penitence in him,' which are themselves inspired by 'the loving righteous-ness' – 'the softening and enabling grace'[6] – of God.[7] Moberly illuminates his meaning here by making an analogy (from below) between the relations

---

[1] R.C. Moberly, *Atonement and Personality* (London 1901), 52–53.

[2] Moberly, *Atonement and Personality*, 71–72.

[3] Moberly, *Atonement and Personality*, 56.

[4] Moberly, *Atonement and Personality*, 61. Moberly appeals here to the Parable of the Wicked Servant (Matthew 18:32–35).

[5] Moberly, *Atonement and Personality*, 58–59.

[6] Moberly, *Atonement and Personality*, 61.

[7] Moberly, *Atonement and Personality*, 59.

of a parent and their naughty child on the one hand, and God and the human sinner on the other. Parental love refuses to identify the child wholly with its naughtiness; and while it cannot wear the aspect of forgiveness so long as the miscreant 'is wholly self-identified with its passion,' it eagerly meets the first glimmer of regret with a loving embrace.[8] At this point Moberly speculates that, to some extent, it may be that 'it was really the goodness and love of the parent which, in the child who reflects the parent's character and influence (as his features and tone)[,] constitutes the child's own primal possibility of yearning and repentant love.' He implies that however true this is of the parent and child, it is certainly true of God and sinner.[9] This concept of compassionate love as the creative matrix of repentance, which Moberly develops here, is one that will reappear at several different points in the subsequent, century-long discussion of forgiveness.

The case of parent and child, however, is not the only kind of case. There is also the case of the victim and the oppressor who treats him with 'outrageous wickedness' and remains impenitent. Here 'I [the victim] do not stand to him [the oppressor] in the place of God. I have, materially, no power to control his wickedness. I have no responsibility for his moral character. I am not his judge.'[10] As in the case of parent and child, I can and should still recognise the wrongdoer as one who 'though self-identified with wickedness now, ... is capable of identity with goodness.' Then, distinguishing between what he is now and what he might yet become, I can and should 'go out, in thought, in desire, in aspiration, in prayer, on his behalf, towards that restoration, in him, of the true self, for which he himself never dreams of praying nor hoping,' and ready to take hold of opportunities for corresponding acts.[11] However, unlike the earlier case, here I must disclaim all right not to suffer, submitting myself to God's discipline.

In *The Christian Experience of Forgiveness* (1927), H.R. Mackintosh both agrees and disagrees with Moberly. He agrees that forgiveness, properly conceived, does not neglect or condone wrongdoing. Indeed, he argues that a genuine act of forgiveness is at once one of mercy *and* of judgement (and is therefore compatible with punishment)[12] – thereby following Wilhelm Herrmann (than whom 'no modern thinker has made a more profound study of forgiveness, human and Divine')[13] against Albrecht

---

[8] Moberly, *Atonement and Personality*, 64.

[9] Moberly, *Atonement and Personality*, 66.

[10] Moberly, *Atonement and Personality*, 67.

[11] Moberly, *Atonement and Personality*, 69. Moberly appeals here to the martyrdom of St Stephen (Acts 7:59).

[12] H.R. Mackintosh, *The Christian Experience of Forgiveness* (London 1927), 24, 25, 27, 44–45, 99, 160.

[13] Mackintosh, *Christian Experience*, 44.

Ritschl, who represents 'the modern prevalence of the notion that love and anger exclude each other.'[14]

Nevertheless, Mackintosh describes as 'really sub-Christian,' Moberly's idea that (God's) forgiveness is correlated to forgivableness and that it is 'conditional, subject to revision, [and] in a real sense precarious and asymptotic.'[15] Against the Augustinian-Scholastic notion of divine grace as primarily a reformative power culminating in a complete state of regeneration that *merits* salvation (including forgiveness?) as a just reward,[16] Mackintosh sides with Luther. Here, God's grace comes in the form of an act of forgiveness – an act of receiving the *un*worthy into fellowship[17] – before it operates as a regenerating power.[18] As such, it is 'free' and 'supernatural,' rather than the product of any natural necessity (i.e., justice).[19] Further, because grace is first of all forgiveness, the kind of regeneration that it brings about is specifically characterised by gratitude and hope.[20] Actually, Mackintosh suggests that the act of forgiveness is not, in fact, the *very* first epiphany of redemptive grace; and that this takes the form of love as 'the creative capacity of pardoning [or forgiveness].'[21] What he means by this is informed by the notion of 'fraternal sympathy' that he draws from Horace Bushnell and James Denney, and which involves an imaginative

---

[14] Mackintosh, *Christian Experience*, 160–162. Mackintosh himself translated the third volume of Ritschl's *Die christliche Lehre von der Rechtfertigung und Versöhnung* (3 vols, 1870–1874) under the title of *The Christian Doctrine of Justification and Reconciliation* (1900). According to Paul Lehmann ('Forgiveness,' in: James F. Childress & John Macquarrie (eds.), *The New Dictionary of Christian Ethics*, [London 1986], 236), Ritschl's attention to forgiveness 'lies behind' Herrmann's consideration of the subject in *The Communion of the Christian with God* (ET 1906; originally published in German in 1886 as *Der Verkehr des Christen mit Gott*) and Mackintosh's 'influential treatment' in *The Christian Experience of Forgiveness* (1927). Ritschl may 'lie behind' Herrmann and Mackintosh in the sense that he stimulated their interest in the topic of forgiveness, but not in the sense that he determined what they thought about it.

[15] Mackintosh, *Christian Experience*, 242.

[16] Mackintosh, *Christian Experience*, 126–135. Moberly (as presented above) is surely right to doubt the good sense of talking about regeneration 'meriting' or 'deserving' forgiveness, because to say that one deserves forgiveness is to say that it is unnecessary. According to Mackintosh, however, the Early Church did think of amendment of life as the basis of forgiveness, and not as the cause of its redundancy (Mackintosh, *Christian Experience*, 126–127).

[17] Mackintosh, *Christian Experience*, 131.

[18] Mackintosh, *Christian Experience*, 144.

[19] Mackintosh, *Christian Experience*, 181. On this point, Mackintosh endorses Ritschl's description of forgiveness as 'synthetic,' rather than 'analytic' (Ritschl, *Christian Doctrine*, 244).

[20] Mackintosh, *Christian Experience*, 265, 255.

[21] Mackintosh, *Christian Experience*, 237.

identification of the victim with the wrongdoer, a certain costly 'bearing' of the wrong done, and a vicarious or substitutionary suffering.[22]

Given that Mackintosh's book was published a mere nine years after the end of the First World War, it would be reasonable to expect his thinking about forgiveness to be shaped by the international hostility fostered by that conflict and by the debate over the Treaty of Versailles' vindictiveness toward Germany. In fact, *The Christian Experience of Forgiveness* barely musters three very passing references to the war and its aftermath. Nevertheless, it is not entirely abstracted from its historical context, in that it is part of The Library of Constructive Theology, which was designed to represent the fundamental affirmations of Christianity 'in the light of modern knowledge' – that is, on the basis of religious experience or consciousness.[23] It would be a mistake, however, to conclude from his appeal to 'experience' that Mackintosh is an unreconstructed nineteenth-century liberal; for the experience that he has in mind is specifically Christocentric. Since God forgives freely and not necessarily, we can only know of his forgiveness 'experimentally,' *a posteriori*, through some concrete, historical event; namely, in the person of Jesus Christ.[24]

No reference to Moberly or Mackintosh is to be found in the brief concluding chapter of Reinhold Niebuhr's *An Interpretation of Christian Ethics* (1935), which carries the title of 'Love as Forgiveness.' Unlike Mackintosh's treatment, Niebuhr's does bear the marks of his sobering socio-political experience, in that he argues, *pace* Tolstoy and all political romanticism, that forgiveness cannot be a substitute for 'social punishment.' The use of force in the maintenance and promotion of justice is a tragic necessity in a sinful world.[25] Nevertheless, the rationale for forgiveness is that 'the evil in the other shall be borne without vindictiveness because the evil in the self is known';[26] and this should shape the manner in which force is used. For the awareness that 'every society which punishes its anti-social members is more responsible for their anti-social conduct than it realizes' should qualify 'the spiritual pride of the usually self-righteous guardians of public morals.' Thus the use of force in the cause of justice will be subject to 'a religious reservation in which lie the roots of the spirit of forgiveness.'[27]

---

[22] Mackintosh, *Christian Experience*, 99, 186–189. Mackintosh refers explicitly to Bushnell's *Forgiveness and Law* (1874). He quotes Denney on this matter, but provides no reference. Elsewhere he refers to Denney's commentary on *Romans* (1900) and *The Death of Christ* (1902).

[23] Mackintosh, *Christian Experience*, vii–viii.

[24] Mackintosh, *Christian Experience*, 174. On this point Mackintosh bears the influence of Herrmann (*Communion*, 47–48).

[25] Reinhold Niebuhr, *An Interpretation of Christian Ethics* (1935; New York 1979), 140–141.

[26] Niebuhr, *Interpretation*, 137.

[27] Niebuhr, *Interpretation*, 141.

Basil Redlich's *The Forgiveness of Sins*, published two years later in 1937, is largely a survey of biblical and patristic literature, passes by Niebuhr entirely, and affords Moberly and Mackintosh only the slightest of glances.[28] Still, in his own way Redlich picks up the theme of the gracious *initiative* of forgiveness that we have already met in the thought of these two latter authors. Although the Old and New Testaments are united in regarding forgiveness as a restoration to fellowship that is conditional upon repentance and confession,[29] the New Testament, according to Redlich, enjoins the offended to be active in wooing the offender back, dealing with him not for what he is, but for what he is capable of becoming.[30] This 'active sympathy'[31] goes by the name of 'forgivingness,'[32] and it is normative for victims: whereas we ought not to forgive those who have wronged us and remain impenitent, we still have a duty to regard them with a forgiving spirit.[33] It is of this, according to Redlich, that St Paul famously wrote in his Epistle to the Romans, 'If thine enemy hunger, feed him; if he thirst, give him to drink: for in so doing thou shalt heap coals of fire upon his head. Be not overcome of evil, but overcome evil with good';[34] and it is as a paradigmatic instance of such a feeding of enemies that the Lord's Supper should be understood.[35] So highly did Jesus rate the importance of this 'forgivingness' that he introduced the notion that God's forgiveness of us is conditional upon it: God can only forgive the genuinely penitent, and the genuinely penitent cannot but regard his own persecutor with sympathetic eyes of 'forgivingness.'[36]

Like Redlich, Vincent Taylor in *Forgiveness and Reconciliation* (1941) approaches the topic of forgiveness from a biblical direction. However, the subtitle of his book, 'A Study in New Testament Theology,' is misleading in so far as Taylor is concerned, not only to articulate a coherent biblical point of view, but also to bring it to bear, critically and constructively, upon 'modern theology.' On the very first page,[37] he makes clear his intention to show that the New Testament does not share the conflation of the concepts of forgiveness and reconciliation that he finds in the work of contemporary theologians such as R.C. Moberly,[38]

---

[28] Basil Redlich, *The Forgiveness of Sins* (Edinburgh 1937), 299, 312.

[29] Redlich, *Forgiveness*, 100–101.

[30] Redlich, *Forgiveness*, 104–105, 111.

[31] Redlich, *Forgiveness*, 149.

[32] Redlich, *Forgiveness*, 104.

[33] Redlich, *Forgiveness*, 298.

[34] Romans 12:20–21.

[35] Redlich, *Forgiveness*, 182–183.

[36] Redlich, *Forgiveness*, 138–139.

[37] Vincent Taylor, *Forgiveness and Reconciliation: A Study in New Testament Theology* (London 1941), 1, 28–29.

[38] R.C. Moberly, *Atonement and Personality* (London 1901).

W.H. Moberly,[39] William Temple,[40] R.S. Franks,[41] R.N. Flew[42] – and Redlich himself.[43] Consistent New Testament usage, according to Taylor, has it that forgiveness comprises 'the covering or removal of the barriers to reconciliation,' whose conditions are repentance and (following Redlich) a forgiving spirit.[44] In fact, Taylor accepts the 'unscriptural' extension of the meaning of forgiveness to include full reconciliation,[45] but argues that attention to the scriptural distinction is nevertheless important.[46] This is so, partly in order to distinguish between the different stages of a complex process, and especially between justification and sanctification (*pace* R.C. Moberly);[47] and partly in order to affirm a Godward aspect to the redeeming work of Christ, and so a mediatorial theory of the Atonement.[48] Quite how Taylor conceives of this is less than crystal clear. It appears that he sees part of the significance of the cross in terms of Christ's obedient and vicarious embodiment of perfect penitence, in which human sinners are drawn to participate by faith, and which thus makes possible God's gracious remission of sins and full reconciliation with him.[49]

3. Philosophy, 1965–1991

In 1927 H.R. Mackintosh wrote that he had asked 'two of the most eminent philosophers in the country' to name any passage in a work of moral psychology that analyses the process of forgiveness, and that 'not a single reference could be given.'[50] Sixty-four years later, on the opening page of his own book on the subject, Joram Graf Haber observes that the 'nature [of

---

[39] W.H. Moberly was the son of R.C. Moberly, and contributed essays on 'The Atonement' and 'God and the Absolute' to *Foundations*, a theological symposium published in 1912. Judging by Taylor's brief quotation of him (Taylor, *Forgiveness and Reconciliation*, 1) – '[forgiveness is] the full restoration of delicate personal relations between friends or between parent and child' – son was like father on this point.

[40] William Temple, *Christus Veritas* (London 1924).

[41] R.S. Franks, *The Atonement* (London 1934).

[42] R.N. Flew, *The Forgiveness of Sins* (London 1916), R.N. Flew, *The Idea of Perfection in Christian Theology* (Oxford 1934).

[43] Redlich, *Forgiveness* (1937).

[44] Taylor, *Forgiveness and Reconciliation*, 17–18, 23.

[45] Taylor, *Forgiveness and Reconciliation*, 31.

[46] Taylor, *Forgiveness and Reconciliation*, 32.

[47] Taylor, *Forgiveness and Reconciliation*, 28. Taylor denies (against Moberly, but with Mackintosh) that 'we are forgiven because we are forgivable' (234).

[48] Taylor, *Forgiveness and Reconciliation*, 32, 269.

[49] Taylor, *Forgiveness and Reconciliation*, 233–236, 270.

[50] Mackintosh, *Christian Experience*, 187. Mackintosh is absolutely discreet about the identities of these philosophers, although in a footnote here he does quote W.D. Ross's translation of a passage of Aristotle.

forgiveness] as a moral response has largely been ignored by moral philosophers'; and he quotes P.F. Strawson's remark in 1962 that 'forgiveness ... is a rather unfashionable subject in moral philosophy.'[51] Haber confirms that this is true, not just of modern times, but of ancient philosophy as well;[52] and he speculates that the most likely explanation is that forgiveness has usually been regarded as a Christian virtue and so beyond the purview of secular philosophers.[53] It is no coincidence, therefore, that one of the few eminent philosophers to have examined forgiveness systematically was an Anglican bishop, Joseph Butler.[54] Haber dates the rise of philosophical interest in the subject from the publication of R.S. Downie's article in 1965,[55] since when there has been an ongoing discussion, carried on largely through journal articles.[56] This change he attributes to the growing interest in the role of feelings – and so of virtues – in moral life.[57]

Haber's own book is the most comprehensive guide to the recent debate about forgiveness among moral philosophers. With Hannah Arendt, Haber agrees that, although 'forgiveness was given its most prominent expression by Jesus of Nazareth,'[58] it may nevertheless be discussed in ethical terms and quite apart from religious dogma.[59] Still, he affirms that what is said about human forgiveness may also be said, by way of Thomistic analogy from below, about divine forgiveness.[60]

With the likes of Butler, Downie, Kathleen Dean Moore, and Jeffrie Murphy,[61] Haber defines forgiveness as an attitude that has to do with the

---

[51] Joram Graf Haber, *Forgiveness* (Savage, Maryland 1991). The quotation of Strawson comes from 'Freedom and Resentment,' *Proceedings of the British Academy* 48 (1962), reprinted in: *Freedom and Resentment and Other Essays* (Oxford 1974), 6.

[52] Haber, *Forgiveness*, 3: 'Neither did the ancients discuss forgiveness, with the exceptions of Plutarch and Seneca. Nowhere in his intricate list of virtues did Aristotle list the virtue of forgiveness.'

[53] Haber, *Forgiveness*. Here he cites Feuerbach's argument that forgiveness takes us into a religious dimension that transcends the ethical.

[54] Haber, *Forgiveness*. The classic *loci* of Butler's consideration of forgiveness are to be found in his *Fifteen Sermons*, first published in 1726, especially Sermon VIII, 'Upon Resentment,' and Sermon IX, 'Upon Forgiveness of Injuries.'

[55] Haber, *Forgiveness*, 1, 17; R.S. Downie, 'Forgiveness,' *Philosophical Quarterly* 15 (1965), 128–134.

[56] Haber's is one of only two book-length treatments of the subject of forgiveness by philosophers. The other is Jeffrie G. Murphy & Jean Hampton, *Forgiveness and Mercy* (Cambridge 1988).

[57] Haber, *Forgiveness*, 1.

[58] In fact, Haber qualifies Arendt: where she wrote of Jesus' 'discovery' of forgiveness, he writes of his supremely 'prominent expression' of it (Haber, *Forgiveness*, 3).

[59] Haber, *Forgiveness*, 3, 7.

[60] Haber, *Forgiveness*, 8.

[61] Joseph Butler, *Fifteen Sermons*, Sermon VIII, 'Upon Resentment'; Downie, 'Forgiveness,' 134; Kathleen Dean Moore, *Pardons: Justice, Mercy, and the Public Interest* (New York 1989), 184; Jeffrie Murphy, 'Forgiveness and Resentment,' in: Murphy & Hampton, *Forgiveness and Mercy*.

overcoming of resentment.[62] He differs from them, however, in denying that this overcoming must be complete for forgiveness to take place.[63] He wants to argue, with H.J.N. Horsburgh,[64] that forgiveness is compatible with lingering elements of resentment.[65] Nevertheless, he resists Horsburgh's proposal that forgiveness be understood to involve both an act of will and an emotional process of purging oneself of resentful feelings, because that still implies that until the process is complete, forgiveness has not really occurred.[66] Further, it implies a 'disconcerting' asymmetry between forgiving and being forgiven. Whereas a wrongdoer naturally supposes that he is forgiven when his victim says that he forgives, that might not be so, according to this way of thinking, if resentment happens to resurface in the victim's heart; and since there can be no guarantee against such reappearance, so it follows that there can be no certainty of being forgiven.[67] Instead, Haber proposes that forgiveness is constituted by the victim's expression (usually, but not necessarily, verbal) of an attitude toward the wrongdoer that involves either the actual overcoming of resentment or a sincere intention to do so;[68] that if the victim subsequently gives up trying to overcome his resentful feelings, then the commitment to forgive is breached, but not annulled; and that it is annulled only if the intention was never sincere in the first place.[69]

Against Jean Hampton, however, Haber denies that forgiveness involves the victim's 'decision to see a wrongdoer in a new, more favourable light ... [as] something other or more than the character traits of which she does not approve.'[70] His objection rests on the grounds that 'we cannot know, with any degree of certainty, who really is virtuous and who is not other than by appealing to a person's behaviour';[71] and that a decision to see the wrongdoer as other than what he is involves deliberate self-deception.[72] As Hampton herself affirms, forgiveness is not an emotional change simply internal to the victim, but one that refers to the wrongdoer.[73] Here Haber follows Murphy in arguing that forgiveness is a virtue only if it is given for a moral reason, and that this makes it quite distinct from therapeutic

---

[62] Haber, *Forgiveness*, 6.

[63] Haber, *Forgiveness*, 6–7.

[64] H.J.N. Horsburgh, 'Forgiveness,' *Canadian Journal of Philosophy* 4/2 (1974), 269–282.

[65] Haber, *Forgiveness*, 21.

[66] Haber, *Forgiveness*, 20.

[67] Haber, *Forgiveness*, 22.

[68] Haber, *Forgiveness*, 6, 40, 51.

[69] Haber, *Forgiveness*, 51–52.

[70] Jean Hampton, 'Forgiveness, Resentment, and Hatred,' in: Murphy & Hampton, *Forgiveness and Mercy*, 84–85.

[71] Haber, *Forgiveness*, 13.

[72] Haber, *Forgiveness*, 14.

[73] Hampton, 'Forgiveness, Resentment, and Hatred,' 36.

forgetting.[74] Bishop Butler was right: resentment is obliged by respect for oneself, for others, for morality, and for the wrongdoer as an appropriate form of protest against intentional injury.[75] Indeed, when warranted, resentment is itself a virtue.[76] Accordingly, a commitment to overcome resentment should only be made – forgiveness should only be granted – for a reason that is consistent with self-respect.[77] Here Haber diverges from Murphy. According to the latter, forgiveness is compatible with self-respect whenever the victim has reason to distinguish the wrongdoer from his wrong – that is, because he repented or had a change of heart, or because he meant well (his motives were good), or because he has suffered enough, or because he has undergone humiliation (perhaps the apology ritual of 'I beg forgiveness'), or for old times' sake (e.g., 'He has been a good and loyal friend to me in the past').[78] Haber, however, argues that only the first reason, repentance, is sufficient. It is not enough that the victim can distinguish the wrongdoer from his wrong; the wrongdoer must do so too. Why? Because otherwise forgiveness amounts to little more than condonation of wrongdoing; but also because only when the wrongdoer repudiates his deed (through feelings of regret and a commitment not to repeat it) is moral community with the victim restored.[79]

Accordingly, the recognition that 'the wrongdoer is "fallen" and is gripped by some self-diminishing power' amounts to a reason to excuse, not to forgive; as Murphy puts it, '"Father forgive them for they know not what they do" goes better as "Father *excuse* them for they know not what they do."'[80] And while it may be true that we ourselves stand in need of forgiveness, this is not (*pace* Murphy)[81] a sufficient reason to forgive, 'because, in the forgiveness situation, our own moral history is not at issue.'[82]

One important thing that this understanding of forgiveness assumes is a prior personal relationship between forgiver and wrongdoer; and this, as R.J. O'Shaughnessy points out and Haber confirms, constitutes one respect in which forgiveness is logically distinct both from the remission of punishment and from an official pardon.[83] Forgiveness is less distinct, however,

---

[74] Haber, *Forgiveness*, 107–108; Murphy, 'Forgiveness and Resentment,' 23.

[75] Haber, *Forgiveness*, 7, 36, 38, 70, 72–73, 81–82.

[76] Haber, *Forgiveness*, 78, 87. Butler argues that resentment is a 'natural passion' that may be virtuous or vicious according to circumstances, but which in itself is indifferent. For biblical support he appeals to St Paul in Ephesians 4:26: 'Be angry, and sin not' (Butler, 'Upon Resentment,' *Fifteen Sermons*, ed. W.R. Matthews (London 1953), 123 (section 3).

[77] Haber, *Forgiveness*, 90.

[78] Murphy, 'Forgiveness and Resentment,' 24.

[79] Haber, *Forgiveness*, 90, 93–94, 96, 103, 110.

[80] Murphy, 'Forgiveness and Resentment,' 20; quoted in: Haber, *Forgiveness*, 109.

[81] Murphy, 'Forgiveness and Resentment,' 32.

[82] Haber, *Forgiveness*, 109.

[83] R.J. O'Shaughnessy, 'Forgiveness,' *Philosophy* 42 (1967), 338; Haber, *Forgiveness*, 16, 61.

from mercy. Haber follows Murphy in endorsing P. Twambley's argument, against Alwynne Smart and Claudia Card, that mercy is not just the judicial mitigation of punishment in a criminal court, but also the plaintiff's waiving of his right over the defendant in a civil court.[84] What this means is that mercy is not restricted to a forensic context, but operates wherever rights are waived – for example, by creditors who release debtors from what they owe. The main difference that remains between mercy and forgiveness is one of specificity: 'In mercy, we waive the right to whatever it is we have a right to. In forgiveness – more specifically – we waive the "right" to resent the wrongdoer.'[85]

Here the question arises as to whether we can waive someone else's right. Or can we forgive only on our own behalf? Haber quotes two of the commentators in Simon Wiesenthal's *The Sunflower* in favour of Dryden's conviction that 'forgiveness, to the injured doth belong.'[86] He also observes that this is the position occupied by John Gingell, and by Ivan in Dostoyevski's *The Brothers Karamazov*, and used by both to argue against the propriety of divine forgiveness.[87] Haber agrees that only the injured have the right to forgive, but argues for an expansion of the concept of 'the injured.' He endorses Horsburgh's distinction between cases where the one who would forgive is intimately associated with the victim, and those where he is not.[88] In the former, the injury to the victim is *also* an injury to his intimate associates, and it is open to them to grant forgiveness for the injury that *they* have suffered (and this, Haber implies, is what justifies divine forgiveness).[89] What is missing from this account, as Haber sees it, is an explanation of why one can forgive only if one has an intimate relationship with the aggrieved. The reason that he offers is that, since forgiveness involves at least the commitment to overcome resentment, and since resentment (as opposed to indignation) is a protest on behalf of *self*-respect, it follows that forgiveness can only be offered for injuries inflicted directly upon oneself or indirectly through one's intimates.[90]

Finally, Haber raises the question of whether wrongdoers' repentance gives them a right to be forgiven, and whether victims have a corresponding duty to forgive. Haber's answer to the first part is negative: if forgiveness

---

[84] Haber, *Forgiveness*, 62–64; Alwynne Smart, 'Mercy,' *Philosophy* 43 (1968), 345–359; Claudia Card, 'Mercy,' *Philosophical Review* 81 (1972), 182–207; P. Twambley, 'Mercy and Forgiveness,' *Analysis* 36 (1976), 84–90.

[85] Haber, *Forgiveness*, 65.

[86] Abraham J. Heschel and Terrence Prittie in: Simon Wiesenthal, *The Sunflower* (London 1972), 131, 173, quoted in: Haber, *Forgiveness*, 45.

[87] John Gingell, 'Forgiveness and Power,' *Analysis* 34/6 (1974), 182; Fyodor Dostoyevsky, *The Brothers Karamazov* (New York 1980), 223–226; quoted in: Haber, *Forgiveness*, 8, 44.

[88] Horsburgh, 'Forgiveness,' 274; quoted in: Haber, *Forgiveness*, 45.

[89] Haber, *Forgiveness*, 8, 47.

[90] Haber, *Forgiveness*, 48.

were strictly earned (or, to allude to the theological discussion in the previous section, 'merited'), then it would be redundant – as Aurel Kolnai has argued.[91] To the second part, he offers a qualified affirmation. On the one hand, if there is no right to be forgiven, there can be no perfect duty to forgive (on every occasion). On the other hand, we are inclined to censure those who withhold forgiveness when granting it would be appropriate, and this suggests that we recognise an imperfect duty to forgive (on some occasions). Where does the force of this occasional obligation come from? The value of moral community, and our duty to strengthen it when we can.[92]

In his book, Haber expressly prescinds from theological issues, although he does mention philosophical discussion about the propriety of divine forgiveness.[93] It is not necessarily that he himself is an atheist,[94] but rather that he thinks that, since the concept of forgiveness is not logically tied to theological ideas, it is sensible to begin with philosophical analysis and only afterwards to proceed, by analogy, to theology.[95] Marilyn McCord Adams takes a subtly and significantly different approach, arguing, not that forgiveness is logically dependent on theology, but that it is nevertheless 'particularly "at home" within a Christian framework.'[96] She begins with a narrative commentary on the debate between Kolnai, Twambley, Murphy, and Herbert Morris. The first three of these are all agreed on the desirability of detaching forgiveness from its traditional religious context. Adams argues, however, that Kolnai only succeeds in transplanting the concept of forgiveness from one religion (Christianity) to another (Morality), in so far as he appeals to a whole-hearted, venturesome, and self-sacrificial love of Value that expresses such an 'attitude of *trust* in the world' as to warrant the risk of forgiving hardened wrongdoers on the mere possibility that they might repent.[97] With regard to Twambley, Adams appears to approve of his dissent from Kolnai's 'obsession with duty and obligation,' and from his preference for a concept of forgiveness that is in some way *earned* by the offender.[98] She also approves of his alternative proposal to take the

---

[91] Aurel Kolnai, 'Forgiveness,' *Proceedings of the Aristotelian Society* 74 (1973–1974), 91–106; reprinted in: Bernard Williams & David Wiggins (eds.), *Ethics, Value, and Reality* (Indianapolis 1978).

[92] Haber, *Forgiveness*, 101–103.

[93] In addition to John Gingell (see note 87 above), Haber mentions Anne Minas, 'God and Forgiveness,' *Philosophical Quarterly* 25 (1975), 138–150, and Meirlys Lewis, 'On Forgiveness,' *Philosophical Quarterly* 30 (1980), 235–245.

[94] Indeed, he implies that he is a theist, when he writes of Gingell and Dostoyevsky that they 'tacitly deny that an injury to man is not also an injury to God – a position I do not share' (Haber, *Forgiveness*, 8).

[95] Haber, *Forgiveness*, 3, 8.

[96] Marilyn McCord Adams, 'Forgiveness: A Christian Model,' *Faith and Philosophy* 8/3 (1991), 278.

[97] Kolnai, 'Forgiveness,' 105; quoted in: Adams, 'Forgiveness,' 281.

[98] Twambley, 'Mercy and Forgiveness,' 88, 90; quoted in: Adams, 'Forgiveness,' 282.

plaintiff's waiving his right over the defendant as paradigmatic, because, since the plaintiff is not morally or legally bound to press or waive his claim, this clears 'moral space for the generosity of forgiveness.'[99] As for Murphy, Adams notes that his moral rehabilitation of resentment is explicitly directed against the prevailing assumption, of Christian provenance, that retributive feelings should always be transcended in pursuit of the deeper values of love and compassion, and that forgiveness is always a virtue.[100] Notwithstanding his championing of the possible morality of retributive emotions, Murphy still endorses some Kantian cautions against acting out of retributive hatred: namely, that since we ourselves are guilty, we lack the moral standing to accuse another; that since we are unable to penetrate the human heart, we are too ignorant to do so; and that since we too need to be forgiven, the Golden Rule obliges us 'to cultivate the ... willingness to be open to the possibility of forgiveness with some hope and trust.'[101]

The burden of Herbert Morris's rather nebulous argument is against Murphy's definition of forgiveness as 'a conscious decisional act,' and in favour of defining it in terms of a process that often involves an empowering 'grace' that transcends our acts of will. This is one of three religious dimensions that Morris discerns in the phenomenon of forgiveness. The second is that forgiveness is 'a mark of a benign universe,' benefitting as it does both giver and receiver; and the third is that it embodies a generosity of spirit that involves a self-transcendence that is 'close to the divine.'[102] Adams proceeds to build on Morris's first 'religious dimension,' arguing for a correlation between one's attitude toward forgiveness and 'the Optimism or Pessimism of one's World View [sic].' Optimists are inclined to forgive, because they see the world as a 'benign' place where Value will ultimately triumph over Disvalue, and where, therefore, 'wrongdoing and even serious injury are not desperate matters.' For Pessimists, on the other hand, injuries are more threatening and protection against them falls entirely to human arrangements. So 'moral rigorism in ethics, and insistence on the moral legitimacy and quasi-obligatory status of retribution' are 'unsurprising concomitants' of such an outlook.[103] The Christian commendation of forgiveness, according to Adams, assumes 'a realistic optimism' about the world. This is based on belief and faith in a God who 'is a Trinity of persons, eternally connected by identity-conferring relationships of self-

---

[99] Adams, 'Forgiveness,' 282–283.

[100] Murphy, 'Introduction: The Retributive Emotions,' in: Murphy & Hampton, *Forgiveness and Mercy,* 2–4; Adams, 'Forgiveness,' 284.

[101] Murphy, 'Hatred: A Qualified Defense,' in: Murphy & Hampton, *Forgiveness and Mercy,* 97–103; 'Forgiveness and Resentment,' 31–32; quoted in: Adams, 'Forgiveness,' 287.

[102] Herbert Morris, 'Murphy on Forgiveness,' *Criminal Justice Ethics* 7/2 (1988), 15–19; quoted in: Adams, 'Forgiveness,' 287–289.

[103] Adams, 'Forgiveness,' 290.

giving love,' who is willing and able to defeat evil utterly both at the cosmic and at the individual level, and who is committed 'to see to it that each created person has a life which is a great good to him/her on the whole.'[104] One implication of this theological belief is that forgiveness is seen as involving a prayerful process of entering into God's point of view. This process includes: 'shifting from a one-dimensional picture of the offender qua offender to a more complex [and compassionate] characterisation'; acquiring deeper insight into oneself as someone with comparable faults and so abandoning self-aggrandizement; coming to recognise that no human being is competent to evaluate or judge another; growing in awareness of God's love and in correlative confidence in one's own worth; and so being liberated to enter into God's love for the offender, to appreciate his 'overwhelming worth,' and to identify with the divine will and power to heal him.[105] As a consequence of seeing things through God's eyes, the victim will commit himself to overcome his retributive feelings.[106] He will also let go of the allied and pernicious notion 'that "everything depends on us" with its correlative zeal for success that outruns human wisdom and power to insure it' and tends to make our pursuit of justice vindictive.[107] Instead, since 'only Divine pedagogy has the power, the insight, and the love for its pupil required to combine success with respect,'[108] he will entrust the offender's reform to God, pray for it, and answer whatever calling he receives to play a limited role in bringing it about. One of Adams' wisest insights is that faith in God and seeing things from his point of view allows an appreciation that some estrangements between victims and offenders are profoundly intractable, that the complete healing of any person is 'a long-term project, requiring no less than the creature's earthly lifetime,' and that in some cases reconciliation in history may not be possible. This is the realism that theological optimism makes possible.[109]

In stark contrast to Adams, Richard Swinburne treats forgiveness in terms that are almost entirely abstracted from religious or theological presuppositions, even though his discussion occurs in the course of developing an account of the Christian doctrine of salvation. His method is first to develop a philosophy of forgiveness and then to work out its consequences for theology.[110] For that reason, our discussion of his contribution appears at the end of this section, rather than at the beginning of the next.

---

[104] Adams, 'Forgiveness,' 290–291.

[105] Adams, 'Forgiveness,' 295–296, 298.

[106] Adams, 'Forgiveness,' 297.

[107] Adams, 'Forgiveness,' 297, 299.

[108] Adams, 'Forgiveness,' 298.

[109] Adams, 'Forgiveness,' 299.

[110] Richard Swinburne, *Responsibility and Atonement* (Oxford 1989). That this is so, is evident in the very structure of the book: Part I (in which the consideration of forgiveness falls) bears the title 'Responsibility,' and Part II is called 'Its Theological Consequences.'

According to Swinburne, a victim is free to forgive unconditionally, but to do so in cases of serious injury is bad, since that would trivialise human goods, the importance of right action, the wrongdoer and his hostile or careless act, and therefore human relations.[111] More specifically, it is good for the wrongdoer that his being forgiven should be dependent upon his making atonement[112] – that is, becoming penitent, offering an apology, repairing the damage as far as possible, and doing penance.[113] Forgiveness is the final act in the process of reconciliation, in which the wrongdoer's atonement is accepted as sufficient, and the injured party undertakes to treat him no longer as the author of the injury. Like Haber, Swinburne regards forgiveness as a 'performative' utterance (e.g., 'I forgive you') or act (smiling in a certain context), which by itself creates a new state of affairs.[114] Victims in general are not obliged to forgive, although doing so in grave cases is a supererogatory good work. Christians, however, are so obliged, since they have accepted forgiveness from God on condition that they forgive others.[115] Provided a wrongdoer has done all that he can to disown his act, and to persuade the injured party of his sincerity, the latter's persistent refusal to forgive cannot prevent the wrongdoer's burden of guilt from being lifted; for the right to refuse forgiveness is limited to cases where atonement is insufficient.[116] However, sometimes – for example, in cases of murder – adequate atonement cannot be made in this life, and forgiveness and reconciliation must therefore wait for the next one.[117]

The bearing of this conception of forgiveness upon the doctrine of the Atonement is that the cross should not be understood in the Calvinist terms of penal substitution, because that has Christ's death result in our being forgiven without our being actively involved in it, and therefore in a trivialising manner. Instead, the cross should be seen in Anselmian terms as God the Son's costly sacrifice of something highly valuable as a gift of reconciliation to God the Father, which humans may then offer as reparation and penance for their sins, and in acceptance of which God may properly forgive them.[118]

In a footnote, Swinburne uses his theory of forgiveness to refute Anne Minas' argument that a good God cannot forgive, since this involves either changing one's moral judgement (it does not), or remitting deserved punish-

---

[111] Swinburne, *Responsibility and Atonement*, 85–86.

[112] Swinburne, *Responsibility and Atonement*, 148–149.

[113] Swinburne, *Responsibility and Atonement*, 81–84. By 'penance' Swinburne means 'a costly gift' that goes beyond what is required by reparation and compensation and constitutes an apology as serious (84).

[114] Swinburne, *Responsibility and Atonement*, 84–85; Haber, *Forgiveness*, 40–53.

[115] Swinburne, *Responsibility and Atonement*, 88.

[116] Swinburne, *Responsibility and Atonement*, 87–88.

[117] Swinburne, *Responsibility and Atonement*, 89.

[118] Swinburne, *Responsibility and Atonement*, 151–154.

ment (but it applies where there is no question of punishment and, besides, there is no obligation to punish), or abandoning a feeling of resentment (forgiveness need not involve feelings at all: 'I can easily forgive that which I do not resent').[119] On this last point, of course, Swinburne could have followed Murphy et al. in making the alternative argument that not all kinds of resentment are unworthy and ought to be abandoned.

4. Theology, 1989–1996

In the same year that Swinburne published *Responsibility and Atonement*, Paul Fiddes' *Past Event and Present Salvation* appeared, offering a very different account of forgiveness and of the Atonement. Whereas Swinburne places forgiveness at the end of the process of reconciliation, Fiddes places it at the beginning; and the reason for this reversal is biblical. Fiddes finds in the Gospels a Jesus who welcomes sinners without waiting for them to repent first; and as an example he cites Luke 7:36–50, where Jesus 'accepts from a prostitute the intimate act of her anointing his feet and wiping them with her hair, without first establishing whether she has given up her trade, and pronounces the forgiveness of God without further enquiry.'[120] Forgiveness is therefore unconditional, but it is not casually so. On the contrary, as modelled by Jesus, [121] it involves a twofold journey on the part of the forgiver as he pursues reconciliation. The first is 'a costly journey of sympathy' into the experience of the offender, at the end of which he can say, 'I forgive you.' But this declaration is an implicit act of judgement, for it brings the offence out into the open; and in challenging the offender to take responsibility, it irritates him, arousing his self-justifying hostility. At this point, therefore, the forgiver must embark on 'the journey of endurance,' in which he bears and absorbs the other's resentment, 'drawing out the venom of his anger.' At the same time, his continuing sympathy 'entices' the offender to accept the judgement. Thus, unconditional forgiveness does not condone the offence, and is active in trying to enable the repentance that is necessary for reconciliation.[122] However, *pace* Swinburne, this repentance is not a kind of payment for wrongs done. It cannot be, for it is impossible to establish with any precision the degree of our responsibility, since 'the

---

[119] Swinburne, *Responsibility and Atonement*, 87 n.8.

[120] Paul S. Fiddes, *Past Event and Present Salvation: The Christian Idea of Atonement* (London 1989), 177.

[121] Fiddes, *Past Event*, 176–177.

[122] Fiddes, *Past Event*, 173–175, 185. Fiddes acknowledges several debts to H.R. Mackintosh in this section.

hidden persuaders are endless in number.'[123] Accordingly, 'we can be as generous in our penitence as God is generous in his forgiveness.'

The implications of this understanding of forgiveness for the doctrine of the Atonement, as Fiddes sees them, are these. First, it, too, tells against Calvin: the cross cannot be an act of propitiation that changes God's attitude from resentment to forgiveness, since God is and was always willing to forgive.[124] Instead, on the cross God makes the twofold journey, offering forgiveness, making manifest the viciousness of sin, enduring the resentment of sinners at their being exposed, but all the time wooing them with his sympathetic love.[125] The cross does bring about an 'objective' change in God, but this is not a change from wrath to love. Rather, in the crucified Christ, the ever-loving God gains 'that experience of the human heart that gives him a way into our hearts.'[126]

Like Fiddes, L. Gregory Jones makes his approach to the subject of forgiveness definitely theological: 'I contend that forgiveness is most adequately understood within a Christian theological framework – and more specifically, within the doctrine of the Triune God ....'[127] Jones explicates what he means here by 'most adequately understood,' when he writes later that such a framework is necessary 'to sustain practices and understandings of forgiveness that are neither co-opted by a "therapeutic" lightness nor undermined by violent and sinful darkness.'[128] How, then, does the nature of the triune God bear on the matter of forgiveness? Since this God is characterised by 'self-giving love,' it is in this that human beings created in the divine image find their 'life.'[129] It also follows that non-violence is ontologically prior to violence, and that the corresponding way to live in a world of conflict is by forgiveness.[130] Indeed, this is the way of the triune God himself; for, in light of the doctrine of the Incarnation, we may say of God what is true of Christ, who 'refused ... to abandon humanity as enemies but sought ... to transform us into friends.'[131] Jones' reading of the

---

[123] Fiddes, *Past Event*, 179, 183.

[124] Fiddes, *Past Event*, 96–104, 178.

[125] Fiddes, *Past Event*, 175–176, 178, 185.

[126] Fiddes, *Past Event*, 178. For this reason, Fiddes reckons that God (uniquely) has the right to forgive sins committed against others: 'because he is the sympathetic Creator who shares the lives of his creatures, experiencing the agony of all those who suffer and receiving their hurt as his own' (Fiddes, *Past Event*, 185).

[127] L. Gregory Jones, *Embodying Forgiveness: A Theological Analysis* (Grand Rapids 1995), xiii.

[128] Jones, *Embodying Forgiveness*, 98.

[129] Jones, *Embodying Forgiveness*, 61.

[130] Jones, *Embodying Forgiveness*, 88. Jones draws here from John Milbank, *Theology and Social Theory* (Oxford 1990), 411.

[131] Jones, *Embodying Forgiveness*, 119, 120, 260, 267. Jones also adopts an opaque, Athanasian view of the Incarnation, when he writes that God overcomes the human propensity

reconciling work of God in Christ owes much to Barth. In the Incarnation, God, rather than waiting for the prodigals' return, graciously takes the initiative and journeys into 'the far country' in search of them.[132] And on the cross, God, who is by right Judge of all, permits himself to suffer judgement instead and for the sake of those who deserve it.[133]

This Christology and Atonement theology shape Jones' discussion of forgiveness by emphasising the element of the victim's compassion – a fellow-feeling that forbears from self-justifying recrimination, and which is therefore able to take the initiative in trying to bring reconciliation about. If the divine Judge can be so moved by compassion to withhold himself from damning those who persecute him, how much more should human victims forbear from damning their fellow-sinners, and seek instead to pioneer reconciliation with them. Although it is true that repentance prepares us to receive forgiveness, it is also true that forgiveness enables repentance.[134] Jones, however, throws virtually all his weight on the priority of forgiveness, quoting not Fiddes but Bonhoeffer: 'Christ made peace with us while we were yet enemies.'[135] Appealing to Jesus' example, and especially to his indiscriminate table-fellowship, he claims this to be a point at which Christianity distinguishes itself from Judaism.[136] Jones argues that not to

---

for violence in the death and resurrection of Jesus by 'binding it up into' his own trinitarian life (Jones, *Embodying Forgiveness*, 113, 119).

[132] Jones, *Embodying Forgiveness*, 118 and n.29.

[133] Jones, *Embodying Forgiveness*, 123–124. Jones, following Barth's view of the cross as the place where 'the Judge [is] judged *in our place*' (my italics), adopts a penal substitutionary concept of the Atonement. Unfortunately, he is more inclined to quote Barth here than to make better sense of his very paradoxical, certainly confusing, and probably confused account. As for Barth's own treatment of forgiveness, its development within a forensic account of the Atonement proceeds in terms of a court-room acquittal. In *Die Kirchliche Dogmatik*, IV/1: *Die Lehre von der Versöhnung* (Zürich 1953), the forgiveness (*Vergebung*) of sins receives a few pages of attention in the course of a lengthy subsection entitled 'Des Menschen Freispruch' ('The Acquittal of Man'). To acquit someone, however, is not the same as forgiving him; the acquitted might well have been innocent (and not just lucky), whereas the properly forgiven must, by definition, have been guilty. In the English edition (*Church Dogmatics*, IV/1: *The Doctrine of Reconciliation* [Edinburgh 1956]), Geoffrey Bromiley sometimes translates *Freispruch* as 'acquittal' (e.g., 574, cp. *Kirchliche Dogmatik*, IV/1, 640), and sometimes as 'pardon' (e.g., in the title to subsection 61.3). This introduces yet another concept. A pardon either remits the punishment of the guilty or declares the convicted innocent; it is not the same as either acquittal or forgiveness.

[134] Jones, *Embodying Forgiveness*, 16, 126. The notion of the reversibility of repentance and forgiveness is borrowed from Bonhoeffer, *Spiritual Care*, trans. J.C. Rochelle (Philadelphia 1985), 44.

[135] D. Bonhoeffer, 'Christ's Love and Our Enemies,' in: Geffrey B. Kelly & F. Burton Nelson (eds.), *A Testament to Freedom* (New York 1990), 287; quoted in: Jones, *Embodying Forgiveness*, 21.

[136] Jones, *Embodying Forgiveness*, 102, 121. Like Fiddes, Jones invokes the story in Luke 7:36–50 (Jones, *Embodying Forgiveness*, 160–161).

grant forgiveness priority is to imply that it is *earned* by repentance,[137] and that in order to be 'a free gift of grace,' forgiveness must be unconditional.[138] This, however, does not follow. The fact that I must do certain things before you may forgive me, does not mean that my doing those things *binds* you to forgive me. What is permissible is not yet obligatory. Nevertheless, Jones prefers to think of repentance as necessary, not to win forgiveness, but to 'appropriate' it and to embody it in our relations with others.[139]

This priority of forgiveness brings Jones into explicit conflict with several of the philosophers that we have encountered. According to Jeffrie Murphy, the ignorance of his impenitent persecutors gave the crucified Jesus reason to pray his Father to *excuse*, but not to *forgive*, them. This Jones dismisses as a 'rather pathetic attempt to correct what he [Murphy] takes to be Jesus' philosophical sloppiness,' thereby implying that Jesus was possessed of a rather unlikely philosophical precision.[140] While agreeing with Murphy and Jean Hampton that resentment (or, as he prefers it, 'righteous anger') can be a virtue,[141] Jones insists that it be located in the 'craft' of forgiveness, lest it ossify into hatred and the desire for revenge.[142] This, however, puts him at odds with part of Hampton's argument for 'moral hatred' toward evildoers,[143] in so far as she supposes that some heinous wrongdoers are too 'morally dead' to be redeemable, and that in these cases moral hatred should be sustained without relent. Although ready to accept that this places her 'outside the proper sphere of Christian faith and charity,' she argues that 'Jesus himself was prepared, on the basis of their behaviour, to judge some people as "rotted" beyond hope and fit only for the fires of hell,' and that his injunction to love one's enemies was not intended to apply in every case.[144] Jones responds by agreeing with Hampton's affirmation of

---

[137] Jones, *Embodying Forgiveness*, 144.

[138] Jones, *Embodying Forgiveness*, 146.

[139] Jones, *Embodying Forgiveness*, 146, 195.

[140] Jones, *Embodying Forgiveness*, 214.

[141] Jones, *Embodying Forgiveness*, 247. He sides, however, with Joram Haber in denying that forgiveness should be *defined* as the overcoming of resentment (Jones, *Embodying Forgiveness*, 233 n.41).

[142] Jones, *Embodying Forgiveness*, 247. He notes here that St Paul's enjoining the Ephesian Christians to be angry without sinning, is followed by an injunction to 'get rid of all bitterness, wrath, anger, fighting, and slander, together with all malice. Be kind to each other, tenderhearted, forgiving each other, as God has forgiven you in Christ' (Eph. 4:31–32).

[143] Jones, *Embodying Forgiveness*, 248–251. Hampton invokes the example of Jesus, and especially Matthew 10:34–36, in support of her views about moral hatred: 'Jesus does appear to encourage us to sustain opposition to our moral opponents, and not to reconcile ourselves with them for as long as they remain committed to their bad cause' (Jean Hampton, 'The Retributive Idea,' in: Murphy & Hampton, *Forgiveness and Mercy*, 149). She is quite aware, however, of the New Testament's injunctions that we be generous in making moral judgements about other people, and she endorses them (Murphy, 'Retributive Idea,' 149–151).

[144] Murphy, 'Retributive Idea,' 153.

the doctrine of hell (as a necessary implication of the gravity of human moral choices), while at the same time asserting the possibility of hell's ultimate emptiness.[145] However, even if hell does acquire some permanent residents, that will be the result of God's inscrutable judgement, not ours. In the meantime, 'we humans are forbidden to repudiate anyone ultimately.'[146] On the contrary, 'we are called, in imitation of the Triune God, ... to *hope* that all will be saved, and to pray and love others [including *all* of our enemies] accordingly.'[147] Not only is such conduct appropriate to the limits of our knowledge and judicial competence, it is also the only sure way of preventing our anger at our enemies from ossifying into hatred, that is, 'into a persistent desire for their ... destruction.'[148]

Like Murphy, Richard Swinburne regards forgiveness as properly *following* repentance in its various forms, not preceding it. It is the final act in the process of reconciliation, not the first one. Jones affirms Swinburne's concern that sin be taken seriously and therefore that wrongdoers be involved in removing it, but argues that this involvement occurs in response to a forgiveness that is already on offer.[149] Among the clearer of his other objections are these: that Swinburne fails to take seriously Jesus' initiating forgiveness; that he neglects the way in which our status as sinners-forgiven-by-God obliges us to forgive fellow-sinners; that he focusses on the elimination of individual guilt rather than the restoration of communion; that by making the efficacy of Christ's work dependent on our offering it to God, he makes forgiveness something that we achieve; and that he lacks an adequate sense of the Spirit's work of showing us how to embody forgiveness in our concrete situations.[150] Three of these complaints missfire. First, Swinburne explicitly affirms the special obligation of Christians to forgive. Second, it is not true that Swinburne is more concerned about individual guilt than the restoration of communion. One of the main points of his emphasis upon the need not to trivialise sin, and for the wrongdoer to be actively involved in repenting, apologising, and doing penance, is precisely to ensure that the reconciliation that takes place is one in which the parties take each other

---

[145] Jones, *Embodying Forgiveness*, 252–254.

[146] Jones, *Embodying Forgiveness*, 255.

[147] Jones, *Embodying Forgiveness*, 258–259.

[148] Jones, *Embodying Forgiveness*, 263.

[149] Jones, *Embodying Forgiveness*, 152, 154, 155 ('Christians ought to be people who, precisely because of the forgiveness of Sin [*sic*] that Christ has already announced and enacted, seek to become holy people through embodied practices of forgiven-ness and repentance'), 156.

[150] Jones, *Embodying Forgiveness*, 155, 156–157. It is not obvious to me what Jones means when he writes that 'Swinburne's understanding of forgiveness and repentance collapses Jesus' life, death, and resurrection into an account of the atonement. In so doing, he loses the integral significance ... of how and why Jesus' nonviolent, forgiving love leads him to the cross; ...' (Jones, *Embodying Forgiveness*, 155).

and their relationship seriously. In treating the case where the victim refuses to forgive even in the face of proven repentance, Swinburne's focus on whether or not the 'individual' wrongdoer's guilt remains, expresses a perfectly reasonable (and pastoral) concern with whether his liberation from the burden of subjective guilt must depend entirely on the victim's mood. Third, in saying that God forgives us only after we have offered Christ's sacrifice as penance, Swinburne is saying, not that our action alone is sufficient to win forgiveness, only that it is necessary. Even in his account, human work still waits upon divine grace.

The priority of forgiveness in Christian practice, according to Jones, is based not only on the divine example of Christ, but also on the Christian's self-understanding as a sinner already forgiven by God.[151] This leads Jones to cross swords with Joram Haber, who reckons that our own need to be forgiven is a bad reason to forgive someone else, because in *this* situation 'our own moral history is not at issue.'[152] He charges Haber and 'much modern moral philosophy' with an excessively myopic focus on isolated situations of wrongdoing and guilt.[153] In my opinion, however, Haber is right. The fact that I too depend on forgiveness should make me compassionate toward you, and ready to forgive. But the integrity of any reconciliation between us, and indeed your own moral growth, requires that you repent (so Swinburne). Thus, in so far as my forgiving you comprises a word or gesture of absolution, signifying that all is once again well between us, I ought not to do it before you have demonstrated sincere remorse. In sum, on this point I prefer Basil Redlich to Jones; for Redlich correlates God's forgiveness of us, not with our actual *forgiveness* of others, but with our *forgivingness* toward them, that is, with a compassionate *readiness* to forgive.

One of the most distinctive features of Jones' treatment is his conception of forgiveness, not just as the absolution of guilt, but as 'an embodied way of life' or, better because more progressive, 'craft,' whereby one learns to live in communion. Here the meaning of 'forgiveness' is broadened out to denote the life-long process of being reconciled 'with God, with one another, and with the whole Creation.'[154] It is also identified with character-transforming practices such as confession, repentance, reconciliation, and excommunication, which are themselves formed and sustained by the other basic Christian practices of baptism and the eucharist.[155] This description of forgiveness in terms of concrete social practices is a salutary corrective to modernity's focus on the isolated acts of individuals, and to Western

---

[151] Jones, *Embodying Forgiveness*, 15 (where Jones quotes from Bonhoeffer's sermon, 'On Forgiveness,' in: Kelly & Nelson [eds.], *A Testament to Freedom*, 262), 47.

[152] Haber, *Forgiveness*, 109; quoted by Jones, *Embodying Forgiveness*, 212.

[153] Jones, *Embodying Forgiveness*, 213.

[154] Jones, *Embodying Forgiveness*, xii, 88, 227.

[155] Jones, *Embodying Forgiveness*, 165–166.

Christianity's privatisation and spiritualisation of confession and forgiveness.[156] Nevertheless, it is surely obfuscating to conflate forgiveness with the
process of (universal) reconciliation, since this suggests that the former is
sufficient for the latter by obscuring the role of repentance altogether. Jones,
however, is unwilling to distinguish clearly between the different moments
of the process of reconciliation, or the different meanings of 'forgiveness,'
arguing vaguely that the latter takes different forms in different situations:
'For example, forgiveness might entail something much closer to "excuse"
in one situation or at one point in the overall context of a relationship,
whereas it might look closer to "retributive punishment" in another situation
or at another point in that relationship.' He betrays an appropriate sensitivity
here to the accusation 'that my description simply substitutes vague
exhortation for rigorous conceptual analysis,' but he maintains that 'the
objection is relevant, though its force is misplaced [*sic*].'[157] On the
contrary, I fear that the objection is both to the point and cogent.

Miroslav Volf is considerably more precise than Jones, in spite of his
declaration that he has little interest in analysing 'the sequence of steps in
the cycle of reconciliation.'[158] In fact, however, he does present a very
definite sequence. In light of the action of Jesus on the cross, the first act in
the process of reconciliation is one of 'self-giving' on the part of the
victim.[159] This is then specified as an 'opening up' of the self,[160] a 'making
space' for the wrongdoer, which identifies him in his humanity and takes
place *before* any judgement is made about him.[161] The victim's will to make
this identification is the fruit of his acknowledgement that the line between
the innocent and the guilty is not as sharp as it usually seems:[162]

> From a distance, the world may appear neatly divided into guilty
> perpetrators and innocent victims. The closer we get, however, the
> more the line between the guilty and the innocent blurs and we see an
> intractable maze of small and large hatreds, dishonesties, manipulations,
> and brutalities, each reinforcing the other.[163]

---

[156] Jones, *Embodying Forgiveness*, 37, 38, 143, 164.

[157] Jones, *Embodying Forgiveness*, 229.

[158] Miroslav Volf, *Exclusion and Embrace: A Theological Exploration of Identity, Otherness, and Reconciliation* (Nashville 1996), 120 n.13. Three notes later he also declares that he
'will eschew all attempts to explain the "logic" of redemption ... I am interested here in
elaborating on the social significance of some aspects of what happened on the cross, not in
explaining why and precisely how it happened' (125 n.16).

[159] Volf, *Exclusion and Embrace*, 23.

[160] Volf, *Exclusion and Embrace*, 47.

[161] Volf, *Exclusion and Embrace*, 29.

[162] Volf, *Exclusion and Embrace*, 81, 84.

[163] Volf, *Exclusion and Embrace*, 81. See also 124: 'But no one can be in the presence of
the God of the crucified Messiah for long without ... transposing the enemy from the sphere of

The basic acknowledgement of human solidarity in sinfulness fuels the victim's will to identify with his oppressor, which grows into 'the will to embrace,' that is, the will to be reconciled. This 'will to embrace,' however, is not 'the embrace itself' or 'full reconciliation.' Whereas the first is unconditional, the second 'cannot take place until the truth has been said and justice done.'[164] This truth-telling and justice may well involve punishment, and until they are achieved 'wrath against injustice' is appropriate;[165] but since this wrath is qualified by the will to be reconciled, the justice it seeks will be kept from vindictiveness.[166] When the truth is told and justice is done, but not before, wrath should be put aside, the wrongdoer embraced, and the past forgotten.[167] However, Volf, like Marilyn McCord Adams, acknowledges that some ruptures cannot be fully repaired in history, and that some injuries are greater than can be owned by the perpetrator and forgotten by the victim. As a consequence, the most that is sometimes possible in this world is forgiveness, not embrace:

Forgiveness ... leaves a distance between people, an empty space of neutrality, that allows them either to go their separate ways in what is sometimes called 'peace' or to fall into each other's arms and restore broken communion. 'Going one's own way' is the boldest dream many a person caught in the vortex of violence can muster the strength to dream.[168]

We have before us, then, a definite sequence, the whole of which constitutes the process of reconciliation: the victim's identification with the wrongdoer, the will to embrace, righteous wrath or resentment, the telling of the truth, the doing of justice, the relinquishing of wrath and of the memory of injury, the declaration of forgiveness, and, according to how far the grievance has been forgotten, either a 'peaceful' parting of the ways or a reconciling embrace. As with Fiddes and Jones, the initiating act is the victim's and it is one of grace. However, whereas both Fiddes and Jones identify this as the

---

monstrous inhumanity into the sphere of shared humanity and herself from the sphere of proud innocence into the sphere of common sinfulness.'

[164] Volf, *Exclusion and Embrace*, 29.

[165] Volf, *Exclusion and Embrace*, 224.

[166] Volf, *Exclusion and Embrace*, 123, 223. Volf's debt to Reinhold Niebuhr here is explicit.

[167] Volf, *Exclusion and Embrace*, 131.

[168] Volf, *Exclusion and Embrace*, 125–126. Sometimes, however, 'going one's own way' is not merely *faute de mieux*, but the only appropriate outcome. For example, during the conference on 'Burying the Past: Justice, Forgiveness, and Reconciliation in the Politics of South Africa, Guatemala, East Germany, and Northern Ireland,' which was held in Oxford during 14–16 September 1998, Ulrike Poppe, the dissident twice imprisoned in communist East Germany, asked what it would mean for her to be 'reconciled' with the man who had informed on her and who now lived on her street. She never knew him before and she certainly didn't want to know him now. Why should she?

complete act of 'forgiveness,' Volf joins Redlich in effectively distinguishing
forgiveness into two parts: the will to embrace (Redlich's 'forgivingness'),
and the embrace itself (Redlich's 'forgiveness'). As with Swinburne, the
performative act (typically in the form of the pronouncement, 'I forgive
you,' but maybe in the form of an embrace) communicating that the past
will no longer disturb the present, waits upon the repentance of the
wrongdoer, in so far as this is involved in truth-telling and is part of the
point of justice. But Volf shrewdly distinguishes between the act of forgiveness and full reconciliation, joining Adams in recognising that the will to
embrace – the desire for full reconciliation – may have to bide its time,
patiently but hopefully, until the eschaton.[169] Volf's articulation of the
process of reconciliation into its constituent parts, and his arranging them in
a definite sequence, is surely much more illuminating than Jones' tendency
to telescope reconciliation into an undifferentiated 'forgiveness.'

Nevertheless, Jones' attempt to retrieve forgiveness from the privatised
world of interior spirituality answers what seems to be a widespread concern.
Two books by German theologians that were published after *Embodying
Forgiveness* but betray no debt to it, take it upon themselves to combat the
'cheap grace' of a forgiveness abstracted from concrete, social life. In *The
Return of Splendor in the World: The Christian Doctrine of Sin and
Forgiveness*, Christof Gestrich follows Bonhoeffer in attributing the decline
of the Christian church in Western Europe in large part to the preaching of
forgiveness without discipleship.[170] He perceives a lethal gap between
rhetoric and reality:

> A considerable difference has emerged between the dogmatic, traditional
> claim that the power of the forgiveness of sins can renew our whole
> existence and our *experiences* with the church's way of imparting grace
> or forgiveness. We often get the impression that the words expressed in
> church are inadequate because they seem to be higher and more glorious
> than what actually goes into our life.[171]

In response, Gestrich proposes that we follow Ephesians 2:14ff. and see
forgiveness as the reconciliation of hostile parties who, in light of Christ's

---

[169] Volf, *Exclusion and Embrace*, 139. Some crimes are so heinous that they should not be
forgotten, nor their perpetrators fully embraced, in this life. However, if 'we remember now
[we do so] in order that we may forget then' (Volf, *Exclusion and Embrace*, 139).

[170] Christof Gestrich, *The Return of Splendor in the World: The Christian Doctrine of Sin
and Forgiveness*, trans. Donald Bloesch (Cambridge 1997), 275–276, 280. This was originally
published as *Die Wiederkehr des Glanzes in der Welt* (Tübingen 1989). I should note here that
another theological volume has recently been added to the burgeoning literature on forgiveness
by a student of Gestrich's, Joachim Zehner, under the title of *Das Forum der Vergebung
in der Kirche: Studien zum Verhältnis von Sündenvergebung und Recht* (Gütersloh 1998).

[171] Christof Gestrich, *Return of Splendor*, 269. Author's italics.

atoning death on the cross, have abandoned all pretensions to self-justification. In this way, forgiveness will involve, not merely absolution, but 'the commitment of the members of Christ's body to a shared life.'[172] More specifically, Gestrich thinks of forgiveness as a vicarious or substitutionary practice, in which the forgiver identifies himself with the wrongdoer and 'bears the consequences of the act for which the other person should have assumed responsibility because the other person cannot assume this responsibility.'[173] As for repentance, he writes that it

> represents a complex divine-human event and that on the human side alone, various acts are part of this event which occurs partly *before* and partly *after* our awareness and experience of being accepted by God's grace. Thus the claim that the proper order is 'first repentance, then grace' is just as wrong as the opposite claim that 'repentance always comes only after the reception of grace.'[174]

This fits exactly with Redlich's and Volf's conception: *before* repentance stands the grace of 'forgivingness' or 'the will to embrace'; *after* repentance comes the grace of 'forgiveness' or 'the embrace itself.'

Although Geiko Müller-Fahrenholz shares Gestrich's opposition to 'cheap' forgiveness, he attributes its trivialisation to the Reformation's 'verticalist reduction,' that is, exaggerated concentration on the divine-human relationship.[175] Müller-Fahrenholz swings to the opposite extreme, however, by insisting on a thoroughly secularised interpretation of forgiveness, partly because he does not consider religious language necessary for a proper understanding, and partly for the sake of being intelligible to 'our contemporaries.'[176] At one point, he does acknowledge that 'the transforming power of a deep faith commitment can and does enable people to transcend defensiveness, hatred and fear';[177] but when, in an appendix, he offers a 'theological' interpretation of practical exercises in forgiveness, this actually comprises a piece of social ethics that makes no use of strictly religious concepts at all.[178] Moreover, Müller-Fahrenholz appears to endorse

---

[172] Gestrich, *Return of Splendor*, 281–282.

[173] Gestrich, *Return of Splendor*, 291, 294–296, 329.

[174] Gestrich, *Return of Splendor*, 272.

[175] Geiko Müller-Fahrenholz, *The Art of Forgiveness: Theological Reflections on Healing and Reconciliation* (Geneva 1997), 12–13, 15. This is a revised, English version of *Vergebung macht frei: Vorschläge für eine Theologie der Versöhnung* (Frankfurt am Main 1996).

[176] Müller-Fahrenholz, *Art of Forgiveness*, 17, 34, 43.

[177] Müller-Fahrenholz, *Art of Forgiveness*, 34.

[178] Müller-Fahrenholz, *Art of Forgiveness*, 104, 105–106. Müller-Fahrenholz seems to think that the use of a notion of repentance makes his interpretation 'theological'; but as he employs it, this notion makes no reference to specifically religious ideas such as God, the after-life, final judgement, etc.

the erroneous idea that the appreciation of secular moral endeavour requires the depreciation of eschatology, when he writes that 'it goes without saying that no Christian church can ever want to renew the mediaeval claim to possess the "keys to the kingdom of heaven": ... Most people could not care less about this sort of kingdom.'[179] Albeit more ambiguously, Gestrich also appears to shy away from any substantial eschatological reference. He closes *The Return of Splendor* with the words: 'In view of the working of grace that sustains us in our limitations and *in our life as a whole*, Christians can also echo this sentiment of the philosophical idealists: God will supply whatever goes beyond our strength. He has already supplied it. Of course, not "there," but "here."' A footnote makes clear that this 'there' refers to the 'place' of 'eternal reward and peace.'[180]

At one point in his book, Gestrich refers to a German contribution to New Testament studies that bears on our topic, namely, P. Fiedler's thesis that the historical Jesus never granted anyone forgiveness of their sins.[181] Gestrich offers the reasonable response that Jesus' unconditional welcoming of the not-yet penitent into his table fellowship was indeed an act of forgiveness, albeit non-verbal.[182] In the Anglo-Saxon world, E.P. Sanders has posed a further challenge to the New Testament consensus, which is also germane to our concerns. This challenge comes in two slightly different forms. In *Jesus and Judaism*, Sanders argues that the historical Jesus did not call for *national* repentance in view of the imminent coming of the kingdom of God,[183] although he is careful to make clear that he is 'not arguing that Jesus did not "believe in" repentance ...'[184] This appears to assume a sharp distinction between corporate and individual repentance, which, as several critics have objected, is not sustainable.[185] Later, in *The Historical Figure of Jesus*, Sanders clarifies and modifies his meaning. In spite of misleadingly provocative assertions such as, 'Jesus was not a preacher of repentance,'[186] he tells us that what he is claiming is not that Jesus disapproved of repentance, but that he offered entry into his kingdom to any who would accept and follow him, even 'though they had not technically "repented," and though they had not become righteous in the way required by the

---

[179] Müller-Fahrenholz, *Art of Forgiveness*, 42.

[180] Gestrich, *The Return of Splendor*, 337 and n.84.

[181] P. Fiedler, *Jesus und die Sünder* (Bern 1976).

[182] Gestrich, *The Return of Splendor*, 271–272.

[183] E.P. Sanders, *Jesus and Judaism* (London 1985), 106–113; Sanders, *The Historical Figure of Jesus* (London 1993), 230–237.

[184] Sanders, *Jesus and Judaism*, 112.

[185] See, for example, Bruce Chilton & J.I.H. McDonald, *Jesus and the Ethics of the Kingdom* (London 1987), 40. N.T. Wright makes the same point, while arguing more broadly that Jesus *did* call for corporate, national repentance (*Christian Origins and the Question of God*, Vol. 2: *Jesus and the Victory of God* [London 1996], 256).

[186] Sanders, *The Historical Figure of Jesus*, 230.

law.'[187] What this amounts to, then, is the significant (but hardly radical) point that Jesus recognised forms of repentance that were more informal and implicit than those required by religious convention, and that the disciples' decision to follow Jesus was as much an implicit act of repentance as his acceptance of them was an implicit act of forgiveness.

5. Political Ethics, 1995–2001

In treating forgiveness, Geiko Müller-Fahrenholz puts greater emphasis than Christof Gestrich upon the role of repentance and its constituents (confession, reparation, and compensation). The reason for this is that he has in the forefront of his mind crimes of a heinous and grand-scale, political nature – genocide, war crimes, state terrorism – that cannot be simply passed over, if there is to be lasting peace within and between national communities.[188] Müller-Fahrenholz's political orientation is symptomatic of the recent interest stimulated in the political roles of repentance and forgiveness above all by South Africa's Truth and Reconciliation Commission (TRC), and to a lesser degree by the efforts of formerly communist countries in Eastern Europe to deal with their oppressive pasts in the wake of the collapse of the Soviet empire.[189]

The classic work on politics and forgiveness, however, was gestating long before 1989, and was published in the year that the TRC was set up. The historical foci of Donald Shriver's *An Ethic for Enemies* all lie earlier in the twentieth century – hostility between America and Germany in the two World Wars, between America and Japan in the Second World War, and between black and white Americans during the Civil Rights Movement of 1955–1968. In this account, forgiveness does involve empathy for the enemy's humanity, but not the excusing of his misdeeds;[190] it does exclude punishment that serves vengeance, but not when it aims at restitution.[191] In Shriver's hands, forgiveness does not come cheap, even if reconciliation is its heart's desire: 'forgiveness is interdependent with repentance. Absent the

---

[187] Sanders, *Historical Figure*, 235, 236.

[188] Müller-Fahrenholz, *The Art of Forgiveness*, x, 25, 26, 28, 97.

[189] For evidence of intellectual cross-fertilisation between these two sets of events, see Timothy Garton Ash's excellent articles on the TRC and on Eastern Europe: 'True Confessions,' *The New York Review of Books*, 17 July 1997, 33–38; and 'The Truth about Dictatorship,' *The New York Review of Books*, 19 February 1998, 35–40.

[190] Donald W. Shriver, *An Ethic for Enemies: Forgiveness in Politics* (New York 1995), 8, 28, 67.

[191] Shriver, *Ethic for Enemies*, 8.

latter, the former remains incomplete, conditional, in a posture of waiting.'[192]
Unlike Gestrich,[193] Shriver believes in the fact of collective responsibility:

> Every citizen, as well as every leader, enters a political community as an
> heir to its past. Each has a right to be proud of some of it and an obligation
> to be ashamed of some of it, even if it is centuries in the past. All have
> this obligation as humans who wisely admit to themselves and others that
> they did not have control of the beginnings of their lives; that circum-
> stance preceded their response to circumstance; that they responded under
> veils of ignorance and partial awareness which are the lot of all humans;
> that they learned to be the more responsible as they listened to their
> neighbours, acted with them, and viewed the results of those actions; and
> that, while they had no choice about counting themselves part of a
> collectivity, neither are they ever to deny their part in its choices.
> Ongoing loyalty to that collectivity, in fact, demands that they shoulder
> their implication in its past record of both virtue and vice.[194]

If there is collective responsibility, then there can be valid acts of representative repentance and forgiveness, performed by political leaders.[195] Here
Shriver comes into open conflict with Joram Haber's banishment of the
notion of third-party guilt, responsibility, and forgiveness, and with the
individualistic anthropology that underwrites it.[196]

He also comes into implicit conflict with some of the commentators in
Simon Wiesenthal's *The Sunflower* (which is not surprising, since Haber
drew upon this work in formulating his own position).[197] Commenting on
Wiesenthal's story of his own experience of being asked, as a Jewish prisoner
in a Nazi concentration camp, for forgiveness by a dying SS officer, Eva
Fleischner and Dennis Prager both insist that we can only forgive those
injuries done to ourselves, and not those done to other people.[198] (They also
claim that this is a characteristically Jewish point of view, and that Christians

---

[192] Shriver, *Ethic for Enemies*, 210.

[193] Gestrich, *The Return of Splendor*, 252: 'the assertion of a collective guilt is always
questionable. This concept must be avoided.' In a footnote, Gestrich appeals for support to
Paul Tillich, *Systematic Theology* Vol. 2 (Chicago 1957), 58–59.

[194] Shriver, *Ethic for Enemies*, 106–107.

[195] Shriver, *Ethic for Enemies*, 91, 107–116.

[196] Shriver, *Ethic for Enemies*, 113.

[197] Simon Wiesenthal, *The Sunflower: On the Possibilities and Limits of Forgiveness* (New
York 1997). This classic of Holocaust literature comprises Wiesenthal's story together with
commentaries by a range of intellectuals – Jewish, Christian, and other. *The Sunflower* was
originally published in Paris as *Die Sonnenblume* (Paris 1969). The first ET appeared the
following year (Paris), and a second in 1976 (New York). In 1997, stimulated in part by the
recent atrocities in Bosnia, a revised American edition appeared with many new commentaries.

[198] Wiesenthal, *The Sunflower*, 141, 216.

are generally more profligate in their distribution of forgiveness.)[199] Prager extends the point by drawing out the implication that where, as in murder, the victim is dead and so unavailable to forgive, the crime is unforgivable.[200] Echoing Haber's argument, however, Christopher Hollis qualifies Prager in suggesting that it is not only the immediate victim who has the power to forgive, but also those who are in some intimate or significant way related to him.[201] In my own opinion, this is correct, provided that it is understood that any single case of wrongdoing will involve several distinct injuries to different parties (the victim, the victim's intimates, and God) that each require discrete acts of forgiveness, and that one act of forgiveness cannot cover them all. Such discrimination has received a measure of front-line corroboration in one of the hearings of the Amnesty Committee of South Africa's TRC. Here, Dawie Ackermann, whose wife had been murdered in an indiscriminate attack on a church during a Sunday service in 1992, found himself asked for forgiveness by the three black perpetrators. Fighting back his tears, he responded: 'I forgive you unconditionally for the hurt you have caused me ... But I can't forgive you the sin you've done. Only God can forgive you for that.'[202] All injuries are complex. Some are so complex (involving, say, millions of victims murdered by thousands of perpetrators) that it is appropriate to say that they are unforgiveable – *comprehensively, by surviving human beings, in history.*

In accordance with this analysis of an injury and its forgiveness into their several parts, I think it is true to say that even God cannot *comprehensively* forgive injuries suffered by his creatures. To that extent, I agree with Abraham Heschel when he writes, 'even God Himself can only forgive sins committed against Himself, not against man.'[203] Nevertheless, whenever one of his human creatures is sinned against, God himself suffers in three respects: first, as a Paternal and Fraternal intimate of the immediate human victim, He suffers indirect harm; second, as divine Benefactor to the wrong-doer, He suffers the direct harm of contempt when the latter squanders an opportunity for doing good and so misshapes himself; and third, as Paternal

---

[199] Wiesenthal, *The Sunflower*, 139, 216–220. Prager: '[A]side from the divinity of Jesus, the greatest – and even more important – difference between Judaism and Christianity, or perhaps only between most Christians and Jews, is their different understanding of forgiveness and, ultimately, how to react to evil' (216); 'I have never heard a Jew say that God loves an evil person' (219); 'the Christian doctrine of forgiveness has blunted Christian anger' (220).

[200] Wiesenthal, *The Sunflower*, 217.

[201] Wiesenthal, *The Sunflower*, 169. So, while Wiesenthal was not among those to whom this particular SS officer had done harm, he did belong to the racial group that SS officers in general were dedicated to annihilate.

[202] This scene is recorded in 'Getting Away with Murder,' a BBC TV documentary about the TRC, which was presented by Michael Ignatieff and originally broadcast on 1 November 1997 as part of the 'Correspondent' series.

[203] Wiesenthal, *The Sunflower*, 166.

and Fraternal intimate of the misshapen wrongdoer, he suffers further indirect harm. Beyond forgiving sins against himself, God can also encourage
human victims to forgive by reminding them of their own sinfulness, thereby moving them to have compassion for their oppressors and to assume a
forgiving spirit or intention, thereby enticing the latter to repent, thereby
enabling the former to forgive in the conclusive sense of declaring that trust
has been restored. Further still, by raising the dead, God can also facilitate
the forgiveness of injuries that could not be realised in history, either
because the victim was murdered, or because time ran out before he could
work his way through resentment to compassion, or because it expired
before the perpetrator could recognise the wrong he had done.

If only the victims have the right to forgive, it follows that no one has the
right to forgive on *their* behalf without their consent; and 'no one' here
includes the leadership of the political community to which the victims
belong. As Joyce Mthimkulu said of those who had applied to the TRC for
amnesty for their killing of her son, 'They are not asking forgiveness from
us, the people who have lost their loved ones. They are asking forgiveness
from the government. They did not do nothing [*sic*] to the government.
What they did, they did to *us*.'[204] Yet Joyce Mthimkulu was not entirely
right; for in killing her son, the murderers had put themselves at odds with
the whole community, attracting the reasonable suspicion that what they
had done once to one person, they might do again to others. Through one
particular crime, they had come to present a general threat. So the government did have something appropriate to forgive: the threat posed to the
national community as a whole.

Nevertheless, it still seems to me incorrect to talk straightforwardly of
amnesty as a political form of forgiveness, as some of the contributors to the
recent symposium, *Burying the Past: Making Peace and Doing Justice after
Civil Conflict*, appear to do.[205] Amnesty is an undertaking by a regime not to
prosecute certain people for crimes that they have committed. Like forgiveness, it steps down from a hostile posture. Unlike forgiveness, however, it

---

[204] Recorded in 'Getting Away with Murder.'

[205] See, for example, Jean Bethke Elshtain, 'Politics and Forgiveness,' in: Nigel Biggar
(ed.), *Burying the Past: Making Peace and Doing Justice after Civil Conflict* (Washington, DC
2001), 53; and Tuomas Forsberg, 'The Philosophy and Practice of Dealing with the Past: Some
Conceptual and Normative Issues,' in: Biggar (ed.), *Burying the Past*, 61. Martha Minow
observes that, in practice, political forgiveness usually takes the form of amnesty, exemption
from punishment, and 'too much forgetting.' That is why her own preferred way of dealing
with 'political' atrocities runs somewhere *between* vengeance and forgiveness through a
mixture of trials, truth commissions, and reparations; Minow, *Between Vengeance and
Forgiveness: Facing History after Genocide and Mass Violence* (Boston 1998), 15, 20, 28,
118. She allows, however, that *after* the truth has been established and convictions secured
through a trial, forgiveness might find appropriate legal expression in a suspended sentence, an
executive pardon, or clemency in light of humanitarian concerns (26). In my view, however,
none of these are legal *expressions* of forgiveness, only legal *analogies*.

does so, not because of compassion for the wrongdoers, but because it reckons that they no longer pose a threat to future peace – and that therefore the offended community can 'trust' them again. Further, the commitment to grant amnesty is often made under a certain political duress; and the actual granting of it need not be made dependent on any expression of remorse by the perpetrators. The fact that these no longer pose a threat to the community may have nothing to do with any inner transformation or repentance on their part, and everything to do with a change in political circumstances.[206] If we speak of amnesty as a kind of forgiveness, we speak only by way of a weak analogy.

What applies to political 'forgiveness' also applies to political 'repentance.' What sense does it make for a British prime minister in the 1990s to apologise for the irresponsibility of a British Government in the 1840s? How can an Irish cardinal ask forgiveness from the British people on behalf of his own for injuries suffered at the hands of Irish terrorists?[207] Tony Blair was not responsible for failing to act sufficiently to alleviate the Irish Famine, and Cardinal Daly was not responsible for the IRA's campaign of violence since the early 1970s. If we have acts of repentance here, we have them only in an analogous sense. Neither Blair nor Daly were taking responsibility for, and repenting of, something that they themselves had done. What Blair was doing was publicly repudiating an instance of culpable negligence by the British state that had become, for many Irish people, emblematic of the British. In his apology he was saying, in effect, this: 'Although there is continuity at various levels between the British state today and the British state then, there is discontinuity in the moral evaluation of Britain's handling of the Irish Famine (and, given the Famine's status as a token, of Ireland as a whole). We British today recognise that we failed to do what we should have done. We therefore publicly accept your judgement upon us, and distance ourselves now from ourselves then. Thereby we hope to assure you that our negligence in the past does not betoken our negligence in the present or in the future.' Likewise, Daly was saying something like this: 'We, the vast majority of Irish people, publicly repudiate what some have perpetrated in our name. We do not want you to confuse us with them, nor the current and future relations between our peoples to be distorted by such confusion. Know that

---

[206] This was the case with the paramilitary convicts who were released early from prison in Northern Ireland, because the organisations to which they belonged had committed themselves in the 'Good Friday' Agreement of April 1998 to pursue their political ends by exclusively peaceful means.

[207] Cardinal Cahal Daly asked forgiveness from the British people in a homily delivered at Canterbury Cathedral on 22 January 1995 (following a similar, but much less celebrated request to the Irish people made by the Archbishop of Canterbury, George Carey, in Christ Church Cathedral, Dublin on 18 November 1994).

we agree with you in your moral evaluation of republican violence, and that therefore you can trust us.' This deliberate repudiation of deeds done or left undone by *other* members of our people, is strictly an expression of regret, rather than one of remorse. It is indeed a political act of apology *rather than* a personal one of repentance.

6. Empirical Studies, 1985–1998

In the Introduction to *Dimensions of Forgiveness: Psychological Research and Theological Perspectives*, Everett Worthington observes

> that the scientific study of forgiveness began only recently. Before 1985, only five studies investigating forgiveness have been identified. In the thirteen years since then, more than fifty-five scientific studies have been conducted to study forgiveness and to help people learn how to forgive.[208]

Worthington ascribes this rise in interest to a variety of factors, including the publication in 1984 of Lewis Smedes' highly popular book, *Forgive and Forget: Healing the Hurts We Don't Deserve*.[209] Worthington's own book represents the first in a series of symposia, funded by the John Templeton Foundation, 'on research into the scientific foundations of effective living – how positive mindsets and virtues enhance the lives of individuals and, ultimately, the well-being of society.'[210] This general self-description immediately indicates two problematic features of some of the material in *Dimensions of Forgiveness*. First, the implication that the *foundations* of forgiveness are scientific, rather than ethical or theological, suggests a certain materialist reductionism. Unhappily, this is confirmed in Worthington's own piece, where he speculates about 'the neurobiological foundation' of his model for promoting forgiveness and about some of the 'mechanisms' that occur during forgiveness and its refusal; where he refers to 'the mechanics of fear conditioning'; where he talks about the attitude of forgiveness being created by the cooperation of 'the body and brain' (as distinct from

---

[208] Everett L. Worthington (ed.), *Dimensions of Forgiveness: Psychological Research and Theological Perspectives* (Philadelphia 1998), 1. Chapter 8 of this book consists of an annotated bibliography of material dating back to 1968, together with a helpful subject index.

[209] Worthington (ed.), *Dimensions of Forgiveness*, 2; Lewis B. Smedes, *Forgive and Forget: Healing the Hurts We Don't Deserve* (New York 1984).

[210] Worthington (ed.), *Dimensions of Forgiveness*, ix. According to Michael McCullough, Julie Exline, and Roy Baumeister ('An Annotated Bibliography of Research on Forgiveness and Related Concepts,' in: Worthington (ed.), *Dimensions of Forgiveness*, 193–194), the Templeton Foundation's interest in forgiveness stems from its prominence in Sir John Templeton's *Worldwide Laws of Life* (Philadelphia 1997).

the human subject); and where he adopts the objective of creating 'a super-potent sequence of stimulus events – a treatment [for unforgiveness] so powerful that *all* people respond positively to it.'[211] To be fair, Worthington allows such mechanistic language to mingle freely with the language of volition (e.g., the 'commitment' to forgive),[212] but he shows no awareness of the tension between them.

The second problematic feature of *Dimensions of Forgiveness* is its prevailing individualism. Forgiveness is often conceived here entirely as a process internal to the psyche of the victim. According to Kenneth Pargament and Mark Rye, it is about overcoming 'negative emotions' and opening oneself to the pursuit of peace.[213] According to Worthington, forgiveness is quite distinct from reconciliation in being *intra*personal rather than *inter*personal: 'Forgiveness happens inside an individual; reconciliation happens within a relationship ... Forgiveness and reconciliation are obviously related, but separate, processes.'[214] Robert Enright and Catherine Coyle agree: 'Reconciliation is not to be confused or equated with forgiveness ... Genuine forgiveness is voluntary and unconditional. Thus, it is not motivated by pressure from a third party, nor is it dependent on the apology or recognition of wrongdoing on the part of the offender.'[215] Lewis Smedes agrees too: 'Forgiveness is individual; reconciliation is social .... Forgiveness is unconditional; reconciliation is conditioned by the offender's response to the forgiver.'[216] Again, to be fair, *part* of forgiveness is indeed a process internal to the psyche of the victim, and involves the acknowledgement that one is made of the same fallible stuff as the wrongdoer, the overcoming of resentment in so far as that is an expression of wounded pride, and the consequent birth of compassion or empathy. Further, it is quite true to say, as Worthington, Enright, Coyle, and Smedes do, that there can be (part of)

---

[211] Everett L. Worthington, 'The Pyramid Model of Forgiveness: Some Interdisciplinary Speculations about Unforgiveness and the Promotion of Forgiveness,' in: Worthington (ed.), *Dimensions of Forgiveness*, 108, 112 (author's italics), 113, 127.

[212] Worthington , 'Pyramid Model,' 125.

[213] Kenneth I. Pargament & Mark S. Rye, 'Forgiveness as a Method of Religious Coping,' in: Worthington (ed.), *Dimensions of Forgiveness*, 63.

[214] Worthington, 'Pyramid Model,' 129.

[215] Robert D. Enright & Catherine T. Coyle, 'Researching the Process Model of Forgiveness Within Psychological Interventions,' in: Worthington (ed.), *Dimensions of Forgiveness*, 141–142. Enright founded the International Forgiveness Institute in Madison, Wisconsin in 1994 (www.forgiveness-institute.org). He also co-edited a collection of essays on forgiveness that is more broadly interdisciplinary than Worthington's, and which contains a very useful 'Comprehensive Bibliography on Interpersonal Forgiveness': Robert D. Enright & Joanna North (eds.), *Exploring Forgiveness* (Madison 1998).

[216] Lewis B. Smedes, 'Stations on the Journey from Forgiveness to Hope,' in: Worthington (ed.), *Dimensions of Forgiveness*, 345–346.

forgiveness without reconciliation[217] – for example, the victim can free herself from excessive resentment even if the wrongdoer refuses to repent, and sometimes merely 'going one's own way' is the most that is possible (Miroslav Volf) or even the only appropriate outcome.[218] On the other hand, these 'therapeutic' accounts of forgiveness completely neglect the dimensions of culpability and justice. As a result, resentment is seen simply as a 'negative emotion' that disturbs and distorts the individual victim and needs to be overcome, rather than as an attitude that, duly governed by compassion and the desire for reconciliation, insists on caring for the wrongdoer by holding him accountable and seeking a just peace that is born of his repentance. My objection here is close to Gregory Jones' criticism of Smedes' *Forgive and Forget* for its assumption of a world where people hurt each other only 'despite their best intentions,' and not where they do it maliciously and culpably. As a result, Jones argues, Smedes' 'therapeutic' account 'internalises and privatises forgiveness ...; it also virtually ignores issues of culpability and repentance .... Forgiveness becomes a means of being "healed of your hate" ...'[219]

Notwithstanding its unresolved methodological tension, and the limitations imposed by its prevalent individualism, *Dimensions of Forgiveness* does do the service of presenting empirical evidence that 'religion' helps to promote forgiveness by reminding victims of their own participation in universal finitude, frailty, and guilt;[220] and that 'people who are more religiously involved continue to place more value on forgiveness than their less religious counterparts.'[221]

---

[217] Worthington, 'Pyramid Model,' 129; Enright & Coyle, 'Researching the Process Model,' 141; Smedes, 'Stations on the Journey,' 346.

[218] It makes less sense to say, as Worthington does ('Pyramid Model,' 130), that there may be reconciliation without forgiveness. What he means here is a mere *modus convivendi* or accommodation, which is not the same as full-blown reconciliation. Smedes is right: 'reconciliation cannot happen without forgiveness' ('Stations on the Journey,' 346).

[219] Jones, *Embodying Forgiveness*, 49. As I see it, therefore, Martin Marty's defence of Smedes against Jones misses the point (Martin E. Marty, 'The Ethos of Christian Forgiveness,' in: Worthington (ed.), *Dimensions of Forgiveness*, 25). Jones is not arguing against a therapeutic approach as such, but against an approach that avoids the issue of culpability, and so the need for repentance, confession, apology, and reparation; and also one which supposes that my own peace of mind may be complete even though I stand in a relationship of estrangement with another.

[220] Pargament & Rye, 'Forgiveness as a Method of Religious Coping,' 68. Worthington does not recognise the role of religion in fostering acknowledgement of one's own guilt – except at one point where, lapsing into religious language, he refers to the realisation of actual culpability as 'a specific epiphany' ('Pyramid Model,' 124).

[221] Pargament & Rye, 'Forgiveness as a Method of Religious Coping,' 66, 68, 75; R.L. Gorsuch & J.Y. Hao, 'Forgiveness: An Exploratory Factor Analysis and its Relationships to Religious Variables,' *Review of Religious Research* 34 (1993), 333–347 (summarised in McCullough et al., 'An Annotated Bibliography,' 236–238).

7. Conclusion

No author is absent from the story he tells, and I have not pretended to be absent from this one. Hitherto, however, my own views have found expression only in sporadic commentary. Now, I shall draw this survey to a close by making clear the position from which it has been made – and which it has helped to establish.

Forgiveness, as I see it, comes in two parts. The first comprises the victim's overcoming of vindictive resentment, the growth of his compassion, and the formation of his intention to restore some kind of 'friendship' with the wrongdoer. This part of forgiveness precedes the wrongdoer's expression of repentance, and is unilateral and unconditional. However, because what it intends has yet to be realised, it remains incomplete. Its completion waits upon the declaration, verbal or otherwise, of 'absolution'; that is, the moment when the victim declares that he will no longer view the wrongdoer in the light of his misdeed and that their relationship may proceed as before. This second part of forgiveness *is* conditional. It depends upon the wrongdoer's demonstration of sincere repentance, precisely because it takes seriously both the wrongdoer and his relationship with the victim.

The initial part of forgiveness, then, does not involve forgetting the injury. On the contrary, out of care both for the wrongdoer and for the integrity of any future 'friendship' with him, that should be remembered; and it should be remembered with the resentment appropriate to a deliberate act of disrespect or unwarranted hostility. Nevertheless, qualified by compassion and a desire for restored 'friendship,' such resentment will not be vindictive. It will be the anger without sin, of which St Paul wrote to the Ephesians (4:26).

The final part of forgiveness, however, does involve a commitment on the part of the victim to 'forget' the injury. Since memory is often beyond the will's command, this cannot be a promise never to remember. It can, however, be a resolve at least not to allow the memory of past injury to jaundice future relations with resentment. In so far as it is based on the assumption that the offender's repentance is sincere, this commitment is conditional: if there is a further offence of a similar kind, it should be withdrawn. Still, this conditionality does not mean that the wrongdoer is robbed of all assurance of forgiveness; only that he is withheld assurance of unconditional absolution.

I have said that the first part of forgiveness involves the victim's intention to restore some kind of 'friendship' with the wrongdoer. Exactly which kind will depend partly on the nature of the antecedent relationship, and partly on what degree of restoration is possible in the time available and circumstances attendant. Former intimates might aim at 'reconciliation,' whereas fellow-citizens need aspire to nothing more than 'accommodation,' and strangers to a mere cessation of hostilities and a 'peaceful' parting of the ways. Sometimes, of course, the end of warfare is as much as even intimates can realistically hope for, given the gravity of the injury involved.

Are some injuries unforgivable? Yes – but only comprehensively, by surviving human beings, and in this life. If there is a God, and if the dead will be raised, and if there is life beyond history, then intractable resentment may yet be tamed by love, stubborn impenitence yet wooed by it, and murderers may yet receive absolution from their victims. Note that this *provisional* kind of unforgivableness grants victims no licence to ossify into bitterness and hatred.

So victims, then, are not obliged to forgive their oppressors? The answer to this is, 'Yes and No.' Humble and honest awareness of the fact of their *own* fatedness and frailty, and of their *own* need for forgiveness, does oblige victims to foster compassion for their fellow-sinners; but it does not oblige them to grant absolution in the absence of repentance. Are victims obliged to grant absolution to sincere penitents? Yes, they are, but this does not mean that penitents deserve absolution; for what obliges the victim is not the morally admirable repentance of the wrongdoer, but the truth about himself and the duty to will what is good.

Can there be third-party forgiveness? No, but intimates of a victim may forgive injuries of their own that are bound up with the victim's. So is there no such thing as 'political' forgiveness? Yes there is, in that a community may forgive the general harm that is done to it indirectly through a particular victim's injury. Beyond this, contemporary political leaders may 'forgive' historical harms done to their communities, but only analogously, and only if they have good claim to be broadly representative of their people. Executive pardons, remissions of punishment, and amnesties are not legal expressions of forgiveness, only legal analogies; for they do not necessarily express compassion for the wrongdoer, or constitute responses to his penitence.

What part does Christian theology play in all this? The concept of the creaturely nature of human being reminds victims of the weakness that they share with wrongdoers; the concept of original sin reminds them that the latter also stagger under the burden of historical fate; and the concept of the universality of sin reminds them that they stand to offenders, not as the righteous to the unrighteous, but as one set of sinners to another, equal in need of forgiveness. Add to this, Jesus' habit of keeping table-fellowship with the *un*worthy, and its constant reenactment in the rite of the eucharist, where the Lord persists in sharing the food and drink of implicit forgiveness with those about to betray him, and it becomes obvious why theologians have been more ready than philosophers to assert an initial, unilateral, unconditional, gracious, generous part of forgiveness. Then trinitarian theology, with its affirmation of the basic relationality of things, can help to counter any privatising, 'therapeutic' tendency to collapse the whole of forgiveness into this unilateral part, by pointing out the intended goal of restored 'friendship' and its reciprocal requirements. Finally, faith in the providence of God and hope for the resurrection of the dead enables a humane acceptance of the historical limits of the growth of compassion and penitence, of the granting of absolution, and of the achievement of reconciliation, but without authorising any desperate relaxation into inordinate resentment.

Contributors

Pamela Sue Anderson is Senior Lecturer in Philosophy at the University of Sunderland. Her publications include *A Feminist Philosophy of Religion* (Oxford 1998).

Nigel Biggar is Professor of Theology in the University of Leeds. His books include *Good Life: Reflections on What We Value Today* (London 1997).

Jane Craske is a minister of the East Didsbury Methodist Church in Manchester, and Lecturer at Hartley Victoria College, Manchester. Together with Clive Marsh she authored *Methodism and the Future: Facing the Challenge* (London 1999).

Christopher Jones is Chaplain and Fellow of St Peter's College, Oxford.

Alistair McFadyen is Senior Lecturer in Theological Studies at the University of Leeds. His publications include *Bound to Sin: Abuse, Holocaust, and the Christian Doctrine of Sin* (Cambridge 2000).

Todd Pokrifka-Joe is a Ph.D. student in the University of St Andrews.

Marcel Sarot is Interim Director of the Netherlands Research School for Systematic Theology and Religious Studies, and teaches Philosophy of Religion at the University of Utrecht, The Netherlands. His publications include *Living a Good Life in Spite of Evil* (Frankfurt am Main 1999).

Karin Scheiber is a Ph.D. student in the University of Zürich, Switzerland.

Nico Schreurs is Professor of Christian Doctrine at the Tilburg Faculty of Theology, The Netherlands. He is the author of several monographs in Dutch.

Peter Sedgwick is Assistant Secretary (Home Affairs) to the Church of England Board for Social Responsibility. He is the author of *The Market Economy and Christian Ethics* (Cambridge 1999).

Peter Selby is Bishop of Worcester. He is a former Professorial Fellow in Applied Theology at Durham University where he wrote his most recent book *Grace and Mortgage: The Language of Faith and the Debt of the World* (London 1997).

David Self is the Team Rector in the parish of St Paul's, Bristol. He has contributed to Robert Llewellyn's book, *Circles of Silence: Explorations in Prayer with Julian Meetings* (London 1994).

Alwyn Thompson is Research Officer for the Centre for Contemporary Christianity in Ireland of ECONI (Evangelical Contribution on Northern Ireland). He edited *Border Crossings* (Belfast 1999).

Deborah van Deusen Hunsinger is an ordained minister in the United Church of Christ and Assistant Professor of Pastoral Theology at Princeton Theological Seminary. Her publications include *Theology and Pastoral Counseling: A New Interdisciplinary Approach* (Grand Rapids, Mich. 1995).

Fraser Watts is Starbridge Lecturer in Theology and Natural Science at the University of Cambridge. His publications include *The Efficacy of Clinical Applications of Psychology: An Overview of Research* (Cardiff 1990).

Haddon Willmer is Emeritus Professor and former Head of the Department of Theology at the University of Leeds. He currently is Research Tutor of the Oxford Centre for Mission Studies. His publications include *20/20 Visions: The Futures of Christianity in Britain* (London 1991).

Index of Names

Editors of multi-author volumes are included only when the reference is to the whole volume, and not to a particular contribution.

Index of Subjects